ESCAPE
OF THE
GUILTY

ALSO BY RALPH ADAM FINE

Mary Jane Versus Pennsylvania
The Great Drug Deception

ESCAPE
OF THE
GUILTY

Ralph Adam Fine

Dodd, Mead & Company

NEW YORK

Published by Dodd, Mead & Company, Inc.
79 Madison Avenue, New York, N.Y. 10016

Distributed in Canada by
McClelland and Stewart Limited, Toronto

Manufactured in the United States of America

Designed by Berta Lewis

First Edition

Library of Congress Cataloging-in-Publication Data

Fine, Ralph Adam, 1941–
   Escape of the guilty.

   Bibliography: p.
   Includes index.
   1. Criminal justice, Administration of—United States.
I. Title.
KF9223.F35   1986   364'.973   86-8946
ISBN 0-396-08590-3

To Kay and Matt, Al and Esther, and
to a very special Aunt Min—and
in loving memory of my parents,
Justice Sidney A. Fine and Libby Fine
of New York.

This book is also dedicated to the
many hardworking men and women—
judges, prosecutors, defense lawyers,
as well as police, parole and
probation officers—who are trying
to make the system work.

CONTENTS

PREFACE

The Untold Story

I STARTED THIS BOOK a year and a half ago. At about that time, I received a small package from the Wembley Tie Company. It wasn't a tie but a coffee mug emblazoned with the words, "I've told the untold story." I have yet to figure out why the Wembley people sent me that cup or how it even fit in with whatever promotion they were running at the time. Yet, sitting on my desk all these months, it provided a fitting spur for this book because although other judges are frustrated by the law's inability to control crime, none has written a book about it.

The legal profession is, more than any other, a profession of words. Words fertilize legal concepts and give them nourishment. While there are thousands of volumes replete with judicial decisions and professional articles dealing with some of the subjects covered by this book, they contain words for the profession. Insofar as the general public is concerned, the story this book relates is largely untold, even though the news media frequently report the more sensational elements of its underlying theme. While I bring to the story insights germinated by the light of my experience, I have used no secret information and have betrayed no confidences. Everything I describe here has happened on the public record and has, so to speak, been free for the reporting.

That the story told here has been largely *un*reported makes the revelations in this book even more significant, since change can only come after knowledge. Simply put, while all of us know *something* is wrong with the criminal justice system, few of us know what. *Escape of the Guilty* takes us on a journey of discovery and shows why our streets are unsafe and why the sanctity of our homes is at risk. It explains what we can do to recapture our liberty from the predators among us.

I expect this book will be controversial. Many of my colleagues in the law—judges, professors, and practicing attorneys—believe that "despite some flaws," our criminal justice system works fairly well. I disagree. *Escape of the Guilty* was born out of my frustrations with the criminal justice system: a system that is so bewebbed with gossamer distinctions and so mired in expediency that—with some exceptions as of late—it seems more intent on finding reasons to let admittedly guilty criminals escape punishment than in doing justice for society.

In *The Sleepwalkers,* Arthur Koestler tells how the Pythagorean Brotherhood slew Hippasos for leaking the existence of irrational numbers (such as the square root of two or the diagonal of any square), which—because they could not be precisely measured—struck at the heart of the Brotherhood's philosophy. Some, whose vision is obscured by a similar parochialism, may view me in that light and see this book as a threat to the criminal justice brotherhood. Yet mathematics was strengthened by Hippasos's revelation, and I hope the law will be strengthened, not weakened, by the story this book tells.

The Code of Judicial Conduct promulgated by the American Bar Association encourages judges to write about "the law, the legal system, and the administration of justice" because, as explained by the Code's official commentary, as "a judicial officer and person specifically learned in the law, a judge is in a unique position to contribute to [their] improvement." Wisconsin's Code of Judicial Ethics is similar. In the words of Judge Irving R. Kaufman, former Chief Judge of the United States Court of Appeals sitting in New York and one of the drafters of the ABA Code, judges "have the duty to speak on matters that affect the judicial system because the public interest cannot be served by silence." It is in that spirit, in the spirit of making everyone better informed about our system of criminal justice, and with the hope that we can one day protect all of our people from the ravages and fear of crime, that I dedicate this book to my associates of the bench and bar throughout this nation. I trust that they will take whatever disagreements some of them may have with my conclusions in the spirit I offer them. Ideas in a free society are strengthened by the tempering fires of controversy.

We are not willing to discredit constitutional doctrines for the protection of the innocent by making of them mere technical loopholes for the escape of the guilty.

—UNITED STATES SUPREME COURT JUSTICE
ROBERT H. JACKSON IN *Stein* v. *New York,*
1953

ESCAPE
OF THE
GUILTY

ONE

Full Circle

THERE IS NO freedom without order, and there is no order without law. Our criminal justice system promises to give us order and thereby preserve freedom. Yet today, millions of Americans live in a society where terror is their constant companion; we are not free. An incredible third of our nation's families have been touched—some mangled—by the lawless. I have been a judge since 1979, and I can tell you that we are largely impotent in our battle with crime.

It is a pleasant fall evening. You and your family decide to go out to dinner. It'll be nothing fancy—just a quick trip to the neighborhood's favorite little restaurant. Before you leave, you lock your house or apartment. You may be a bit leery about crime. After all, your friend next door was burglarized two weeks ago, and rumor has it that the young mother up the block was either raped or robbed or both.

But you're not going to be gone too long, so you're not very concerned. Crime is something that always seems to happen to the other fellow. If you're careful and take sensible precautions, there's no need to worry. So you lock your door, and you may even leave a light on to make any would-be burglar think you're home.

Dinner was terrific, and everyone had a good time. When you arrive home, you find the front door jimmied. The place is a mess. The contents of closets and drawers are scattered all over the house. The word *strewn* takes on a new and sickening meaning. Although you know it will be hours before you can clean it all up, you see immediately that this keepsake, that memento, is

1

gone. Days will pass before you will be able to remember everything that has been taken. Right now, however, all that is a mere
abstraction. You feel violated, degraded, frustrated, and angry.
Crime has hit home.

If you are lucky, they will find the burglar. Perhaps a neighbor saw someone suspicious. Maybe a check with the local pawn-
shops will turn up something. Most likely, however, the burglar
will go uncaught, and your possessions will be gone forever.

Let us assume, however, that a suspect *is* caught—perhaps
trying to pawn your grandfather's mother-of-pearl cravat pin.
Assume also that the police do everything right: the arrest is made
legally, and the suspect is advised of his rights before he makes
any statement.

The suspect will be taken to a police station for booking. In
those places like Wisconsin where prosecutors screen cases (that
is, decide what charge, if any, should be lodged against a suspect), he'll be brought before a prosecutor for charging. In some
places, the prosecutor is a district attorney or one of his or her
assistants. In other places, the prosecutor is called a state's attorney or county attorney. The prosecutor's role—whatever the title—is the same: to represent the government in its case against
the person accused of violating the law. Since, in your city, cases
are screened by prosecutors before a person is charged with a
crime, the assistant district attorney will examine the police reports and perhaps interview you and the pawnshop owner, as
well as the suspect. If the suspect is interviewed, he can have his
lawyer present. If the suspect wants a lawyer to help him and
cannot afford to hire one on his own, a taxpayer-paid lawyer will
be assigned.

In Wisconsin, this power to appoint lawyers for suspects too
poor to hire them is the responsibility of a state public defender.
Usually, the appointed lawyer will be a member of the public
defender's staff. Occasionally, he or she will be one of many private lawyers who have volunteered for these criminal cases. In
Wisconsin, their pay is barely what is needed to cover office over-
head.

You learn that the suspect is twenty years old. He has had
one conviction since he turned eighteen, the age when, in the
eyes of the law, he became an adult. The conviction is for something called "receiving stolen property." It sounds like something
dishonest pawnbrokers or coin dealers do, and you ask about it.

The assistant district attorney explains that while the maximum penalty for burglary is a ten-year sentence, receiving stolen property can either be a nine-month misdemeanor, if the property has a value of $500 or less; a two-year felony, if the property is worth more than $500 but less than $2,500; or a five-year felony, if the property is worth more than $2,500. She tells you that the suspect's prior conviction was the result of a plea bargain: he was originally charged with burglarizing a home not far from where you live. He took some silverware, a TV set, a stereo, and a few old coins.

He was allowed to plead to a reduced "receiving stolen property" misdemeanor charge because it was his first adult crime and, in the words of the assistant district attorney, "he wouldn't get prison time, anyway." When you express surprise at the misdemeanor part because you thought all that stuff would be worth more than $500, she says, "Oh, well, it doesn't really make that much difference. I guess you can say we only charged him with receiving *some* of the stolen property; the part that was worth less than the $500. It's one of the little fictions we use to move cases. You wouldn't want us to have to try all these cases, would you?"

At this point, you're still pretty numb. Your house has just been ransacked, and all this is new to you. You feel you should protest, but you don't know what to say. So you just nod. It is a noncommittal nod. You instinctively feel that something's wrong.

The odds are, of course, that this case will "plead," too. That is, that the defendant, his lawyer, and the assistant district attorney will work out a deal of leniency in exchange for the defendant's guilty plea. Between 75 percent and 90 percent of all felony charges are "pled out." The figure is even higher for misdemeanors. Most of the time, the victim is never even notified of the deal, let alone consulted. Your discussion with the prosecutor may be the last time you hear about "your" burglary. If you ask, you will probably be told the twenty-year-old was given probation again. The prosecutor explains that she, the defense lawyer, and the judge did not want to send him to prison and turn him into a "hardened criminal" for just a "property crime." The burglary is more than a "property crime" to you, however, and you wonder why the criminal justice system cannot protect you and your neighbors.

The most visible part of the criminal justice system is the trial. Although few criminal cases actually go to trial, it is the keystone to all our freedoms. Here, unlike the situation in many countries of the world where the government can lock people up on almost any pretext or none at all, no person may be punished for a crime unless he either pleads guilty (or its equivalent) or is found guilty by a jury of his fellow citizens.

Trials are run by set procedures and rules. Lawyers for each side attempt to persuade the jury (or judge, if the right to a jury trial is given up) that their version of the facts is correct. They do this by presenting evidence: either the testimony of witnesses who tell what they have personally seen or heard, or tangible items that may, in some cases, speak more forcefully than the most articulate witness.

After each side presents its evidence, the judge instructs the jury on the legal principles that must guide its consideration of the case. One critical jury instruction concerns the burden of proof. Under our system, no defendant in a criminal case has to prove anything. He does not have to testify. He does not have to call witnesses. He does not have to introduce any exhibits. The government must do all the proving in a criminal case, and the proof must satisfy the jury that the defendant is guilty beyond a reasonable doubt before it may find the defendant guilty. In forty-five of the fifty states, a jury verdict in a criminal case must be unanimous.

The jury trial is the last vestige of citizen control over any important governmental function. In a criminal case, the jury can disregard the law and acquit someone who is clearly guilty, and there is nothing the trial judge—or a whole bench of appellate judges—can do about it. And that is the way it should be. For in the final analysis, the jury is the community's conscience.

Although the trial is what usually comes to mind when we think of the criminal law, it is, as we shall see, but a small part of the process. Before we look at where we are and why the system is not working, we must first examine the past.

Our criminal justice system has evolved, sometimes slowly, sometimes fitfully, over the course of a thousand or more years. The journey in search of our legal heritage must start in England at around the turn of the first millennium, for our legal system here in the United States is a child of English law, and that law is old indeed. Although our system has become independent of its parent, the beginnings are there.

Imagine for a moment what it must have been like to live thousands of years ago among the lawless, where only the strong could be free, where you could own only what you were able to defend, and where you would remain alive for only as long as no one stronger wished you dead.

Life in a lawless society is intolerable. Even the strong are subject to ambush; they too will, if they are able to survive, grow old and weak. So, gradually, codes of conduct developed. Often, these codes or rules were nothing more than a recognition of the clan's pecking hierarchy: the chief would enforce a modicum of fairness and preserve some semblance of order. The group, however, was still at risk from marauding neighbors.

In time, the groups grew and, as clan lines blurred and their members became more diverse, the chief's personality was no longer an effective peacekeeper. Something had to take its place. Nurtured by the fertilizer of need, the rudimentary buds of criminal justice systems began to sprout in every place where *homo sapiens* walked erect.

The watershed year of our jurisprudence is 1066, the year William of Normandy vanquished Anglo-Saxon England and King Harold at Hastings. Like any other conqueror, William sought to bring his new subjects under his central authority. He and his successors, however, recognized that building upon—rather than destroying—Anglo-Saxon tradition and custom would beguile the task. Their tools were the itinerant royal officers—nascent judges, really—who extended the royal presence into even the most remote forest-shielded villages. As they struggled to resolve myriad disputes, they applied familiar concepts based on that Anglo-Saxon tradition and custom. In short, they recognized legal principles common to the whole country, what was later to be called the Common Law. Theoretically, at least, these judges were not making new law; they were, rather, deriving their decisions from what had always been the law.

Justice under the pre-Conquest Anglo-Saxons had been swift. Criminals caught red-handed were executed on the spot. Those who were able to escape immediate apprehension were chased down and then executed. Anyone witnessing a crime was required to raise the "hue and cry," that is, to summon his neighbors to catch and punish the malefactor. Governmental authority was so tenuous and nebulous that private revenge by a victim's family members was encouraged. This, of course, led to Hatfield/McCoy-type blood feuds, which only increased the general lawlessness. For a period of time, an offender could buy immunity from retaliation by his victim's family. These fines, called *wergild* ("man's price"), varied with the victim's social standing. It cost more to kill a big shot than it did someone else. There was a twist to the *wergild* concept, however. The man with higher social standing (and, therefore, a higher *wergild*) was subject to a higher fine should he offend the peace.

As legal historians Frederick Pollock and Frederic Maitland point out in their massive exploration of English law up to the end of the thirteenth century, it soon became clear that a system of money payments would have to "give way before a system of true punishments." Not only were the early punishments "true," they were devastating. Mutilation—the loss of hands and feet under Henry II and emasculation and exoculation under his great-grandfather William the Conqueror—combined with brutal forms of execution were routine. Pollock and Maitland explain the word *exoculation* from the comfort of their Victorian society, saying, "We use too mild a word if we speak of 'blinding.' The eyes were torn out."

The form of penalty was generally discretionary with the judge, who was guided by the king's personal preferences. Again, as Pollock and Maitland put it, the felon could hardly "complain if a foot was taken instead of his eyes, or if he was hanged instead of being beheaded." By the thirteenth century, death had generally supplanted mutilation as the preferred penalty for felons. Petty larceny was sometimes punished by whipping and sometimes by taking the thief's ear. In some locales, the thief would have his ear nailed to a post and would then be given a knife to cut himself free. Third offenders—those who had no more ears to lose—went to the gallows. In that rough time, when criminals were viewed as vermin fit for extermination, those who had lost limbs or ears in an honorable way, such as in battle, would often get a letter of explanation from the king to carry as a safe-conduct pass. All in all, it must have been an unsettling period in which to live. It was a time when being inconspicuous and inoffensive were life-saving qualities.

While the annealing influences of time and maturity would

ultimately temper the harshness, progress was slow. Yet there was a primordial awareness—almost a groping, if you will—that guilt or innocence should be impartially determined *before* punishment. Initially, this responsibility was placed in the hands of God in a "trial" or a testing by ordeal or oath.

The Anglo-Saxon ordeal tested the accused in one of four ways: by hot iron, by hot water, by cold water, or by morsel. The first required the accused to carry a piece of red-hot iron in his hand for nine steps. The second required that he plunge his hand, either to the wrist or to the elbow depending on the circumstances, into a cauldron of boiling water. The healing of the burns was a providential sign of innocence. In the ordeal by cold water, a bound suspect was tossed into the drink. If the pure water accepted him—that is, if he sank—his soul was revealed to be unsullied by guilt. Contrary to modern myth, many persons who were declared innocent by the cold-water ordeal were fished out before they drowned. In the ordeal by morsel, the accused passed if he was able to swallow a piece of dry bread or hard cheese. If the food stuck in his throat, he was guilty. These forms of the ordeal were abolished following the fourth Lateran Council in 1215.

A later variant of the ordeal, apparently introduced by the Norman conquerors, was trial by battle. It pitted the accused against his accuser. If the accused won the fight, his innocence was vindicated. Here again, however, victory was thought to be the result of divine intervention and not of the comparative strengths of the parties.

"Trial" by ordeal is, obviously, a distinct improvement over a mob's summary execution. Indeed, many were "acquitted" by the technique. Nevertheless, the ordeal hardly comports with modern notions of justice. Less jarring to our sensibilities were the procedures involving the oath.

One method of testing by oath was to permit the accused to solemnly swear that the charge was untrue. In our own coarse age, when lies and even perjury are considered by too many as appropriate political, social, and economic tools, this may seem like an easy way to avoid punishment, but our early English forebears took their oaths quite seriously. After all, temporal pain and punishment were minor when compared to the threat of eternal damnation.

Generally, the accused was permitted to contest the accusation on his own oath alone for only minor charges. A second form of trial by oath was necessary if circumstances required a stronger showing of innocence: the accused would have to bring in oath helpers, known as *compurgators*. The number varied with the type of crime. These neighbors and friends, all free men of good repute, did not testify about what had happened; they were not witnesses as we know them today, and they knew nothing of the facts. Rather, their task was to swear that the accused was truthful. If he was truthful, his denial was true—or so the syllogism went.

The oaths were complex and highly structured. One slip from the prescribed form was a clear sign of guilt. Indeed, Pollock and Maitland tell us that in the twelfth century the oaths were generally so elaborate that "rather than attempt them, men would take their chance with the hot iron."

The trial-by-oath witnesses testified according to a prescribed formula; they were not asked questions or cross-examined. If they adhered to the rubric, their oaths were accepted. If not, their oaths failed. Again, the fact-finding burden was on God.

A third form of the trial by oath used actual witnesses to the event. This, of course, is closer to the modern-day concept of a trial, in which jurors must evaluate the often-conflicting stories of persons who have seen or heard something relevant to the issues being tried: "I saw the defendant shoot the cashier," for example. These situations, however, were fairly limited and were usually restricted to disputes concerning transactions for which witnesses were needed. Thus, official witnesses from the local community were required for the sale of goods or cattle. They would testify about what they saw if the sale was later challenged or if the purchaser was charged with theft. A present-day echo of this all-but-forgotten procedure is the witnessing of a Last Will and Testament. After you die, if there is a dispute about whether you actually signed the Will or about your state of mind at the time, those who witnessed your signature will be called to testify. In the ninth and tenth centuries in Anglo-Saxon England, children were often used as witnesses and, in a practice that reflects the barbarous time, they were scalded with hot water to burn the events into their memories.

For a long time, the bringing of criminal charges was a private affair. Prosecution was left to the person whose relative was killed or whose cattle was taken. Moreover, these cases were handled by local courts, which were dominated by the local noble or landowner. All this began to change in the latter half of the twelfth century, when Henry II felt that his central authority was sufficiently strong to prevail over countervailing local interests.

A first move was the incremental expansion of the "King's Peace." Crimes committed during coronation festivities or various religious holidays or on the King's four major highways (built by the Romans many centuries earlier) were considered to be affronts to the King and a violation of his peace. Alleged violations of the King's Peace were tried in the King's court, irrespective of the victim's status. Thus, for example, if John was killed during Pentecost, his brother could bring charges against the alleged killer before the King's judges in the King's court.

Initially, royal jurisdiction over crimes was limited to the narrow areas implicating the King's Peace. However, since justice was usually more even-handed in the King's court than it was in the local courts, persons lodging criminal accusations understandably began to allege that the offense was a breach of the King's Peace, even though technically it may not have been. The King's judges, eager to expand their jurisdiction on behalf of the Crown, permitted this early exercise of "forum shopping" without further scrutiny.

Almost concurrently with the expansion of the Crown's jurisdiction over criminal cases, the government started to assume part of the prosecutorial function, which, as we have seen, had previously been left solely to private initiative. The King's traveling judges went from village to village convening what, in modern terms, could be called grand juries. Groups of citizens were placed under oath and asked to tell who had committed what crimes since the judge had last visited them.

Unlike present-day grand jurors, who merely evaluate evidence presented to them by a prosecutor (or, in the case of so-called "runaway grand juries," evidence they dig up), these citizens were, loosely, witnesses who related what they knew or what was common knowledge in the community. This was the accusation. Those they fingered in front of the King's judge, like their modern counterparts indicted by a modern grand jury, still had to face trial. At this point in history, trial was by ordeal. If the instigator was the victim or—if the victim was dead—his relative, the ordeal was by battle.

Charges lodged by these grand juries were serious. Prior to

their institution, a person acquitted by ordeal or by oath was thought to be innocent and was able to resume his normal life. A person acquitted following an accusation by one of these groups of citizens, however, suffered the severe penalty of exile. He was forced to go to the nearest port and await the first ship that could remove him from England. A man without a country in those days was almost a man without the means to sustain life. The severity of the punishment reflected, in a very real sense, a recognition that testing by ordeal was not a particularly accurate method of determining the truth. In short, if your neighbors swore that you were guilty, you were probably guilty irrespective of whether your burns healed or you were able to defeat your accuser in battle.

These grand juries mark the first time government was involved in the prosecution of crime. But government did not gain a monopoly on it, and it would not, in England, for another 650 years. Indeed, private criminal prosecution was preferred and would be given the first crack for several hundred years. Private prosecution was last used in England in 1818 when a man accused another man of raping and murdering his sister. The accused rapist challenged the brother to battle; after the courts said the brother had to fight the defendant, he dropped the charge. A year later, Parliament abolished both private criminal prosecution *and* trial by battle.

Private criminal prosecution persists in a rudimentary form in Wisconsin. It is as old as Wisconsin statehood. Several years ago such a private prosecution was initiated in my court. More recently, a young woman was upset that the district attorney in Milwaukee would not prosecute two members of the Green Bay Packers she claimed had raped her. She sought to have a judge authorize the issuance of criminal charges against them.

This remnant of citizen involvement in criminal prosecutions reflects Wisconsin's populist history. It is a check on the largely unfettered discretion about whether to prosecute enjoyed by our state's district attorneys. It may very well be unique to Wisconsin, and it is rarely used even there. Nevertheless, it can work as a safety valve in the event of perceived lax law enforcement.

This is important; when people believe the criminal justice system cannot or will not control crime, we see the return to earlier methods of "law enforcement"—feuds, mob action, and the like. Unfortunately, as the case of Bernhard Goetz and the public's reaction to it tell us, more and more people think they must take the law into their own hands to see that justice is done.

At two-thirty in the afternoon of January 26, 1981, thirty-four-year-old Bernhard Goetz was walking along the Canal Street subway station platform in New York City. He had just purchased about a thousand dollars' worth of equipment for his electronics business. Three muggers jumped him. One was caught by a nearby policeman as he tried to push Goetz through a plate-glass window. Sixteen years old, the mugger ultimately pled guilty to a misdemeanor. He served four months of a six-month sentence. According to friends, Goetz, like many crime victims, was devastated by the attack and by the criminal justice system's weak response. He tried to get a permit so he could carry a gun but was turned down. Less than four years later, Goetz had a gun and would use it.

On December 22, 1984, Goetz was again riding a New York City subway. According to his story, four young men approached and demanded five dollars. Goetz pulled a revolver from his belt and fired. "I have five dollars for each of you," he reportedly said as he emptied his .38-caliber pistol, hitting each of his attackers. One of them is apparently permanently paralyzed from the waist down. All four had arrest records, including burglary and armed robbery; three were carrying sharpened screwdrivers at the time.

Goetz's action, which resembled that of the fictional Charles Bronson character in the 1974 movie *Death Wish,* instantly hit a nerve in a public frightened of crime and outraged at the criminal justice system's inability to handle it. In the movie, Bronson, torn by the rape and murder of his wife and daughter, stalks deserted streets luring would-be muggers to their doom. Audiences cheered lustily as each thug was blown away by Bronson's oversize handgun. The movie was, for its hundred or so minutes, a refuge from the fear and a tonic for the helplessness the moviegoers all felt.

Goetz, a real-life "Death Wish" figure, had done what the public knew the criminal justice system would not and could not do: he had hurt three predators and had taken one out of commission. Thousands applauded. In January 1984, syndicated columnist Mike Royko, himself a mugging victim, probably reflected the sentiment of most of his readers when he wrote, "I'm glad Goetz shot them. I don't care what his motives were or whether he has all his marbles. The four punks looked for trouble, and they found it. Case closed." A retired New York City fire chief, who had once been mugged while in uniform, agreed: "This guy rendered a service. He is our John Wayne." Even before Goetz turned himself in, the outspoken civil rights group, the Congress of Racial Equality, offered to pay for his legal defense.

Not everyone supported Goetz, of course. New York Governor Mario Cuomo blasted those who would circumvent the law: "That vigilante spirit that says justice will be done—that impatience with our system of justice—that's not unusual. It's dangerous and it's wrong." Royko's rejoinder to this response was that the justice system simply wasn't working. "Just take a seat in any big city's criminal courtroom," he told his readers, "and watch the dismay on the faces of the victims as judges lightly slap the wrists of meat eaters. More thugs than victims are grinning at the end of a typical day in court."

Bernhard Goetz, of course, is but one fairly recent and well-publicized instance of a citizen taking the law into his own hands either out of fear or from frustration. For example, on the same day Goetz surrendered to the Concord, New Hampshire, police, a forty-six-year-old hit-and-run motorist in New York City was beaten by a mob in a way reminiscent of the ancient "hue and cry." According to a United Press International report, the man had just killed a thirty-one-year-old woman as she stepped from her car onto a Harlem street in New York at two in the morning. A cab driver saw what happened and cut the man off about a block away. A group of about ten men, led by the young woman's boyfriend, descended on the man and kicked and punched him for several minutes until he was rescued by a passing police squad.

Instant "justice" is not only the province of an enraged mob in Harlem or a lonely, frightened, gun-toting mugging victim in a graffiti-marred subway. Men in three-piece suits walking on sunny and fashionable Fifth Avenue in New York also resonate to the instincts of our ancestors. This is how a woman named

Suzanne Geller described the scene in her July 1, 1983, letter of complaint to *The New York Times.* As we shall see, she triggered some energetic responses.

> Early in the afternoon of Tuesday, June 30, one of those clear, comfortable summer days when Fifth Avenue feels like the most exciting city street in the world on which to walk, I was stunned by what is frequently called "an incident," a very sad incident.
>
> Crossing south on 51st Street, I heard a lot of shouting behind me. I turned and saw two men fighting in the middle of the crosswalk. In a fraction of a minute, several pedestrians came to the rescue of the victim of a robbery attempt and forced the perpetrator to the ground.
>
> My respect for the responsible citizens was short-lived. As the would-be robber was held down, he was kicked, punched, stomped and beaten. I watched in horror and heard myself scream, "Stop—stop beating him—stop!" Against the noise of the traffic and ever-increasing mob, this was no more than a whisper. The attack was brief, and when the wounded man was pulled to his feet, the observers clapped and cheered.
>
> The hatred and anger and violence of the well-groomed "responsible" citizens was more frightening than the attempted robbery. To observe the display of uncontrolled animal-like behavior of the attache-case carriers and the support of the crowd left me feeling sick and ashamed.

A week later, *The New York Times* printed a rejoinder:

> I'll bet I felt a lot more "sick and ashamed" than Miss Geller last evening when my sunglasses were snatched from my shirt front on a crowded Columbus Avenue. I was powerless to do anything about a group of eight to 10 so-called kids. . . . It wasn't so easy swallowing the humiliating helplessness, and it wasn't so easy getting to sleep. In fact, I kind of hope to find myself in a "well-groomed" mob like the one Miss Geller saw. . . . I'd like to get in a few kicks myself.

Losing a pair of sunglasses to rowdy teenagers is, of course, minor compared with the murders, rapes, robberies, and burglaries that plague this nation. Yet this man, like Bernhard Goetz in 1981 and millions of crime victims throughout this country, had lost more than property; he had lost his security, his human dignity. Those losses, I am certain, ate at his stomach for a long time. Yet had his attackers been caught, their experience with the justice system would have encouraged further criminal activity rather than deterred it. Another *New York Times* reader responded to Geller's letter with a call to action:

> At a time when the Police Department is understaffed and the criminal justice system is overburdened and ineffective, we must rely more and more on our fellow citizens to come to our defense when we are attacked by street criminals. . . .
>
> If law abiding citizens would fight back with increasing frequency, the muggers of New York would realize that they continue their criminal ways only at the risk of grave personal injury to themselves.

With increasing frequency, citizens *are* fighting back. Several years ago, a truck driver and storefront minister in Buffalo, New York, raised the "hue and cry" against the man he believed had abducted and raped his ten-year-old daughter.

Willie Williams's daughter was taken from her apartment at four in the morning. Twelve hours later, she escaped and fingered a thirty-two-year-old man as the rapist. Williams and twenty-four friends went after the man, who not only had a prior rape conviction but was also out on bail for another sexual assault. According to press reports, the man was savagely beaten. Then, in what the Buffalo police describe as a "fit of rage," Williams plunged a knife into his stomach, wounding but not killing him. The stabbing was filmed by a local television station that had a crew in the area to interview neighbors about the abduction and rape.

Williams, like Goetz, became an instant hero. Although the local district attorney tried to remind people that "the reason we have a whole system of laws is to prevent vigilante-style justice," most sided with Williams. Indeed, Buffalo's mayor said he would have done the same thing if anyone had raped his two preteen daughters. One person, apparently less sanguine about the effectiveness of the criminal justice system than the district attorney, complained that the authorities "should have let that mob rip" the accused "limb from limb."

After centuries of struggle, our legal forebears were able to substitute the rule of law for the lawless instincts of the jungle.

It was not easy, however, to suppress a victim's natural desire for personal revenge. Indeed, during the transition, as one of Henry IV's judges tells us from the yellowed pages of history, a murderer was dragged to his execution by "the dead man's wife and all his kin." This shift from personal revenge to public justice is now complete, but the law's impotence is forcing some in our society to revert. Simply stated, we have so polluted the stream of justice by plea bargaining, by unwarranted leniency, and—in the words of the late Supreme Court Justice Robert H. Jackson—by the discrediting of appropriate "constitutional doctrines for the protection of the innocent by making of them mere technical loopholes for the escape of the guilty," that some citizens, contemptuous of the system's palliative powers, avoid it. A recent survey indicates that almost half of all Americans keep guns in their homes for *protection,* and that one in ten carries some sort of weapon for the same reason. In a very real sense, we are coming full circle. It is a dangerous trip, however, for when people take the law into their own hands, it leaves society lawless and subject to the whims of the strong.

Come with me, as we see what is wrong and what we can do to set it right.

TWO

Compromises With Crime

FIFTY YEARS AGO, Franklin Delano Roosevelt stood on the Capitol steps and took the oath of office for his second term as President of the United States. As he looked out over the nation, he spoke of poverty's terrors. "I see," he said, "one-third of a nation ill-housed, ill-clad, ill-nourished."

That was January 20, 1937, and our country had still not emerged from more than seven years of the dark, debilitating Depression. Today, even the 15 percent who are below the so-called poverty line have far better lives than did their counterparts of the thirties, but crime has ballooned with a deadly malignancy. Indeed, it was during the sustained prosperity of the 1960s and the Great Society public welfare programs that were engineered in that era that crime rates rose the fastest.

Our population has grown some fourfold since 1937, from approximately 60 million then to 235 million today. Yet there are now nine times as many reported rapes, nine times as many reported robberies, and eleven times as many reported burglaries. Although some of the increase can be pegged to better reporting, there is no doubt that we are a nation tormented by crime and the fear of crime.

Crime is, as CBS commentator Bill Moyers noted some years ago, a "terrorism" that "threatens our way of life." Sensing the pulse of America, he added,

> Desperately we crave victories over it, occasions on which to embrace one another in relief that civilization may yet will out. Until then, every compromise with crime is surrender and invites a plague.

Unfortunately, we compromise with crime every day—and we *are* enduring the plague as, on the average, one American is murdered every twenty-five minutes, one is raped every seven minutes, one is robbed every fifty-nine seconds, one is assaulted every forty-nine seconds, and one suffers a burglary every nine seconds.

The major compromise with crime is plea bargaining. Plea bargaining is that bushel basket of practices that are used to encourage guilty pleas from criminal defendants. In exchange for a guilty plea to one or more crimes, a prosecutor promises to reduce the charges to which a defendant will plead (for example, receiving stolen property from burglary), to dismiss or not issue other charges, or to recommend a lenient sentence. It is no wonder that a 1973 report of the U.S. National Advisory Commission on Criminal Justice Standards and Goals concluded,

> Since the prosecutor must give up something in return for the defendant's agreement to plead guilty, the frequent result of plea bargaining is that defendants are not dealt with as severely as might otherwise be the case. Thus plea bargaining results in leniency that reduces the deterrent impact of the law.

Deterrence is, of course, further disabled as the criminal brags about his "deal." One Houston assistant district attorney told Albert W. Alschuler, a law professor who has extensively studied plea bargaining, that "clearly the most important part of our job lies in making defendants think they are getting a good deal."

The permutations of plea bargaining are as varied as snowflakes. The end result, however, is far less pretty. It is, as one early state supreme court called it, "a direct sale of justice." Plea bargaining is rooted in expediency. In return for a break, the criminal agrees to not make waves, to take a slap on the wrist and move on. Plea bargaining ignores the importance of disabling the criminal from his predation; in effect, it makes punishment into merely a cost of doing business. Dean Roscoe Pound of the Harvard Law School studied plea bargaining in the 1920s and called the practice a "license to violate the law."

I offer several fairly recent examples from Wisconsin that are, unfortunately, typical of what happens in courts all over this country every single day.

• Several years ago, a man in his mid-thirties was accused of holding up a gas station and threatening to shoot the operator. The armed robbery was plea bargained down to theft and, despite his having just previously served some eleven and a half years in an out-of-state prison for complicity in the murder of a police officer, he was sentenced to a one-year term at the Milwaukee County House of Correction. A little over a year later, the man was in court again. This time, he was charged with four armed robberies, two of them committed while wearing a mask to conceal his identity.

The maximum possible sentence for armed robbery in Wisconsin is twenty years. Wearing a mask adds another possible five years. As before, the new cases were plea bargained: two of the armed robberies were dismissed, and the man pled guilty to two. The judge, who recognized that the defendant was, in his words, a "dangerous man," imposed a fifteen-year prison term on each of the two convictions, but, following the prosecutor's plea bargaining recommendation, he ordered that the sentences run *concurrently;* that is, he decreed that the imprisonment clocks would run simultaneously. Indeed, at the time he was sentenced, Wisconsin was so generous in its "good time" credits that the defendant, if he earned them all, faced a maximum imprisonment of just seven and a half years—less than two years per armed robbery. Eligible for parole after only six months, he was released in 1984 after serving four years of his term. In March of 1986, he was arrested by federal authorities for selling heroin to an undercover officer and for offering to get a half-kilogram (just over a pound) more in exchange for $16,000.

• A defendant who was already charged with a five-year felony of conspiracy to manufacture methamphetamine was accused of committing five foodstore and pharmacy robberies, three—and possibly four—of them while armed with a gun. Four of the charges were dropped in exchange for his guilty plea to the fifth. He pled guilty to the drug charge and was sentenced to three years in prison. He was given a concurrent five-year sentence on the robbery conviction. In a very real sense, he received a pass not only on four of the robberies but on the drug conviction as well. If he earns all of his "good time" credits, he will be back on the streets after a little more than three years. Again, he would be eligible for parole—at the parole board's discretion—after just six months.

• A twenty-one-year-old man was accused of jumping into the victim's car and, at knife point, taking the car and his money. The police alertly spotted and pursued the stolen auto; the man rammed their squad car, injuring one of the officers. The original charges of armed robbery and endangering safety by conduct regardless of life (a five-year felony) were plea bargained: the defendant denied his guilt but accepted conviction on the armed robbery count. (As we will see later, this is one of the many little fictions some courts permit in order to facilitate plea bargaining.) He pled guilty to a reduced misdemeanor charge of injuring a person by "reckless driving." He received a three-year suspended sentence and three years probation for the armed robbery and a suspended one-year sentence plus two years probation, with the requirement that he serve ninety days at the Milwaukee County House of Correction during nonworking hours for the reckless driving conviction. The sentences were ordered to run concurrently.

• A young man was known as the "shadow burglar" because he eluded capture while committing over fifty burglaries. When he was finally caught, he agreed to plead guilty to six counts of burglary, one count of attempted burglary, and one count of theft in return for not being charged with the additional forty-five burglaries. Although the assistant district attorney, in presenting the deal to the judge, recommended "long term incarceration," the judge praised the twenty-one-year-old man for his "cooperation" and sentenced him to six ten-year terms on the burglary charges, a five-year term on the attempted burglary, and nine months on the theft. But he ordered that they run *concurrently*. The burglar received, in effect, one sentence for eight convictions and more than fifty crimes. This is typical for the spree criminal: the more crimes committed in a short period of time, the less likely he or she will be punished for each. If the "shadow burglar" earns all of his "good time" credits, he will be released from prison in less than five and a half years—one and a quarter months per crime. If he is paroled earlier (as most felons are), he will be out on the streets and probably into people's homes sooner than that.

Many plea bargains occur in sexual assault cases. The ostensible reason is to spare the victim from the additional trauma of having to testify about her or—occasionally—his degrading experience. Although there are times when the victim will accept having the assailant slapped on the wrist in order to avoid reliving the horrible event at a trial, many victims want to see their rapist receive appropriate punishment and are willing to help. As in the following example, many cases are plea-bargained nevertheless.

The defendant was charged with first-degree sexual assault, which is defined by the statute as "sexual intercourse with another person without consent of that person by use or threat of use of a dangerous weapon." The crime is a twenty-year felony in Wisconsin. At the preliminary examination, the seventeen-year-old victim testified that she had met the thirty-one-year-old defendant at a bar and that, by putting a knife to her throat, he had forced her to go upstairs to his apartment. Once there, he forced her to undress. This is how she described her ordeal in response to questions by the assistant district attorney:

Q: Where was the knife when he told you to take off your clothes?

A: In his hand. And then when I took my clothes off, he said "Lay down" and laid the knife beside him on the bed on a little table beside him, and then—then he said—then he say "Give me a blow job."

Q: What did you do?

A: Then I gave it to him. I wasn't going to give it to him. He said "I ain't playing with you." Then he picked that knife up and put it right here. Then I just put my head down and started doing it.

Q: Okay. What happened next?

A: And then he told me—then when he—then we was doing it about five or ten minutes. Then he says—then I say "I'm tired." Then he said—then he say "Keep doing it 'til I tell you to stop." And then he got up. He went to the drawer and got a rubber.

Q: And what did he do with it?

A: And he put it on and then he said "get up top of me and fuck me." Then I got up top of him. He said, "I ain't playing with you. I slap the shit out of you." That's when he jumped up and got the stick from over his bed.

Q: What did the stick look like?

A: I don't—it was like a little head on the top, and it was real pointy at the end.

Q: How long was the stick about?
A: About like that.
Q: Show me with both your hands.

At that point the victim demonstrated how long the stick was, and the lawyers agreed that it was about two feet long. Her story continued:

Q: What did he do with the stick?
A: He had it in his hand like this. Then he say and then I was feeling like beginning to cry. He said "You drop a tear, I bust you upside your damn head with this stick." Then I was going to cry. Then I was crying like this, and he said "You just drop a tear." That's when he picked that knife up and had it like this, and he had the stick in his hand like this.
Q: Now, he had the knife next to your neck, is that right?
A: Yup.
Q: He had the stick in his other hand?
A: Right.

According to the girl, the knife was eight inches long and had a four-inch blade. She related what happened next.

A: I got on top of him and stuck his thing in me.
Q: You've got to tell the judge what you mean by "his thing."
A: His penis in my vagina."

She finally escaped when he went to the bathroom:

> And he told me to wait in the kitchen, "You better not try nothing" and when he used the bathroom I ran and grabbed my coat and ran down the steps and he ran to the door on the top of the steps with the knife butt naked, and I ran out the door and it was two men sitting in a van and told them "Take me for help, this man just raped me."

Despite all of this, the case was plea-bargained moments before a jury was to be selected for the trial. The charge was reduced to third-degree sexual assault (the five-year felony of nonconsensual sexual intercourse), and the judge gave the defendant two years probation, plus incarceration evenings and weekends for the first sixty days.

One common plea-bargain variation to which I have already alluded is where the prosecutor promises the defendant and his lawyer that he will recommend a lenient sentence in return for a guilty plea. Although the judge is not bound by the recommendation, it usually carries great weight. If the judge goes along with the recommendation *because* of the plea bargain, the criminal gets a lesser punishment than the facts warrant. If the judge would have imposed the recommended sentence—or one close to it—in any event and irrespective of the plea-bargain, the defendant will *believe* that he is getting a break. In either case, in the reality of a break or its perception, the criminal justice system's credibility is weakened.

Consider incest, where victims have always had a hard time getting justice. Incest is a triple crime: the victim is raped, her psyche is damaged if not destroyed, and, of course, the family is ravaged. For too long, however, incest has been treated differently from other serious crimes. In a forceful letter to the editor of *The New York Times,* Philadelphia Common Pleas Judge Lois G. Forer complained about what she saw as the trivialization of incest by doctors and lawyers:

> Prosecutors who demand long prison sentences for thieves frequently recommend psychiatric probation for the incest/rapist, arguing (1) he is not really a criminal because it was only his daughter, (2) the father is supporting the family, and (3) the child has been examined by a doctor, who reports that she was not injured.

Judge Forer, who as an attorney represented child victims, disputed these rationales and reiterated what should be obvious but is all too often obscured:

> Incest is a serious problem. It is also a serious crime. It should be dealt with seriously. No rapist should be permitted to return to the home where the child victim is. No woman should be coerced into having sex with her daughter's rapist under the rubric of therapy.

Nevertheless, another Pennsylvania judge actually dismissed an incest case saying that it was a "family affair" whose resolution was best "kept in the home." Similarly, in a recent Cincinnati case, an eight-year-old girl was sexually assaulted a number of times by her uncle and her mother's boyfriend. The men were allowed to plead guilty to four reduced charges and were placed on probation for three years in addition to a ninety-day jail term.

The judge explained that the little girl had "consented" and that, after all, it was "in the family." According to an Associated Press dispatch, the men's confessions "indicated that the child was not forced to participate but was reluctant to continue at times."

The pattern of what Judge Forer justly condemned is revealed by the story of a man with whose crimes it took the legal system more than ten years to cope. First, to use Judge Forer's word, it "trivialized" them. Then it plea bargained some of them away.

In September 1979, a forty-year-old father appeared in court charged with the twenty-year felony of first-degree sexual assault for having had intercourse with his seven-year old daughter. There were apparently no problems of proof; according to the criminal complaint, he admitted it. Yet over five months later, the case was plea bargained down to incest, a ten-year felony. The sentence: he would have to spend three years on probation and serve five consecutive weekends at the Milwaukee County House of Correction. The sentencing judge made cooperation with a psychotherapist a condition of probation. At the time, the psychotherapist worked for one of Milwaukee's many companies providing private counseling.

This was not the first time the man had gotten into trouble for sexually abusing a child: nine years earlier, he had received two years probation for sexually assaulting another young girl. Nor would it be the last.

The man's three years of probation expired on April 21, 1983. According to the official probation discharge sheet, dated August 30, 1983, he had "satisfied all conditions" of his probation. Nevertheless, on June 6, 1983—ironically, two months *before* the discharge report—he was back in court, charged with two counts of sexual assault. According to the complaint, he had intercourse with the young daughter again. She was now eleven. The investigating detective reported that the little girl told him she had been assaulted "on numerous times in the past." The man was also accused of raping his older daughter, aged nineteen. Like her younger sister, the nineteen-year-old told the detective that her father "has done this to her on numerous occasions prior to this time." The maximum penalty for the first charge was twenty years; the maximum penalty for the second charge was ten years, because the victim was older.

Like the earlier time, there were apparently no problems of proof: not only did the older daughter testify at the sentencing hearing, but the defendant had admitted the crimes. Yet here again, the case was plea bargained. In return for the defendant's guilty plea to both charges, the assistant district attorney recommended imprisonment for two to three years, followed by probation, although he understood that the crimes were "two of the most serious offenses in the State of Wisconsin."

The assistant district attorney told the judge that he recognized that there might be

> some people who may say a two to three year recommendation is not severe enough, that the defendant should be sentenced to 20, 30 years in prison, but I think if we do that we would essentially be locking the defendant up, throwing the key away and not really giving him any chance.

The defense lawyer argued for probation and more counseling. In support of his argument, he called to the witness stand a psychotherapist from the company that had previously treated the defendant.

The psychotherapist testified that he had been seeing the defendant two to three times a week ever since three days after the initial June 6 court appearance, and that he and another therapist were seeing the family about once a week. He proposed that the sessions continue and advised against any incarceration. The defense lawyer then asked:

> All right, what—from what you know of [the defendant], um, and you were recently made aware of a 1970 conviction of—of, um, taking liberties with a minor that was not a member of his family, do you know anything about [his] background that would lead you to believe he was a danger to anyone else in the community other than his family?

The psychotherapist replied, "No, sir."

On cross-examination, however, he admitted he could not be certain that the man would not, again, sexually assault someone.

The older daughter also testified at the sentencing hearing. Her brief testimony is important for what she did not say as well as for what she did say. This is how she responded to her father's lawyer:

Q: Now you were—you are one of the victims in the case that brings him before the court, is that right?
A: That's right, sir.
Q: All right. Now you were in court when I outlined a sentencing recommendation for the judge to follow, were you not?
A: Yes, I was, sir.
Q: Did you hear what I outlined?
A: I don't remember.
Q: Well, did you hear what I said?
A: Yes.
Q: All right. And what I basically said, to save time, is that I want your husband, or I'm sorry, I want your father to stay in—in Milwaukee and whatever time he is going to do—at the House of Correction rather than going to prison. Do you remember me saying that?
A: Yes, sir.
Q: Okay. Now, which would you rather have happen to your father?
A: I don't want him to go to prison. I—I've seen movies and stuff and it doesn't look too good.
Q: Are you—would you be afraid of your father if he was in the House of Correction?
A: No.

The assistant district attorney then asked her a few questions:

Q: Your father has assaulted you on a number of occasions, isn't that correct?
A: Yes, sir.
Q: And he has done the same thing to [your younger sister], isn't that correct?
A: Yes, sir.
Q: And those assaults were pretty frightening for you, weren't they?
A: Yes, sir.
Q: And you do know that in the past when your dad got in trouble like this he didn't go to prison, he was given a chance and given probation to try to get his head together. Correct?

A: Yes, and it didn't work out too well.

Q: And now in this case here, notwithstanding what he did to you, you still think he should be given another chance?

A: I—you know I don't—I don't want him to be sent to prison, you know, but I don't want him to be in the house—in our house anymore.

Q: Okay. Is that because you're fearful not only for it happening to you again but to your sister?

A: Yes, sir.

Q: Okay. When—when your dad came back into the home last time, did you have some concerns then that this stuff might start happening again?

A: I—I had some concerns, but I didn't think it would happen again.

A psychologist employed by the Wisconsin Division of Corrections called by the prosecutor criticized the probation/therapy plan proposed by the defendant's lawyer:

> I have a couple of concerns with it. One, I think it does in fact diminish the severity of the offense. While testing [the defendant], I noticed something that was very clear to me in that there's a definite manipulative quality in terms of how he perceives what he has done. That concerned me. While I am clearly empathetic [sic] with him in terms of his remorse, I do feel that we would be remiss in our duty if we did not chastise him at this point.

Then later, in response to questions posed by the defendant's lawyer, she touched on the therapeutic value of punishment:

> [In prison] he would have the opportunity to understand that his behavior cannot go unaccounted for. He would have to recognize himself that he has become a criminal. At the House of Correction, having talked to many men and women while there, they tend to see themselves in a transitory state where they are not really considered criminals. In prison, you realize that you are, in fact, a criminal. This is part of the punishing attitude that I am—I am addressing at this time, something I think [the defendant] needs to appreciate. . . . The value of the prison again, I say, is that I think [he] needs punishment.

The judge, of course, was not bound by the prosecutor's recommendation. Nevertheless, he gave the defendant a prison sentence of, in effect, three years and ten months, to be followed by five years probation.

No one but the judge will ever really know whether the defendant actually received a light sentence in return for his guilty plea. Nevertheless, the perception of plea bargain–induced leniency is almost as corrosive as the reality.

Plea bargaining, of course, requires judicial participation. In Wisconsin, for example, no prosecutor may dismiss or reduce a criminal charge unless the judge agrees, and no judge, in any state, is required to give the sentence worked out by the prosecution and defense. If the rule were otherwise, of course, we would rarely need judges. Most criminal charges are resolved by pleas, and if judges were bound by the plea deals and had to impose the recommended sentence, the sentencing function could, in the great bulk of cases, be taken over by clerks who could use a rubber stamp like this:

Sentence Imposed

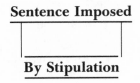

By Stipulation

Most judges, for reasons we will explore later, go along with plea bargaining. No case highlights this more than the story of the so-called "Milwaukee Three."

The late 1960s and early 1970s were turbulent times in this country. In the summer of 1968, Hubert Humphrey—then Vice President of the United States—kissed a television screen that had just shown his nomination for President by the Democratic convention meeting in Chicago. Outside his hotel room, hundreds of radicals fought with police; some of the bystanders, caught in the maelstrom, were battered by both sides. The war in Vietnam and increasing tension between the races had polarized this nation. Dozens of groups—some famous, others not—coalesced around charismatic leaders and author Tom Wolfe chided those he termed the "radical chic" for their spiritual and financial support of thugs and hoodlums. One of these groups, the paramilitary Black Panther party, was born in 1966. Its paradoxical goals of feeding and educating black children and armed terror attracted support from many disenchanted black youngsters all over the country. Almost immediately, there were violent confrontations with authorities.

On a late September night in 1969, a month before Black Panther chieftain Bobby Seale would be ordered bound and gagged in the middle of his riot conspiracy trial in front of Chicago Federal Judge Julius J. Hoffman, and two and a half months before Chicago Panther leaders Fred Hampton and Mark Clark would be killed in a police raid, three young Panthers were driving alongside a Sears parking lot on the north side of Milwaukee. A young patrolman, walking his lonely beat, saw the Volkswagen approach. Suddenly, a flash of gun metal caught his eye. In a move that may have saved him his life, he dropped to the ground. A shotgun blast tore through the air where he had been standing.

As the car sped off, the officer relayed its license number over the police radio. In a few minutes, the car was spotted by a police squad, and after a brief struggle, Jesse Lee White, Booker T. Collins, Jr., and Earl Leverette were arrested. The three were charged with attempted murder under Wisconsin's "party to a crime" statute, which makes those who help someone else commit a crime as guilty as the person who actually commits it. The maximum penalty: imprisonment for thirty years.

The arrest of the "Milwaukee Three," as they soon came to be called, was a natural lightning rod for the young and the not-so-young self-proclaimed radicals in that era of disenchantment. Groups rallied round, and there were the *de rigueur* rallies.

The protests culminated in a six-hour festival the Sunday preceding the trial's start. The event, as poignantly described by *Milwaukee Journal* reporter Walter W. Morrison, was a mélange of flea-market capitalism and songs praising revolutionary terror, flavored with the smells of barbecuing chicken and marijuana. Three weeks earlier, a young physics researcher had been killed when a terrorist bomb destroyed a University of Wisconsin building in Madison, Wisconsin. In its September 7, 1970, issue, *Time* magazine told its millions of readers,

> A group called "the New Year's Gang" claimed responsibility for the bombing and promised more explosions unless its

demands are met by October 30. Among them: removal of ROTC, the release of three Milwaukee Black Panthers charged with shooting a policeman and, pathetically, elimination of parietal hours for freshmen women.

It was a time of tension and turmoil.

Jury selection began Monday morning, September 14. Outside the courthouse, demonstrators chanted, "Free Bobby! Free The Three! Overthrow the Bourgeoisie!" "Bobby" was Bobby Seale.

One of the three men, twenty-five-year-old Leverette, was able to make his $5,000 cash bail. The others were held in custody. That afternoon, Leverette—who, the evidence would later show, was the car's driver—skipped town. The trial of White and Collins continued.

On September 22, 1970—one year to the day after White and Collins were arrested—a jury found each of them guilty of attempted murder as "party to a crime." White had, according to the evidence, shot at the patrolman from the Volkswagen's front seat while Collins sat in the back. Immediately after the jury returned its verdict, a lawyer representing the two men asked that the sentencing be put over "for a couple days to allow us to further confer with our clients." The judge replied that he found "no reason or no necessity for so doing" and that he intended "to dispose of this matter this evening." He added, "I will hear any recommendations which you may have, however." The defense lawyer, in a brief statement, asked for leniency:

> Your Honor, as far as Jesse White is concerned, the Court is familiar with the past criminal record of Jesse White. The record contains no felony convictions. It contains, I believe, two misdemeanor convictions. The criminal record of Jesse White is far from extensive.
>
> As far as the record is concerned for Booker Collins, Jr., he has been convicted, as far as I know, of one city disorderly conduct charge in his past history. Besides that, Booker has a distinguished war record. He has spent over a year in Vietnam, receiving the Purple Heart. He was put in for a Bronze Star for his service in Vietnam. Because of the absence of this criminal record, further because of his distinguished military service on behalf of his country, I believe this Court should take those matters into consideration in this case.

I have known Booker and Jesse. I have worked with them now on this case. I know both of the men, and at all times they have been totally cooperative with counsel; and I know them to be of the highest character.

I know the charge they have been convicted of is, of course, the most serious—one of the most serious crimes that are in the books that they have in the state. However, I think the Court should take into consideration that this is not the type of case where we are dealing with two men with extensive criminal records. You are dealing with two men, Your Honor, both very young men—one man 20, one man 24—I'm sorry, I have both ages wrong, 21 and 22. Both are very young men.

I believe to give these men the maximum penalty in this case would be doing not only a disservice to them but also a disservice to the community. I don't believe that under the circumstances and history of these two men, that that kind of penalty would be called for in this case.

I also have been advised by both Jesse and Booker Collins that they wish to exercise their right of allocution.

Allocution is the term given to a defendant's last statement before sentencing. The moment of allocution is one of those clock-stopping times in life when the air hangs heavy with silence. In an ideal world, of course, no human should ever have sway over another. But an ideal world is a world without crime. As long as men and women violate the rights of others, their own freedoms will be circumscribed by strangers.

The judge asked the defendants to step forward. Jesse White spoke first:

Defendant White: First of all, I want to say the jury did convict us of a crime that we didn't commit, and the long past history in America of never showing a Black man in this country no type of justice in the past 400 years. When we first was kidnapped off the street and charged with the charge of attempted murder, which we knew nothing about, we started experiencing the same thing that our ancestors and grandmothers and parents have been experiencing since Black people first been in this country, this injustice, you know; and the way I see it, every Black person in America today is nothing but a slave because ain't no justice in this country.

The Court: I don't consider that allocution in connection with this matter. Mr. Collins, do you have anything you want to say?

Defendant Collins: Right.

Defendant White: Can I say what my feeling—

The Court: If you have something that is not in that vein, you may address your remarks to the Court concerning sentencing in this matter but not political or sociologically oriented.

Defendant White: I'm not saying something political. I'm just speaking what I think is true.

The Court: I'll hear from you, Mr. Collins.

Defendant Collins: Well, first I agree with him along the lines of injustice. This is what we have experienced, and like you said the trial is not political; but everything else out there attests that it is, you know, because like the tight security, the bond being raised and everything, saying that the trial is political because we don't receive any justice. They don't have any evidence to convict us. They convict on any type of evidence they want to throw together and convict a Black man. It's enough to convict a Black man.

The Court: I've heard enough of that, too. There are many, many, many thousands of your people who would violently disagree with you, as does this Court. This jury found you guilty of what this Court considers to be not merely proof beyond a reasonable doubt but proof beyond all possible doubt.

Then it was the district attorney's turn. He disputed the defendants' claim of a frame-up and recounted the extensive investigative efforts that preceded his charging them with attempted first-degree murder. "I think one of the most tragic aspects of this case," he concluded, "is that by these false claims these persons have developed support among a few; and it has been the tragic aspect, a gross misleading of society to the belief that this was not other than what the jury found. In other words, a cold-blooded, virtually fiendish attempted assassination of a City of Milwaukee police officer." He then made his recommendation:

> As the Court is aware, the defendants did not testify, and I'm sure that the Court will give that appropriate consideration. Other than that, I think a very substantial sentence is called for.

The judge agreed and sentenced each of them to the thirty-year maximum.

I have told all of this at some length because the story of the

"Milwaukee Two" contrasts with what happened to the car's driver, Earl Leverette. Leverette, who had skipped bail after a lunch break in the midst of jury selection on the first day, was finally caught in the fall of 1971. Compared to what had happened a year earlier, everything was sweetness and light. The tensions were fewer, and Leverette was permitted to plead no contest to the charge of attempted murder. His lawyer told the judge that "there has been some conversation and discussion with the District Attorney's office" and they had agreed "that if Mr. Leverette were to change his plea from not guilty to one of no contest to the charge in this case, that the District Attorney's office of Milwaukee County would not prosecute Mr. Leverette for bail jumping, a charge that would arise out of his non-appearance at an earlier trial scheduled in this matter, and that on the acceptance of the no contest plea, it would recommend to the Court that a period of incarceration—a sentence of incarceration be imposed, leaving the term of that sentence to the discretion of the Court."

After the judge satisfied himself that the defendant knew what he was doing, the assistant district attorney made his formal recommendation:

> It's been the position of the State since the inception of this matter that it was an out and out attempt at an assassination of a policeman. The defendant here in court today did not take a passive role in the attempted assassination of Officer Schroder; he was the operator of the vehicle. I think that is sustained unequivocally by the evidence.
>
> He operated that vehicle so as to position it for the person who fired the shot. He moved it from the center southeast bound lane of the highway into the curb lane, and the vehicle slowed to two to three miles per hour. That, in the State's opinion, is the effort of the defendant and his companions to give the shooter of the weapon the best possible shot at the officer as opposed to that taken from a speeding vehicle or a vehicle moving at what can be characterized as a normal rate of speed along a city street.
>
> The fact that Officer Schroder is not dead is somewhat within the realm of miracles in my opinion. The weapon fired at him contained a charge of double O buck, as evidenced by the empty shell contained in it, and it was confiscated a few moments later. Double O buck is, I think common knowledge, a large projec-

tile, a number of large projectiles contained within a shotgun shell. The effects of striking a human being with such a charge from a weapon of the sort of State's Exhibit No. 1 I think can be concluded as fatal.

I find that that type of conduct is such that anyone who would engage in it, would aid and abet a person who fired the lethal shot, is the type of conduct that the State must demand that the person guilty of it be incarcerated. I ask the Court to incarcerate this defendant for a period of time within the Court's discretion. I would ask the Court to carefully reflect upon the heinousness of this crime; the defendant's involvement therein not as a passive participant; the act of helping position the gun platform as it were for an accurate shot at a human being, at an officer of the law.

When it was his turn, Leverette's lawyer disputed that Leverette had slowed the car to permit an accurate shot. He pointed out that—as with White and Collins—Leverette had a minimal prior record. He also asked the judge to consider that his client had entered a plea of no contest to the charge. When Leverette had nothing to add before being sentenced, the judge reviewed testimony from the earlier trial concerning Leverette's role in the shooting. He said he agreed with the prosecutor's "appraisal of that characterization of the offense herein involved." He then listed the factors he would consider in passing sentence:

- the defendant's age (he was twenty-four at the time of the shooting; the others were twenty and twenty-one);
- his lack of a prior felony record (the others did not have felony records either); and
- the fact that he had served a year for the resisting arrest charge arising out of the same incident (the others had also).

Finally, he came to the apparent crux of the matter: "and most substantially the fact that this defendant, by the proffered change of plea which has been accepted by the Court has not in any way controverted the testimony adduced nor has he gambled with the conscience of a jury in the trial of this matter." He sentenced the defendant to a term of not more than ten years.

It might seem strange to use failure to gamble "with the conscience of a jury" as a basis for a lenient sentence to the man who, according to a view of the evidence shared by both the prosecutor and the trial judge, had helped White get an accurate shot by carefully maneuvering the car *and* who had jumped bail. Nevertheless, this payoff for a guilty plea—and, perhaps in some cases, a concomitant penalty for going to trial—was and is the policy in many criminal courts. *New York Times* reporter Sam Roberts thus recently described a New York judge's way of "moving cases." A man appearing before the judge was accused of criminal possession of heroin and cocaine. "I'd give him a year on each count, concurrent, if he takes it today," the judge told the defense lawyer, "one to three consecutive if he doesn't."

Most judges won't admit to punishing a defendant who goes to trial. Others, however, are not shy about it. In the late sixties, for example, Washington, D.C., Federal Judge John J. Sirica— the man whose tenacious pursuit of Watergate brought down President Nixon—sentenced an eighteen-year-old man to five to fifteen years in prison for holding up a bus driver with a toy pistol. Although convicted by a jury, the young man continued to maintain his innocence. This obviously annoyed Judge Sirica, who, in passing sentence, commented, "If you had pleaded guilty to this offense, I might have been more lenient with you."

The court of appeals, in a decision written by then Chief Judge David Bazelon, one of the country's most articulate liberal jurists, sent the case back to the trial court for resentencing. In part of the decision not joined in by his colleagues, Judge Bazelon slammed plea bargaining as an unnecessary interference with a defendant's right to trial. He pointed out that we would surely not condone a system where defendants were fined for exercising their constitutional rights on the one hand or, on the other, bribed to give them up. Why, he asked, do we then accept a system where defendants are either punished for going to trial or—looked at from the other side—rewarded with lenient sentences for not going to trial? "The answer," he deduced, "may well lie in the tendency to define due process by past process." He meant that we often accept the familiar without rational analysis out of mere force of habit; this is the "paml shade" syndrome we will look at in Chapter 5. The whole question, however, goes back to fundamental fairness: whether we will, as a civilized society, enforce criminal laws fairly and impartially, with decisions based on what is just—what is just for the accused, for the victim, and for the community—rather than expedient.

Unjust leniency for others can, understandably, stick in the craw of those who have been treated with just severity. A decade after the car driver in the "Milwaukee Three" case was rewarded for his admission of guilt, Jesse White was back in court—my court. He was asking for a reduction in his thirty-year sentence, and his argument was basically this:

1. I am guaranteed a right to a jury trial by the United States and Wisconsin constitutions.
2. I should be able to exercise that right without being afraid that if I lose I will be punished merely because I chose to go to trial.
3. The other judge obviously gave Leverette a break because he had not, in his words, "gambled with the conscience of a jury."
4. Since I got thirty years and Leverette only got ten years, I was punished for exercising my constitutional right to a jury trial.

I agreed with White's argument that no one should be punished simply because he or she wishes to go to trial. Nevertheless, I denied his request. As the shooter, he was clearly the most culpable of the three, and his sentence was appropriate. Furthermore, although the bail-jumping driver benefited from the plea-bargained deal, I did not believe that White had been penalized for going to trial.

White attempted to portray himself as deserving release because he was thoroughly rehabilitated:

> I have thought about things that have happened during the 60s and prior to the 60s and things that could have led to those incidents, and I see certain—whether the court accepts this or not—certain types of brainwashes and so forth that were instilled into the mind of young people and still are, you know, things that I couldn't recognize or I wasn't mature enough to recognize at that time and so forth. The court, if it has anything to do with emotions, which I don't understand too much

about, should have considered those factors, the political factors which were brought on by the education that was being given, to Black people in particular, at that time in the community by various organizations and so forth. The age, you know, I think the court should consider the age of the struggle that was going on within the community and the age of the people in the community that were being—that was called at the time education, but more so brainwashing.

However, the question of whether a prisoner has been rehabilitated is something that a parole board must answer, and so far, apparently, White has not succeeded in persuading its members that he is ready to be released.

White has been in prison for more than a decade. He has seen men who have committed crimes worse than his come and go. In 1983, he again tried to have his sentence lowered—this time to twenty years, the new statutory maximum for attempted murder. The judge to whom the case was assigned denied the request. In an articulate letter in support of his petition, White—with only an occasional misspelling—reported that he has "seen Rapist, Armed Robbers and even Murderours receive time cuts from various courts." His observations are forceful reminders that we are, in Moyers's words, compromising with crime.

THREE

Hands of a Leper

JUDGES IN WISCONSIN, as in most states and in the federal system, are generalists: we hear both civil and criminal cases. Most trial judges did at least some criminal work before assuming the bench, either as prosecutors or as defense lawyers. As children of the system, many accept plea bargaining the way, I would imagine, those who live in a mill town accept pollution of the local river, as a necessary, if unpleasant, evil. They accept plea bargaining because they fear the criminal justice system could not survive without it.

There are exceptions, of course. Scattered across this nation are judges who, like United States District Court Judge Herbert J. Stern of Newark, New Jersey, believe that one should not bargain with criminals. Stern is a former prosecutor. When he was appointed U.S. attorney for New Jersey in 1973, one of the first things he did was to send the following memorandum to his assistants:

> This is to remind all Assistant United States Attorneys that it is my inflexible position that I am opposed to plea bargaining. This has been the position of the office since I first came to it as an Assistant and it remains the position of the office.
>
> When I say "plea bargaining," I mean a situation where the Assistant participates in conversations with the defendant or his lawyer and the judge as to what the sentence will be if the defendant agrees to enter a plea of guilty. In my view, such conversations are in derogation of the spirit of what the entire criminal justice system is all about and I see no necessity, such as an overburdening of criminal calendars, which would justify us in engaging in such discussions and thereby turning the processes of justice into a market place of bargain and sale.

Unlike Stern and most of my federal and state colleagues, my roots are exclusively on the civil side of the law. A 1965 graduate of Columbia Law School in New York, I clerked for a United States district court judge in that city for two years and then served a little less than three years as an appellate attorney in the civil division of the United States Department of Justice in Washington, D.C. I moved to Wisconsin in 1970, wrote a couple of books, and from mid-1974 through 1975, was a news reporter for one of Milwaukee's television network affiliates. I resumed the full-time practice of civil law in 1976, while also hosting a television show called "A Fine Point."

"A Fine Point" was, in a sense, a local version of Phil Donahue's program. In the course of its run from mid-1975 through the summer of 1978, the show explored a variety of topics, ranging from the controversies surrounding the Kennedy and King assassinations to transsexuality. My guests included such national figures as economics Nobel laureate Milton Friedman, writers Elie Wiesel and Paul Erdman, John and Maureen Dean of Watergate fame, ERA opponent Phyllis Schlafly, and atheist activist Madalyn Murray O'Hair. I even had a fellow on the show who claimed to be a hit man for the mob. It was a fairly popular show, and no doubt the exposure it gave me helped me in my 1978–79 campaign for a vacancy on the Wisconsin circuit court.

Lawyers in Wisconsin become judges in two ways. If a judge retires or dies in the middle of his or her term, the governor appoints a successor, and the person appointed has to run in the next regularly scheduled election. If a judge retires at the end of his or her term or if the seat has been newly created and is therefore open, there is just an election. Judicial elections in Wisconsin are nonpartisan, and although party affiliation is a significant factor in gubernatorial appointments to the bench, it plays almost no role in the election itself—at least in Milwaukee County.

By and large, judges come from established cliques in the legal community. The largest such group in Milwaukee County is the district attorney's office, with approximately sixty lawyers. Nearly a quarter of the thirty-seven trial judges in Milwaukee have served in that office. My election was different, however. I was elected to the bench without the active support of any lawyer group, much less the criminal bar. I was not tied to the system.

Although I had never been a prosecutor or a defense lawyer,

my first three years as a judge were spent hearing criminal cases exclusively, involving first juveniles and then, after a year, adults. The evils of plea bargaining were apparent immediately.

Most of us have an inner accountability, a conscience, if you will, which guides our actions. Simply put, most of us do what's right because we would feel funny if we did not. For most of us that is enough. That ultimate cynic, H. L. Mencken, once called conscience the "little voice which tells us someone is watching."

Unfortunately, some persons with impaired inner accountabilities will break the law if they believe no one is watching. Witness the dramatic increases in crime during the seven-month period starting in September 1944 when wartime Denmark was denuded of its regular police force and during the 1969 one-day Montreal police strike. As *The Toronto Star* contemporaneously reflected on the Montreal tragedy, "What was really frightening was the way in which normally law-abiding people indulged in looting, brawling and setting fires." Even in ancient, less lawful times, the absence of sanction left not even rudimentary restraint. Until the late thirteenth century in England, the King's Peace died when the King died and could not be reinstituted until a new monarch was lawfully crowned. "Evil-doers were not slow to seize such an opportunity when it came," British legal historian Frederick Pollock tells us. "We read in the English Chronicle," he reports, "under the date of 1135, that on the death of Henry I 'there was tribulation soon in the land, for every man that could forthwith robbed another.' "

Unless they are to wreak havoc on the rest of us, people with impaired inner accountabilities, people whose consciences will not check their antisocial behavior when no one is watching, must be controlled. Some can be controlled by imposing external accountability. That's the theory behind having the criminal law draw certain behavioral boundaries:

"Step over this line and commit a burglary, and you will be punished in this way."

• "Step over that line and commit a robbery, and you will be punished in that way."

And so on. But external accountability through punishment will only deter crime if the sanctions are believable and if they outweigh crime's benefits.

Although some potential offenders may be kept from criminal activity by the threat of punishment, there are others, the recidivists, who can be controlled only by isolating them from the rest of society, what criminologists call *incapacitation* usually through incarceration. Centuries ago, exile was a form of isolation. The ultimate incapacitation is, of course, capital punishment.

If criminal activity may be prevented by deterrence on the one hand and incapacitation on the other, what about rehabilitation? Rehabilitation, which many see as a more humane way of dealing with crime, is a chameleon concept. It is only effective if it either bolsters an offender's inner accountability—his conscience—or enhances the law's credibility not only by giving the offender a taste of prison but by giving him marketable skills—something tangible to lose.

Conscience is a composite trait infused with elements of heredity, upbringing, and environment. As Harvard Professors James Q. Wilson and Richard J. Herrnstein tell us in their book *Crime and Human Nature,* it is generally fixed early in life, and there is not much that can be done to alter its basic structure. Rehabilitation directed at reforming conscience is, to quote Gibbon's remark about education, "seldom of much efficacy except in those happy dispositions where it is almost superfluous." We can, however, give the offender the tools with which he or she can fashion a stake in society, and we can then make the loss of that stake painful. This, as noted Norwegian law professor and criminologist Johannes Andenaes teaches, is the very essence of deterrence: "the risk of discovery and the cost of punishment outweighing the temptation to commit crime." While rehabilitation can thus give a synergistic boost to deterrence, it is powerless unless the system is credible.

The humanity in all of us wishes that programs to rehabilitate criminals—money, jobs, and education—would work without the threat of punishment. How wonderful it would be if crime could be smothered by industry, learning, and love. Yet, unfortunately, attempts at nonpenal rehabilitation have generally failed.

The benchmark analysis of the effectiveness of rehabilitation efforts on criminals was conducted under the direction of criminologist Robert Martinson, who, in the early 1970s, along with two colleagues, evaluated some 231 published studies. Their gloomy conclusion was that "with few and isolated exceptions, the rehabilitative efforts that have been reported so far have had no appreciable effect on recidivism." Five years later, this was confirmed by a study sponsored by the National Research Council of the National Academy of Sciences. Since sugar and honey have failed, the law must use vinegar.

We usually talk about deterrence as a force to encourage conformity with what most of us would agree are tenets of moral law: prohibitions against murder, rape, arson, burglary, and the like. The prerequisites of successful deterrence—sanctions that are credible and sufficiently unpleasant to make their risk outweigh any potential gain from the activity sought to be deterred—are also effective when the so-called crime is antagonistic to moral law. Johannes Andenaes, calling upon his wartime experience in a 1952 article, writes:

> Consider a blacked-out city in an occupied country. The occupier's order has no moral authority at all—on the contrary, he is the enemy and must be resisted. But even so, hundreds of thousands of families take great care each night to prevent the least crack of light from showing. As if guided by an unseen hand, these countless householders go into action as soon as darkness falls. No one defies the order, because everyone knows that there is not enough to be gained to make the risk worthwhile.

"Yes, but they are law-abiding people," you might reply, "and are used to obeying authority." Yet the experience in Montreal confirms that even some law-abiding people will, if they believe no one is watching or that no one cares, act lawlessly. Indeed, merchants recognize this when they place dummy or real TV cameras in their stores in an attempt to prevent shoplifting. If customers know the cameras are fakes, however, there is little external incentive to obey the law.

We know to keep our hands out of a flame because the very first time (not the second, fifth, or tenth time) we touched fire, it hurt. Those who are impervious to pain, because of a nerve disorder, for example, lack this self-enforcing protective mechanism. We now know that those suffering from leprosy lose their flesh not because it rots from their bodies as was once believed but because, unable to feel pain, they receive no feedback from their injuries. Persons suffering from the disease can, for instance, literally strip the skin from a hand in an attempt to turn a jammed doorknob because they simply do not know when to stop. By the same token, many criminals don't know when to stop because plea bargaining distorts the effective transmission of pain signals so vital to deterrence.

A classic example of this was a young man who admitted to three armed robberies of savings and loan institutions. As the result of a plea bargain, he was placed on probation and was sent to the Milwaukee House of Correction for a year with "work release" privileges. During this time, he was driven around town by House of Correction social workers, ostensibly to help him find work. Twice, they took him to savings and loan branches. He robbed both. Four days after he was freed from his "work release" custody at the House of Correction, he robbed another savings and loan. Convicted, the man finally received a thirty-year prison term.

One day, a young man came before me. His lawyer said he wanted to plead guilty to burglary. The prosecutor was a young but experienced assistant district attorney with the intense black piercing eyes of a Russian saint. He told me that in return for the guilty plea, he was recommending probation. He gave no other reasons: his recommendation was the quid pro quo for the guilty plea. A seventy-one-year-old woman's apartment had been ransacked while she was attending church on Palm Sunday. Among the items stolen was her grandmother's wedding ring.

The young man sat in court with stolid, almost sullen eyes. However, he was no stranger to courtrooms: his juvenile record was extensive and included at least five burglaries, some involving his own grandparents. Indeed, he had just been released from Wisconsin's maximum security juvenile reform school three weeks before the Palm Sunday burglary.

I could hardly believe what was being proposed, and I let everyone, including the defendant, know:

> Well, I will tell you right now, unless there are some things
> not revealed by the pre-sentence report, he is not going to get

probation for a residential burglary committed less than a month after he gets out of [the reformatory].

The defense lawyer, an elderly gentleman appointed to represent the defendant by the state public defender, attempted to make the best of what was clearly a bad situation:

> Well, if the Court please, there is a record here, true, as a juvenile. There is a very slim record since he became 18 years of age. All of these crimes are crimes of poverty. They are crimes of property. There is no physical violence against any person. No one has been hurt by reason of this defendant's conduct.

The young man had turned eighteen just three weeks before the burglary, which probably accounted for the "very slim record" during that time.

The defense lawyer was, of course, wrong when he said his client's crimes were crimes of property. Residential burglaries are people crimes. Those whose houses or apartments have been burglarized lose not only their property but their sense of security as well. It is a terrorizing experience that many victims report as a rape of their most precious environment, their homes. I doubted whether the 71-year-old victim would agree that she had not been hurt.

The defendant, of course, said he was sorry, and he used all the right words:

> I would like to say that I'm sorry for committing the crime that I committed and I would like to get the chance of probation to prove to myself, my family and the Court that I would like another chance and try to make, go to school and just get a chance out there again. I would like to do that, be put on probation for this, get supervision and help from them to help me do this, and I think that with the probation that I can.

Sentencing is never fun. It sounds like a cliché to say that sentencing is an awesome responsibility. But it *is* an awesome responsibility that no degree of concern about crime and its victims can make any easier. Like most judges, I try to explain every sentence so that everyone in the courtroom, including the defendant, will understand.

There are four major factors a judge must consider in passing sentence. The first is the nature of the crime. Was it an armed robbery where three people were pistol-whipped, or did someone pilfer a loaf of bread to feed a starving child?

The second consideration concerns the character of the person being sentenced. Is he or she a first-time offender who made a bad mistake and knows it, or a hardened criminal who will continue to prey on victims unless incarcerated for a long time?

The third factor is perhaps the most important and requires an evaluation of how to best protect the public from the defendant. Will the public be protected if he or she is put on probation, or does protection require isolation from the community in a jail or prison?

The last factor combines elements of the first three. First, there must be an evaluation of the impact any sentence will have on the integrity of the criminal justice system. Is the sentence too harsh under the circumstances, or is it too lenient? Society has a right to be assured that the criminal justice system is working properly. Second, what effect will any sentence have on what is called general deterrence? The deterrent effect of our criminal laws is directly related to the certainty of punishment. Potential criminals must know that their crimes will be punished and that there are no free rides. Third, there is the notion of *desert*. Perhaps scholar Charles E. Silberman put it best when he wrote in his highly regarded book, *Criminal Violence, Criminal Justice*, "We punish criminals, in short, because justice, i.e., fairness, requires it; punishment is a way of restoring the equilibrium that is broken when someone commits a crime."

This is how I began my explanation of why this young recidivist burglar was not going to get probation despite the prosecutor's recommendation:

> Here we have a burglary, a residential burglary, a particularly brutal residential burglary, the apartment of a 71 year old woman. The place was ransacked. A gold wedding band which belonged to the 71 year old woman's grandmother was taken. This is a woman who, because of the burglary, is living in constant fear, according to the probation report. It's awful to have this community turned into a series of locked doors, cubby holes and locked doors, behind which people cower out of fear. I think she was going to church when this happened. She was going to church on Palm Sunday.

When I recounted the defendant's prior criminal history and what the system had done about it, it was clear that imprisonment was the only alternative: nothing else had worked. He had committed his first burglary when he was fourteen. At fifteen, he took some $3,000 worth of coats from his grandmother's home. Apparently nothing was done about these crimes except some "counseling." He stole from his grandmother again when he was still fifteen; this time, it was charged as a burglary, and he was put on juvenile probation. He had put his hand into the fire three times, and three times it had not been hurt. Less than a month later, he again burglarized his grandparents' home. Finally, he was sent to Wisconsin's reform school.

Perhaps by that time it was too late to make the young man believe the system really meant business. After all, the signals had been all to the contrary. He had stayed in the detention facility for about a year, and almost immediately upon his release, he was arrested for two more burglaries. He was returned to the facility, where he had remained until he turned eighteen—a little less than a year. The Palm Sunday burglary occurred some three weeks later.

I announced the inevitable: "It is the sentence of this Court that you be incarcerated in the Wisconsin State Prisons for an indeterminate period of not to exceed eight years." The maximum penalty for burglary in Wisconsin is ten years.

Needless to say, the young man and his lawyer were shocked. They had walked into court that morning expecting another pass—a free ride—because the burglary was his first adult offense. Of course, their expectations had been fueled by the young man's earlier experiences and, consistent with those experiences, the plea bargain.

Our system promises punishment in return for lawless behavior, but it rarely delivers. This gives the lie to that promise. Another clear example of this was the deferred prosecution program attempted in Milwaukee County in battered women cases.

The criminal justice system has long been frustrated by the powerful symbiotic bond between the abused and the abuser. At the time of the abuse, most battered women cry out for help:

"Keep him away from me—make him be good." Yet after time
has passed and the most recent wounds have healed, there is a
rapprochement: a new honeymoon of remorse and courtship.
Unfortunately, and tragically, the cycle repeats as tension first
builds and then explodes in cascades of physical abuse.

Few battered women want their husbands or lovers to go to
prison. Additionally, since the pretrial period is usually a time of
relative calm, many victims refuse to testify, and they will try to
have the cases dropped entirely. Of course, there is usually additional abuse after the threat of criminal sanction is past.

In an attempt to protect battered women and, if possible, to
break the pattern of abuse, the district attorney's office in Milwaukee County tried a deferred prosecution program. In essence, the abuser would agree to a laundry list of conditions in
exchange for not being prosecuted immediately. He would agree,
for example, to join a Batterer's Anonymous group, to attend
alcohol and drug rehabilitation sessions, and to participate in
counseling. He would be told that a violation of the agreement
would result in immediate prosecution. A formal contract to that
effect would be signed, and everyone would leave the prosecutor's office happy, basking in the optimistic glow of expectation.

Unfortunately, the program rarely worked and has now been
abandoned. Typically, the man would violate the conditions of
his contract in small increments. He might take a drink here or
miss a meeting there. His wife or girlfriend, having not yet been
hit and not willing to upset the arrangement by making a moun-
tain out of a molehill, would ignore these initial transgressions.
The abuser got the message: the agreement could be violated
without consequence. Soon, the number and severity of the violations would increase, until ultimately there was new abuse.

In Minneapolis, police tested the theory that it was better for
social welfare agencies to mediate domestic abuse cases than to
arrest the husband or boyfriend. They tried an experiment in
which a third of the abusers were arrested while the others were
either ordered from the house to cool off or were otherwise handled informally. In a six-month follow-up, they found that those
who had been arrested (and who, on the average, had spent no
more than a week in jail) were less likely to repeat their crime.
As a result of this experiment, many cities, including Milwaukee,
now have a policy to arrest suspects in domestic abuse cases.

Another example of how expectations of leniency can fertilize a disregard for rules occurred in a program to monitor defendants while they are out on bail. A defendant was in my court to be sentenced. As a condition of his bail, I had required that, like many others I would release on bail, he meet with the monitoring agency several times a week. The meetings are very important since not only might a missed appointment indicate that the defendant was slipping in his resolve to stay out of trouble while out on bail, but it might also be the first warning that he had left town. The more quickly a warrant could be issued for his arrest, the less potential there was for trouble. Accordingly, I told all defendants that if they missed one appointment, they would be picked up for having violated a condition of their bail.

The defendant, a young man, came to court with a representative of the agency, who presented a letter from the defendant's contact worker praising him for having missed only one meeting. I reminded him of my order that there were to be no misses whatsoever. In an attempt to excuse the defendant, the agency representative explained, "Well, judge, I think I can take responsibility for that. When he came to the program, he was told he had three misses."

I was nonplussed. "You tell them that?" I asked.

"Well, under the guidelines of the program, that's accurate," he explained. "We don't tell them to miss three times, but we tell them their limit is three misses or three no contacts."

I did not see the difference between telling them to miss three times and telling them that their limit was three misses. Although the agency representative told me that the guidelines had been changed as a result of my concern, the mindset reflected by the earlier policy pervades the system and vitiates its credibility. As Professor Wilson has pointed out, the certain and strict enforcement of our criminal laws *will* reduce unlawful activity— ranging from white-collar offenses on the one hand to street crimes and murder on the other—but there must be credibility.

In 1982, voters in Washington, D.C., were fed up with how the courts were treating drug dealers in their community. As a result, they passed an initiative requiring prison terms for most persons convicted of selling drugs. The initiative passed by a two-

and-a-half-to-one margin. Yet, as Ed Bruske of *The Washington Post* related in a series of articles in May 1986, reporting on the newspaper's two-year study of the mandatory sentencing law, things have not changed because the judges and lawyers are, for the most part, using plea bargaining to skirt its requirements. Thus, the law allows addicts who are first-time offenders to receive treatment rather than incarceration. It is an option not available to repeaters. Nonetheless, repeaters often avoid prison because prosecutors will agree, as part of the plea bargain, not to tell the judge about a defendant's prior record. Most judges prefer, in Bruske's phrase, to "rubberstamp" the deal and do not ask. One prosecutor told Bruske that he "felt like I was going behind the voters' backs." A judge was a little more blunt, noting that the ruse was "convenient for plea bargaining, but it's illegal."

The plea-bargaining charade has permitted the circumvention of other mandatory sentencing laws and frustrates society's attempts to impose some credibility. Legislators in both Massachusetts and Michigan, for example, have tried to control the unlawful use of guns. Starting in April of 1975, someone carrying a handgun without a license in Massachusetts faced a mandatory one year in jail. Michigan's antigun law went into effect in 1977 and required that an additional two years be tacked onto any felony sentence if the defendant was carrying a gun at the time of the crime. Prosecutors and judges in Massachusetts took the law seriously, and it worked. The Michigan story, however, as Professor Wilson relates, was different:

> Many judges would reduce the sentence given for the original felony (say, assault or robbery) in order to compensate for the add-on. In other cases, the judge would dismiss the gun count. Given this evasion, it is not surprising that the law had little effect on the rate at which gun-related crimes were committed.

This is the same mechanism which, according to a New York lawyer friend of mine, Robert G. Harley, was apparently at work in Saudi Arabia in the mid-1950s, when the standard punishment for thievery was the loss of a hand. Harley's father was, at the time, an employee of Aramco, and they lived in the company's American compound. Since the Americans thought amputation was barbaric, they rarely reported burglaries. The result, as Harley tells it, was that the Saudis, thus immunized from *any* punishment, stole only from the Americans.

Plea bargaining destroys credibility by making penalty a commodity subject to haggling. It sends another, equally ominous signal by its frequent reliance on legal fictions. We have already seen, for example, how concurrent time merges several crimes into one punishment. Another species of legal fiction is where those in the system either partially or wholly disregard the law, as in the case of the Washington, D.C. drug law we have just discussed.

The great Supreme Court Justice Louis D. Brandeis once observed in another context,

> Our Government is the potent, omnipresent teacher. For good or for ill, it teaches the whole people by its example. Crime is contagious. If government becomes a lawbreaker, it breeds contempt for law; it invites everyone to become a law unto himself.

Shakespeare's Angelo, in "Measure for Measure," expressed it a little more colorfully: "Thieves for their robbery have authority when judges steal themselves." In other words, how can we expect criminals to obey the law when every day they see prosecutors, defense lawyers, and judges ignore the law for the sake of expediency? Consider the use of Wisconsin's law against "joy riding."

It is a felony in Wisconsin to operate a motor vehicle without the owner's consent. Persons who do so are, theoretically at least, subject to two years imprisonment and a $10,000 fine. If the car is abandoned within twenty-four hours and is not damaged, however, the crime is joy riding. Joy riding is a misdemeanor with a maximum period of incarceration of nine months. Although it is a violation of prosecutorial standards to charge someone with a crime that the prosecutor, in a good faith evaluation of the case, believes cannot be proven beyond a reasonable doubt, prosecutors in Milwaukee routinely use this reduced-penalty provision as a plea-bargaining chip even in cases where the car is not abandoned within twenty-four hours or is damaged. Consider the following hypothetical case.

John Doe steals a car from a shopping mall parking lot by

breaking the driver's window and punching out the lock. Two days later, he is stopped by an alert police officer. The prosecutor offers the following deal: "I'll charge you with the joy-riding misdemeanor if you agree to plead guilty. Since this is your first offense, I will recommend probation." By letting Doe plead guilty to a lesser crime, *one he did not commit*, the system is telling him, in effect, that it is okay to ignore the law when it is expedient to do so.

Another example of letting a defendant plead guilty to a crime he did not commit occurred in a case involving an alleged sexual assault by a psychologist on a patient. The abuse of psychologically dependent patients by their therapists is an area of significant concern. As in the case of incest, the rape of someone in therapy inflicts multiple wounds. Significantly, all the studies that have examined the efficacy of deterrence conclude that white-collar professionals are more likely to be deterred by the threat of prison than are street criminals. They are also more likely to know whether the system means business. Accordingly, law enforcement in this area should be firm.

Several years ago, a criminal complaint was filed in the circuit court for Milwaukee County. It charged that during a therapy session, the defendant, a psychologist, "had [his patient] engage in an act of fellatio with him" and that "this was the 3rd time that she had engaged in this type of conduct with the defendant during a therapy session." Now, nonforcible but unconsented sexual intercourse (defined to include fellatio and cunnilingus) is third-degree sexual assault in Wisconsin, a five-year felony that is also punishable by a $10,000 fine. Although he confessed the act to the police, the therapist was not charged with sexual assault. Rather, he was charged with disorderly conduct, a ninety-day misdemeanor that is also punishable by a fine not to exceed $1,000.

Disorderly conduct is a quicksilver offense of which almost every state has a version. As its name implies, it is designed to keep the peace. In Wisconsin, a person is guilty of disorderly conduct if he or she "in a public or private place, engages in violent, abusive, indecent, profane, boisterous, unreasonably loud or otherwise disorderly conduct under circumstances in which the conduct tends to cause or provoke a disturbance." The offense has two elements: first, there must be some sort of unusual conduct; second, the circumstances must be such that the conduct "tends to cause or provoke a disturbance." The criminal complaint charging the psychologist with having his patient engage in fellatio with him alleged that "as a result of this conduct, a disturbance was created."

The assistant district attorney justified charging the psychologist with disorderly conduct instead of sexual assault on the ground that it would be difficult for him to prove that the victim did not consent. *Consent* is defined by the statute as "words or overt actions by a person who is competent to give informed consent indicating a freely given agreement" to engage in the sex act.

Putting aside the issue of whether the consent question should have been left to a jury, *if* the woman "consented" to the acts, *then* there could not have been the requisite disturbance or potential disturbance. In my view, the assistant district attorney used a legal fiction to get rid of a tough case. The doctor also got a good deal. Although the criminal complaint recited that he had, in fact, admitted the acts of fellatio, he was permitted to plead no contest. In return for that minimal concession, he was ordered to undergo counseling and was placed on probation for a year.

Unfortunately, disorderly conduct is looked upon by some prosecutors as a convenient umbrella charge, one they can use in order to have a case plead out, even though they may have to shade the facts a bit. One such case came before me during the year I was assigned to hear misdemeanors. The criminal complaint contained nothing to indicate that it was anything other than a simple, almost typical, disorderly conduct case.

The complaint, as is the usual practice, was the sworn statement of a police officer written by an assistant district attorney. It related in legal jargon what the citizen/victim told the officer: "that she met the defendant and that she and the defendant went to his apartment . . . that while she was present with the defendant she observed the defendant become extremely upset and that the defendant struck the wall with his fist and threw a board that appeared to her to have nails in it and that she became extremely upset and frightened by the defendant's conduct and that she eventually was able to flee from the defendant's apartment." One thing about the complaint struck me as a little odd:

it was signed by a police detective whom I knew from prior experience usually investigated sexual assault cases. Perhaps that knowledge subconsciously fueled my skepticism concerning the whole matter.

The defendant, a gangly young man of twenty-three, came to court to plead guilty to the charge. In order to accept a guilty plea, a judge must first be satisfied that the defendant is pleading guilty voluntarily—in essence, that he knows what he is doing and hasn't been threatened. Additionally, the judge must be satisfied that there is a factual basis for the plea, that is, that there was a crime and that there is sufficient evidence to prove that the defendant did it. This latter protection is designed to prevent innocent people from being railroaded. Although many judges are satisfied with testimony from the investigating police officer, with a prosecutor's statement as to what the investigating officer would say *if* he were called to testify, or with the lawyers' agreement to the facts alleged in the complaint as supplying the necessary factual basis, I always ask defendants to tell me what they did. First, it helps the defendant come to grips with his or her crime, which, in my view, is an important step in the penitential process. Second, as we shall see later, having the defendant recite what he or she did screens out those cases where the defendant is pleading guilty—usually at the lawyer's behest—even though he or she might not have actually committed a crime.

When I asked this young man what he did, he seemed to resist. "You want me to run down the whole story?" he asked.

I replied that I did.

His lawyer quickly interjected. "Your Honor, we can stipulate to the facts of the complaint as the basis for a finding of guilt. What transpired in the complaint are the facts."

However, I told them that "I want to hear it from the defendant."

The young man then, reluctantly, related his story:

> Well, I guess I met some young lady. And this friend of this young lady or something came up and asked me what I was on, or something, if I was high on something. And I told her that I had dropped some acid. And I had dropped some acid, and I guess a certain person was looking for some acid. And I said, "Do you have a ride?" By that time we were out in the hall. This was in a big party. There were a lot of people

and a lot of booze. And we were in the hall; and I guess it just came down to, got kind of involved a little bit, started flirting a little bit. And we went to my apartment down on the second floor. This was on the fourth floor. And I guess I lost my cool a little bit.

The Court: What did you do?
The Defendant: Punched the wall, threw a board.
The Court: Anything else?
The Defendant: That's it.
The Court: What did you throw the board at?
The Defendant: The wall.
The Court: You threw the board at the wall?
The Defendant: Yeah.
The Court: All right. Based on your statement and plea, I find you guilty of disorderly conduct contrary to sec. 947.01(1).

At that point we were ready for sentencing, and I asked the assistant district attorney for his recommendation. I also asked to see the police report, informally known as a "show-up." Trouble percolated as I read the thick document.

The Court: Well, I don't understand this case with respect to the show-up. It came in as a sexual assault case and not until the last page of the show-up is there any discussion as far as I am able to determine—the handwriting is not the best—of the incident which comprises the charge here.

The prosecutor, an earnest man in his late thirties, admitted that the police had brought the matter to the district attorney's office as a rape case but that a reviewing prosecutor had decided to charge the defendant with disorderly conduct instead.

I was astounded. In fact, the matter reminded me of how, just two months earlier, the same assistant district attorney and another defense lawyer had plea bargained a drunk driving case by agreeing that I would not be told that the arresting officer had found the driver facing the wrong way on one of Milwaukee's major interstate highways.

I asked to hear from the victim, who, the prosecutor told me, was waiting across the street in his office. A student at Marquette University, she was a frail, pallid-looking young woman. She told me how she had met the defendant at a party, had gone with him to his apartment looking for some microdots of LSD, and had been forcibly raped. She said that after the rape, the defendant went berserk and threw a board at her. She was able to escape when he let her leave in search of some bandages for a cut on his hand.

The defendant, of course, had already pled guilty. The constitutional protection against double jeopardy probably protected him from a new charge of sexual assault arising out of the same incident, and there was very little that could be done. Although he had been placed on probation for a burglary committed a number of years earlier, had violated that probation with a subsequent "receiving stolen property" charge, and had been placed on probation again for possession of marijuana; and although his record also included convictions for shoplifting and vandalism; both sides, pursuant to the plea bargain, were recommending yet another term of probation for the "disorderly conduct." I was frustrated and angered by the use of the charade to "process" the case. As I told the parties, "the substance of the matter is rape, and it should have been an up or down decision" on a sexual assault charge. Unfortunately, my hands were tied and I could do little but express my dismay at the outrageous plea bargain.

Wisconsin, of course, is not the only place where square pegs are slipped into oversize round holes as part of the plea-bargaining process. As a prosecutor told two researchers working under a National Institute of Mental Health grant, "A lot of fictions are entered into. For instance, with the elements. In order to get within a lesser included offense, people kind of fudge the facts a bit. . . . I've seen some people plead guilty . . . to attempted possession of narcotics, and I think that is pretty hard to do!" Indeed, two Oregon lawyers—one caught with cocaine outside a judge's chambers and the other caught while snorting the powder—were spared felony records as well as professional discipline because they were able to plea bargain possession charges down to the misdemeanor of "attempted possession." As Oregon Supreme Court Justice Berkeley Lent put it in his dissent, "The charade is transparent." Equally transparent was one innovative non-Wisconsin prosecutor's practice of reducing drunk driving charges to "driving with a defective muffler."

"Attempted possession" of narcotics is, I guess, a little like being "almost pregnant." A closely related legal fiction used by many prosecutors is charging only part of the crime. For example, the penalty for welfare fraud in most states varies with the amount taken. Thus, in Wisconsin the maximum penalties increase in steps from six months incarceration ($100 fraud) to ten years ($2,500 fraud). Many of the plea bargains result, therefore, in charging a defendant with fraudulently getting public assistance, "a part of which does not exceed $500," even though the total amount of the fraud might well exceed the minimum necessary to charge a felony. The criminal complaint as thus phrased permits the misdemeanor charge.

Almost irrespective of what charge is brought, however, it was my experience that the district attorney's office in Milwaukee County very rarely asked for *any* incarceration in welfare fraud cases, apparently subscribing to the "cookie crumb" theory of criminal justice: if you catch the cookie thief with his hand in the jar, it is punishment enough if you make him shake the crumbs back into the container. Since a defendant in Wisconsin cannot be imprisoned *and* be made to pay restitution, and since a person in Wisconsin cannot be imprisoned for failure to pay restitution if he can't afford to, an order requiring restitution in lieu of imprisonment is a sham if restitution is not possible. In most welfare fraud cases, meaningful restitution *is* impossible by the very nature of the crime. Failure to punish the dishonest welfare recipient cheats and demoralizes those who *are* honest:

Miss Dishonest: Honey, you shouldn't have told them about your part-time job. I didn't and got an extra thirteen grand before they got wise.

Miss Honest: What happened when they caught you?

Miss Dishonest: Get this! First, they charged me with only taking a piece of it, you know, the first $500 or something like that. My first time caught, you know. Second, the lawyers worked it out so I got probation.

Miss Honest: You didn't get no time?

Miss Dishonest: Nope. Not a day. The judge did tell me I'd have to pay it all back . . .

Miss Honest: Thirteen Gs? How you gonna do that?

Miss Dishonest: Can't. My lawyer says that if I can't pay, they can't make me.

As Johannes Andenaes has written, "The unthinkable is not unthinkable any longer when one sees one's comrades doing it. Why should one be honest when others are not? The risk seems less real, and at the same time, moral inhibitions are broken down." Indeed, the risk *is* less real.

The restitution ploy is used often in plea bargaining even though, in reality, the defendant will never be able to pay. Of course, if he or she is financially solvent, the money can be recovered in a civil lawsuit in addition to any criminal penalties that may be imposed following a conviction. "Restitution," however, usually provides a convenient excuse for everyone involved. "After all," they can say, "our first priority is getting the victim's money back." Memories, of course, fade, and three years down the road, when the defendant hasn't paid a dime of the ordered restitution and the period of probation ends, it will only be dimly recalled that the defendant sat in court and, with an air of sincerity in his or her voice, avoided prison by promising to make the victim whole. Obviously, two people will remember: the victim has learned the system is powerless; the criminal knew it all along.

Application of the "cookie-crumb" concept is not, of course, limited to welfare fraud. Indeed, it is most often used in so-called white-collar-crime cases. As we have seen, professional persons are most likely deterred by the prospect of prison. Yet these criminals are usually able to avoid prison via the restitution/plea-bargaining route. Even if payment is made, returning the crumbs to the cookie jar is but a hollow vindication for society. Often, they are even permitted to plead *nolo contendere* (no contest), which permits them to continue to protest their innocence and avoid most of the stigma of guilt. Thus, Spiro T. Agnew—who had just bartered the vice presidency in return for a slap on the wrist, stood on the courthouse steps and declaimed his no-contest plea to very serious criminal charges as his cloak of innocence. "It is no wonder," wrote former Attorney General Herbert Brownell, Jr., in 1953, "that the public regards consent to such a plea by the Government as an admission that it has only a technical case at most and that the whole proceeding was just a fiasco."

Twenty-seven years after Brownell's observation, Benjamin R. Civiletti, then the attorney general, directed federal prosecutors not to accept no-contest pleas except in extraordinary circumstances. "The acceptance of nolo pleas from affluent white collar defendants," he wrote in July 1980, "as opposed to other types of defendants, lends credence to the view that a double standard of justice exists."

An interesting example of a plea bargain coupled with the acceptance of a no-contest plea took place in Milwaukee at the end of 1984. A psychiatrist was charged by government investigators with billing for work he never did and submitting more than 230 insurance claims totaling some $89,000. The psychiatrist was permitted to plead no contest to misdemeanors, thereby avoiding more serious felony charges, as well as prison, in return for his agreement to repay the overbilling and to have his *corporation* fined an additional $68,000. The judge called the psychiatrist's actions "a significant fraud" and emphasized the need for deterrence: "How do we deter physicians and other similarly employed persons from doing the same thing?" he asked. Nevertheless, the judge followed the deal. The psychiatrist was placed on probation for two years and was allowed to make the payments over the two-year period. Additionally, the judge ordered him to spend his evenings at the Milwaukee House of Correction under a 140-day "work release" arrangement.

If the prosecutor thought he had a case against the doctor that could be proven beyond a reasonable doubt, the deal was unfortunate. Not only did it let a premeditated criminal off the hook with penalties little different from losses he would have suffered if a tax shelter investment had gone sour; it also sent a message to the community that can only weaken respect for the law and cripple deterrence. If, on the other hand, the prosecutor did *not* have a case he thought he could prove beyond a reasonable doubt and was accordingly using the plea bargain to bail out, then the doctor was unnecessarily subjected to what the late Supreme Court Justice Felix Frankfurter once referred to as the "awful instruments of the criminal law." In either case, justice was ill-served by a system of plea bargaining, which, as we will see in the next chapter, has two evil faces.

FOUR

The Faces of Janus

THE OBSERVATION OF eighteenth-century English judge and legal historian William Blackstone that "it is better that ten guilty persons escape than one innocent suffer" expresses the soul of our jurisprudence. It is, appropriately, very difficult to convict someone of a crime.

First, every defendant goes to court protected by the presumption of innocence. The prosecutor, if he or she is to get a conviction, must prove the defendant guilty beyond all reasonable doubt. This is the highest burden of proof known in the law. No one may be convicted on suspicion. The proof must be there, and it must be clear.

Second, unlike the situation in some countries, the accused need not do anything that might assist his prosecution. He doesn't have to explain anything—ever—and he doesn't have to call any witnesses on his behalf. In a criminal trial, the prosecutor must do all the proving; the defendant can sit back and listen.

Third, the prosecution must carry its burden of proof with witnesses whom the defendant and the jury can see and hear, *and* whom the defendant can question: no anonymous sources; no secondhand accusations; no thirdhand reports of tale-bearing gossips. Every story is subject to rigorous cross-examination, which, if done with skill, is highly effective in ferreting out the truth.

Fourth, every criminal trial must be open to the public and to the press. No "Star Chamber" proceedings (so called because the room where that tyrannical English court of the Middle Ages conducted its business in secret was decorated with stars) are permitted. A public trial keeps everyone honest and the proceedings fair. In the words of British philosopher Jeremy Bentham, written almost 150 years ago, "Without publicity, all other checks are insufficient."

Fifth, every person accused of a crime must be told *what* crime. This may seem like an obvious requirement, but during substantial periods of history, the accused never found out what he or she was supposed to have done until brought before the inquisitorial tribunal or, indeed, until shortly before his or her execution. Often, the accused never found out. The same is true in many countries today.

Sixth, crimes must be specifically defined so people will know what is, and what is not, prohibited. No one can be convicted of, for example, "hanging around" or for selling products at "unreasonable" prices.

Seventh, defendants have a right to be tried without unreasonable delay, before the memories of witnesses fade. A speedy trial also prevents defendants—who, don't forget, not only are presumed to be innocent but may actually *be* innocent—from languishing in jail or, if out on bail, from living under the Damoclean sword of uncertainty.

Eighth, since the law is full of traps for the unskilled and the unwary, every person facing incarceration has the right to a competent lawyer whether or not he or she can afford to hire one. Additionally, no one can prevent a lawyer from vigorously representing his client.

Ninth, every defendant has the right to call witnesses on his behalf, if he wants. If for some reason the witnesses will not come to court voluntarily, the government will force them to do so.

Tenth, and perhaps most important, every person accused of a crime has the right to be tried by an impartial jury from his or her own community. In many other countries, guilt or innocence is decided by some government functionary.

In our age, when nonelected government officials control almost every aspect of our lives, the jury is the last bastion of citizen control. Jurors represent community values and use their collective wisdom and common sense in reaching a verdict. A jury may acquit because it believes the defendant is not guilty, because it thinks the law under which he was charged is a bad law, or because it feels the government has done something improper in investigating or prosecuting the case. Most important, a jury may acquit for no reason at all. Whatever the cause, however, an acquittal is final. It may not be overturned.

The many impediments to conviction act as a sieve that strains out all but the guilty. It is a fine-meshed sieve and protects all of us from the heavy hand of government oppression. Unfortunately, however, the sieve has a serious leak.

In the preceding two chapters, we looked at the various ways plea bargaining compromises our system by letting the guilty escape just punishment. Like the Roman god Janus, however, plea bargaining has another face: the face of extortion. Simply put, plea bargaining is too often used as a tool either to encourage or, grimly, to force guilty pleas from those who might not be guilty.

Imagine for a moment that you have been arrested for passing a bad check in the amount of, let's say, ninety dollars or so. You've had some serious problems with the law. Now thirty, you committed your first felony when you were seventeen, and you served a five-year sentence at the state reformatory. Your second felony came several years ago and you were, in effect, placed on probation. Now you face two to ten years on the bad check charge.

You get yourself a lawyer, and the plea bargaining begins. Unfortunately for you, the prosecutor is not one of those "I'll give you three armed robberies for the price of a theft" people. Your state has a law requiring lifetime incarceration for third-time felons, and you both know that he can work it out for you to be sentenced to prison for life if you are convicted on the bad check charge. He wants a guilty plea, and he offers you a five-year sentence if you plead. It's either that or life, he warns with catlike insouciance that is galling and frightening at the same time. After all, he's toying with your future as if it were a stunned mouse.

Five years, of course, is a long time for a ninety-dollar bad check. Although you would be eligible for parole after fifteen years, "life," too, is a pretty long time. You talk to your lawyer, and although he explains the prospects for acquittal on the bad check charge, ultimately the decision of whether to plead guilty and take the five years or plead not guilty and risk a life sentence is yours and yours alone. What do you do?

Kentuckian Paul Lewis Hayes, whose general background I

have just described, faced that dilemma in January 1973. He pled not guilty.

Rebuffed in his attempt to close the case with a guilty plea, the prosecutor had Hayes charged under Kentucky's repeater statute. Hayes was convicted and was sentenced to the mandatory life term.

In appealing his sentence, Hayes argued, in essence, that it was unfair to make anyone choose between the Scylla of a five-year sentence on a guilty plea and the Charybdis of a life sentence following conviction after a trial. Additionally, to uphold the life sentence would, he contended, punish him for demanding something to which he had an absolute right: a jury trial.

The prosecutor didn't think there was anything unfair about it. After all, hadn't Hayes been warned of the possible consequences? This is how the prosecutor put it when he questioned Hayes about it at a later hearing:

> Isn't it a fact that I told you at that time that if you did not intend to plead guilty to five years for this charge and . . . save the court the inconvenience and necessity of a trial and taking up this time that I intended to return to the grand jury and ask them to indict you based upon these prior felony convictions?

In reviewing the case, the Supreme Court agreed with Hayes's basic contention:

> To punish a person because he has done what the law plainly allows him to do is a due process violation of the most basic sort, and for an agent of the State to pursue a course of action whose objective is to penalize a person's reliance on his legal rights is "patently unconstitutional."

Nevertheless, the Supreme Court affirmed Hayes's life sentence.

If the affirmation seems a strange response from a Court that, over the years, has reversed innumerable convictions because of errors made by police officers acting in good faith, the Court's reasoning merely compounds the problem. In the "give and take" of plea bargaining, it explained, there was no "punishment or retaliation so long as the accused is free to accept or reject the prosecution's offer." The Court's logic reminds me of an ingenious contention advanced by a government lawyer in the early 1950s when he argued that a person seeking entry into the United

States and detained on Ellis Island was not in custody because he was free to depart in any direction but west. The late Supreme Court Justice Robert H. Jackson rejoined with, "That might mean freedom, if only he were an amphibian!"

Four years after the *Hayes* decision, the Supreme Court acknowledged that "it had been 'mandated' by the Court's 'acceptance of plea negotiation as a legitimate process.' " It explained its view that the "fact that the prosecutor threatened the defendant (Hayes) . . . did not establish that the additional charges were brought solely to penalize" him. Yet in its haste to insulate plea bargaining from constitutional attack, the Court has conveniently ignored the fact that, but for Hayes's exercise of his constitutional right to a jury trial, he would not have been charged as a repeater and thus would have been exposed to a maximum punishment of ten years and a realistic punishment of substantially less. Hayes was punished by having his exposure increased to a mandatory life sentence the moment he asserted his innocence and demanded that jury trial.

The choice Hayes faced was similar to that offered by the seventeenth-century British innkeeper Tobias Hobson, who gave his guests the selection of any horse in his stable, as long as it was the one closest to the door. In reality, Hayes, like Hobson's lodgers, had no free choice: either offer was unreasonable, especially if Hayes believed himself to be innocent. Indeed, since for a guilty person the choice was between a sure five years or a sure life sentence, it can be argued with some success that only an innocent person would have rejected the prosecutor's deal.

Hayes's dilemma was foreshadowed in a 1967 report issued by the President's Commission on Law Enforcement, *The Challenge of Crime in a Free Society:*

> There are also real dangers that excessive rewards will be offered to induce pleas or that prosecutors will threaten to seek a harsh sentence if the defendant does not plead guilty. Such practices place unacceptable burdens on the defendant who legitimately insists upon his right to trial.

Six years later, the National Advisory Commission of Criminal Justice Standards and Goals agreed:

> Underlying many plea negotiations is the understanding— or threat—that if the defendant goes to trial and is convicted

he will be dealt with more harshly than would be the case had he pleaded guilty. An innocent defendant might be persuaded that the harsher sentence he must face if he is unable to prove his innocence at trial means that it is to his best interest to plead guilty despite his innocence.

Of course, as we have seen, *no* defendant need prove his or her innocence. Rather, the State must prove every defendant guilty of each and every element of the crime beyond a reasonable doubt in order to get a conviction. The National Advisory Commission's perception that plea bargaining *informally* shifts this burden to the defendant—at least in the mind of a defendant subject to the kind of plea-bargaining pressures to which Hayes was subjected—is highly significant. It underscores plea bargaining's war against our most precious cherished tradition: the presumption of innocence.

The *Hayes* case was decided by the United States Supreme Court in 1978. Since then, prosecutors all over the country have used it as a tool with which to extract guilty pleas from hesitant defendants. Their methods have ranged from the direct threat used against Hayes to the interesting variant of a federal prosecutor in Philadelphia telling a twenty-two-year-old woman that her husband and codefendant would face an additional ten to twelve years in prison if she didn't plead guilty. The woman's right to have her guilt or innocence decided by a jury was thus limited by her concern for her husband. What made matters worse was that her lawyer, who advised her to plead guilty, also represented her husband. Her guilty plea was affirmed by a United States court of appeals over a stinging dissent by Judge Herbert J. Stern who called the dual representation "an actual conflict of interest of the gravest magnitude."

The practical implications of the *Hayes* approach can be gleaned from the following scenario involving our old friend, the disorderly conduct statute.

John is in Milwaukee for a convention. It could be any kind of convention: teachers, engineers, salesmen. His wife and small children are at home several hundred miles away. It's a nice night out, so he decides to walk along downtown Milwaukee's main street, Wisconsin Avenue. Bereft of some of his inhibitions because he is in a strange city and is alone, he tries to pick up a young woman. He's not really looking for a prostitute, but he realizes that's what he'll probably get. After all, he muses, how often does he get a chance to be away from home? And besides, he'd like to see what it's like. Tom, the fellow he carpools with back home, told him of a gal he met while at a convention in Kansas City. The more he thinks about it, the more excited he gets.

Bill is also walking down Wisconsin Avenue. Spending the evening with a prostitute is the furthest thing from his mind. He too has a wife and a couple of kids at home and is in Milwaukee for a convention. That afternoon he made a special presentation to his convention group, and he is tired. Wine and a fine meal at The Grenadiers, one of Milwaukee's best restaurants, have made him sleepy. A brisk walk in the cool night air will, he hopes, sufficiently revive him for an early-morning presentation he will make the next day.

A half-hour into his walk, Bill sees a striking red-haired woman in a yellow slicker. She's blowing on her hands as if cold. She's waiting for her boyfriend, he figures as he walks past. She smiles. He returns the smile.

"You gotta light?" she asks.

He fumbles in his pocket. A pipe smoker, he always has matches. Finally, he finds them. She pulls a cigarette from her pocket, which he lights, his hands cupped against the night breeze. Her skin looks soft in the flickering light; her eyes look like those of a doe.

"New in town?" she asks, blowing some of the first puff's smoke in his face.

"Yes, just for a couple of days."

"Convention?"

He nods. "Cold?" he asks.

"Yes."

"Waiting for someone?"

"No."

"Isn't it kinda late to be out?" he asks.

"Is it too late for you?" Her lips end the question in a little curl.

"Almost," he replies, thinking about his busy day tomorrow.

"You look a little lonely," she says quietly.

He smiles. "I guess I am."

He's also a little nervous. She's very attractive, and he's acting like a schoolboy trying to ask the homecoming queen for a date. He is also feeling a little guilty when he lets a momentary thought of his wife and children intrude upon their conversation. He is definitely enjoying himself, and he is beginning to wonder whether she'll come back to his hotel room with him. What the heck, he thinks.

"Can I buy you a cup of coffee?" he asks haltingly.

"I can't," she says coyly.

"Why?"

"I'm working."

There's a long pause as they look at each other.

"Working?" he asks. Then he understands. "Oh."

"Surprised?"

"In a way."

"Why?" Her voice was soft.

"I don't know, you look prettier than most of the—"

"Hookers?" She smiles. "Does that scare you?"

"No."

There's a long pause.

"Well?" she finally asks, taking a last draw on her cigarette before tossing it into the gutter.

"How about a date tonight?" he asks.

"I'm working, you know."

"How much?" he finally asks. She shrugs her shoulders. "I don't have much—I wasn't really expecting this."

"That's all right," she replies softly. "You're nice."

"Twenty-five?"

She smiles and brushes the left side of her hair.

He reaches for her hand. "Come," he says, "I'll get you a cup of coffee first—"

There's a squeal of tires as a black Chevy jolts to a halt. Two big men jump out.

"Police! You're under arrest."

They spread-eagle him against the car, search him, spin him around, and handcuff him. The woman is three feet away, watching with a thin-lipped smile.

"What took so long?" the taller of the two men asks. "I thought you'd never give that signal."

"I dunno—I guess I'm getting tired. It's late. How many more we need to get?"

"Two more."

"Oh, Jesus!" she spits.

A large green wagon turns the corner and stops by the curb. One of the men unlocks the back doors. "Okay, lover boy, in you go."

Bill struggles up the steps. It is not an easy maneuver with handcuffs.

"What's this about?" he finally asks.

"You're under arrest for prostitution. Nine months in jail or a $10,000 fine or both."

"You've got to be kidding."

"This ain't no joke, lover boy." Bill looks around. The woman is standing in the shadows staring at her watch. "Listen," the officer continues, "play ball, and you'll be out tomorrow with a hundred-dollar fine."

"Play ball?"

"Sure. Plead guilty to disorderly conduct, and the DA won't charge you with prostitution and you can go on your way. But don't say anything until I give you your rights."

Bill is so stunned by what has happened, he hardly hears what the police officer is saying. All he can think of is what his wife is going to say if she ever finds out. And his speech! He has to give that speech tomorrow morning! He's got to get out.

". . . and if you cannot afford a lawyer, one will be appointed for you at no charge to yourself. You don't have to answer any of my questions, but if you do you can stop at any time. You can also pick and choose which questions you want to answer. You can answer some or none of the questions. Do you understand the rights I've just given you?"

"I've got to get out. I've got to make a speech—"

"Did you understand the rights I've just read to you?" the officer asks again, interrupting.

Bill nods yes. "Listen," he says somewhat frantically, "I've got to get out. I've got a speech tomorrow morning at 8:30, and besides, I'm supposed to call my wife in less than an hour."

"You should have thought of that before, lover boy. Got any bail?"

"Bail? You've got to be kidding. How much?"

"Two hundred and fifty."

"All I've got is twenty-five or thirty."

"No good. All right, in you go."

Bill clambers up the final step into the police van, assisted by a firm push. The doors slam behind him.

"Welcome," someone says sardonically.

There are three other men in the van, including John, who was picked up an hour earlier. The wagon is closed up and stuffy. It smells of urine. Bill sits like the others, knees spread, elbows on thighs, head in hands—and waits. It'll be forty-five more minutes before numbers five and six are loaded into the van. Number five is an elderly man with a grizzled beard. He reeks of wine. Number six is a young college student who sobs quietly as the wagon heads for the jail. There they will all spend their first night behind bars—all except for the old man. He's a regular and is eagerly anticipating his first good meal in a couple of days.

The little scenario is, of course, fictional. It is a loose composite of many cases I heard when I was presiding over misdemeanor cases that involved the Milwaukee Police Department's decoy operation. Many cities have similar programs to get the "Johns" on the theory that drying up the demand will reduce prostitution. I don't know whether it works or not—although one prostitute testified in a case before me that she and her coworkers of the night are chased from an area rather than arrested when the decoy operation sets up shop. Nevertheless, guilty pleas are elicited from the men by threatening to charge them with the nine-month-and-$10,000-fine misdemeanor "prostitution" (which is committed by someone, male or female, who "offers or requests to have non-marital sexual intercourse for anything of value") if they do not plead guilty to the ninety-day-and-$1,000-fine misdemeanor "disorderly conduct."

The men have been arrested on the prostitution charge, and that means that they must spend the night in jail unless they can post the standard $250 cash bail: no reductions, no checks, no credit cards. Few people, of course, carry that kind of cash, and visitors from out of town have no one to call for bail money. Even those who live in town would probably have no one whom they could call—or, given the circumstances, whom they would want to call—in the middle of the night. So most of them do, indeed, spend the night in jail; for most of them, it will be their first.

Jail is not a pleasant place. It is overcrowded and filled with the sullen and hostile. Screams of the mentally deranged punctuate the dank night. As they await their 8 A.M. meeting with an assistant district attorney, few of the men arrested for prostitution get any sleep. When 8 o'clock finally and mercifully comes, they are led, handcuffed and in chain-gang style, to a small office, where a prosecutor will review their cases. Unlike the prosecutor, who has presumably had a good night's sleep, they are tired, dirty, unshaven, and thoroughly shaken by their ordeal. They were swooped up in the middle of prurient visions, herded like common criminals, photographed, and fingerprinted. They are hardly in any position to think clearly.

The assistant district attorney is not a sadist; he just wants to get his day over with as painlessly as possible. That means he doesn't want any boat-rockers.

Plead guilty to disorderly conduct, he tells them firmly, and you'll be fined $100. Fight it, and we'll take you to trial on the prostitution charge. It's as simple as that—take it or leave it. It's an echo of *Hayes,* although the stakes, obviously, are not as great.

Of course, he's told them that they have a right to a lawyer, and that if they cannot afford a lawyer one will be provided free. He's also told them that they don't have to even talk to him if they don't want to. But the message is clear: make waves, and you face a possible nine-month jail term plus a $10,000 fine. They may not know that no judge would ever impose such a draconian penalty—they've just spent a night in jail, and they can't think straight. They don't want to risk it.

In Wisconsin, once a district attorney charges a defendant with a particular crime, the charge cannot be reduced or dropped unless a judge agrees that reducing or dropping it is in the public interest. If the district attorney refuses to prosecute, the judge can appoint a special prosecutor. That's the theory, anyway. As I've mentioned, most judges everywhere let the prosecutor do anything he or she wants, as long as it gets rid of a case. Essentially, that's what plea bargaining is all about.

One day, when I was presiding over misdemeanors, five men were brought before me. They had been arrested the previous evening following street-corner discussions of varying sexual import with an undercover policewoman posing as a prostitute. None of them was represented by a lawyer. None of them had been able to post the $250 bail, and therefore they had all spent the night in jail. They were haggard, tired men who looked defeated and older than their actual ages. Two of them, as I recall, were from out of town.

They were brought from what's known as the "bullpen"—the place where prisoners coming to court are kept. The assistant district attorney told me that they had agreed with another prosecutor to plead guilty to the disorderly conduct charge. I looked at the men closely; they looked at their feet.

"Do you understand," I explained to them as slowly and carefully as I could after telling them what the disorderly conduct charge was all about, "that though charged with a crime, you stand here innocent, that is, the law presumes that every person accused of having violated the criminal law is innocent until a prosecutor is able to persuade a jury of twelve citizens to their satisfaction beyond a reasonable doubt that the person is guilty? Do you also understand that you are entitled to a lawyer to help you defend against the charge and that if you cannot afford a lawyer, one will be given to you free of charge? Do you also understand that you have a right to see and hear those persons who might be called to testify against you and that you have a right to call witnesses for you and that if they don't want to come, we'll force them to come in and testify for you if that's what you want? Do you also understand that you have an absolute right to a trial, either before a judge alone or before a jury of twelve people from the community and that, if you are convicted, you will not be punished for choosing a trial? That is to say, any sentence I will impose will be exactly the same if you plead guilty today or if you decide to go to trial and are convicted."

They all replied, in one form or another, that they understood what I was telling them. I then asked, as is routine, whether any of them had been promised anything to get them to plead guilty or whether they had been threatened in any way. Two of the defendants said they wished to plead not guilty. One of them explained that he had originally agreed to plead guilty only because the assistant district attorney threatened to charge him with the stiffer prostitution charge unless he did so.

The prosecutor immediately asked for permission to change the disorderly conduct charge to prostitution. I refused, despite the prosecutor's argument that the *Hayes* case immunized that kind of leverage in order to get a guilty plea.

Some time later, the prosecutor renewed his request, and I held a formal court hearing at which the prosecutor's boss, District Attorney E. Michael McCann—a stridently moral man of impeccable integrity—testified. He denied any desire by his assistants to avoid trials, and he indicated that his policy of giving men and women accused of offering or requesting commercial sex for the first time the option of pleading guilty to disorderly conduct was motivated by mercy. He condemned the men who reneged on their agreement with the assistant district attorney for their "duplicity," and he explained that his office would be prejudiced if forced to go to trial on the disorderly conduct charge because, in his words, "we can't prove a disorderly." When I asked him whether he thought it was proper to charge a person with a crime the prosecutor felt he couldn't prove, McCann replied, "That's an interesting question. I think it is perfectly proper." I denied the motion to increase the charge from disorderly conduct to prostitution. As far as I know, the district attorney's office never did take the men to trial.

The district attorney's argument that men who solicit sex for money (the so-called "Johns") should face the same penalty as the women who sell their bodies to them is a good one. The women are the real victims of what some contend is a "victimless crime." Police decoy operations can, if handled correctly and publicized, help. If they are incorrectly handled, however, the operations become mere tools of harassment.

Although District Attorney McCann testified that his charging decisions were prompted by mercy, it is clear to me, at least, that the manner in which the cases are handled leaves the door open for much potential abuse: the possibility of police entrapment compounded by circumstances that tend to encourage guilty pleas irrespective of a person's innocence.

*　　*　　*

A finely tuned criminal justice system will punish the guilty and leave the innocent unmolested. We have already seen how plea bargaining lets many criminals escape just punishment. Since the 1978 decision in *Hayes*, the innocent have been at risk as well.

Hayes was a five to four decision written by the late Justice Potter Stewart. An analysis of its main thesis, a minor paean to all the deals and all the haggling, reveals the meringue upon which it rests:

> Plea bargaining flows from "the mutuality of advantage" to defendants and prosecutors, each with his own reasons for wanting to avoid trial. Defendants advised by competent counsel and protected by other procedural safeguards are presumptively capable of intelligent choice in response to prosecutorial persuasion, and unlikely to be driven to false self-condemnation.

Let us consider that statement, thought by thought.

"Plea bargaining flows from 'the mutuality of advantage' to defendants and prosecutors, each with his own reasons for wanting to avoid trial."

Prosecutors want to avoid trial for a number of reasons. Perhaps the most important reason is that trials are hard work and many prosecutors have heavy caseloads. A case that is "dealt away" is seen as a case that does not have to be tried. As one highly respected Wisconsin prosecutor, a superb trial lawyer and brilliant legal scholar, told me, "Plea bargaining is a concession to the burned out DA. It keeps us on the job for ten or fifteen years when we might otherwise burn out after two to three." There are other reasons as well: the evidence might not be very clear-cut, and the prosecutor may not wish to risk a loss; the defendant is a first offender and is likely to get probation, and it seems a waste of time to go through a trial just for that; and so on. However, the primary reason prosecutors (and defense lawyers and judges) like plea bargaining is, I submit, simply that it makes life easier.

Defendants also want to avoid trial for a number of reasons. Those who are clearly guilty fear that once the judge hears all the grisly details from the victims, the resulting sentence will be more severe than if the judge just heard a dispassionate statement of the facts from the lawyers. Additionally, defendants may fear that the prosecutor will recommend, and the judge will impose, a more severe sentence just because, in the words of *Hayes*'s prosecutor, they both had to endure "the inconvenience and necessity of a trial." Finally, of course, defendants do usually get great deals.

"Defendants advised by competent counsel . . ."

Many defense lawyers rarely, if ever, try cases. They plead their clients guilty. That's the only way they can earn a living given the fact that they usually represent people who either have very little money or none at all. In the latter case, the lawyers are paid by government programs, and the fees are such that taking a case to trial is usually uneconomic. In the former case, a client and his family may be able to come up with $1,000, $2,000, or possibly $3,000. That is a handsome fee for two hours of consultation and a twenty-minute guilty plea; it's a paltry payment for a four-day trial and the needed preparation. As Professor Alschuler has pointed out,

> There are two basic ways to achieve financial success in the practice of criminal law. One is to develop, over an extended period of time, a reputation as an outstanding trial lawyer. In that way, one can attract as clients the occasional wealthy people who become enmeshed in the criminal law. If, however, one lacks the ability or the energy to succeed in this way or if one is in a greater hurry, there is a second path to personal wealth—handling a large volume of cases for less than spectacular fees. The way to handle a large volume of cases is, of course, not to try them but to plead them.

A Boston lawyer he interviewed put it this way: "A guilty plea is a quick buck." One in Alaska was a little more genteel and told National Institute of Justice researchers, "Criminal law is not a profit making proposition for the private practitioner unless you have plea bargaining." The simple fact is, as sociologist Abraham S. Blumberg has pointed out in a 1967 article aptly entitled, "The Practice of Law as Confidence Game," criminal defense lawyers find it more advantageous to cooperate with prosecutors and judges who press for guilty pleas than to zealously represent their clients. After all, they must deal with them on a day-to-day basis.

The client, on the other hand, is a transitory figure who is usually—and quite literally—gone tomorrow. The young boat-rocker who comes into the system with strong ideals and a firm sense of justice quickly learns, in the words of the late longtime Speaker of the House of Representatives Sam Rayburn, that in order to "get along," one must "go along."

In his book *The Best Defense,* Harvard Law Professor Alan Dershowitz relates how one angry chief federal prosecutor in New York yelled at an attorney for some real or imagined transgression of the "go along" code: "You son of a bitch. You're cut off. My office will never deal with you again." As Professor Dershowitz observed, for a defense attorney practicing in the New York federal court where the prosecutor operated, "these words could amount to a decree of bankruptcy."

An interesting example of not rocking the boat occurred before me in a first-offense drunk driving appeal from Milwaukee's municipal court. Wisconsin law permits a defendant unhappy with a municipal court conviction to get a new trial in the circuit court. After the case was called, the defense lawyer said that he had discussed the matter with the city prosecutor's office and that they had "an agreement." The deal was that the defendant would either plead guilty or no contest, and in return the city would recommend the minimum penalties. When I reminded the lawyers that I didn't accept plea bargains and would impose whatever sentence I felt the circumstances warranted whether the defendant pled guilty or not, the assistant city attorney complained that he "was handed the file ten minutes ago" and wasn't ready to go to trial. He told me that the prosecutor to whom the case was assigned hadn't shown up because she had already agreed to the plea bargain. When I wondered why the city attorney's office couldn't be properly prepared for a trial when they knew my views on plea bargaining, the defense lawyer jumped in: "Judge, maybe I can save everybody time here." He said his client was willing to plead guilty irrespective of my policy because, in his words, "I don't want to put the city in an uncomfortable position."

In many cases, unfortunately, institutional pressures arising from the mutual interests of the people who have to deal with each other every day—the judges, the prosecutors, and the defense lawyers—result in a back-scratching daisy chain. When that happens, the system fails because there are few, if any, checks.

There is, however, an additional and serious flaw in Justice Stewart's view that "competent counsel" will prevent the torture of false self-condemnation. Even if the financial aspects of representing most criminal defendants did not chill a lawyer's willingness to take a case to trial, what advice can even an eager and skilled lawyer give to someone in Paul Hayes's position?

"Defendants . . . protected by other procedural safeguards . . ."

What procedural safeguards? Assume for a moment that Hayes was innocent. If he had pled guilty because of the threat, would not that have been the type of "false self-condemnation" that the Court said couldn't happen? After *Hayes,* there are *no* procedural safeguards in any court where the judge permits the prosecutor to up the ante on a defendant who refuses to cave in and forgo his constitutional right to a jury trial.

"Defendants . . . are presumptively capable of intelligent choice in response to prosecutorial persuasion, . . ."

A *presumption* in the law is something which need not be proved. In this case, the "presumption" label is used because, I fear, the statement cannot be proved. How could anyone faced with Hayes's dilemma make an "intelligent" choice? At best, it's a roll of the dice.

"Defendants . . . are . . . unlikely to be driven to false self-condemnation."

This is simply not true. Again, assume for a moment that the Hayes-type defendant is actually innocent. If he succumbs to the prosecutor's threat, he would, by definition, be falsely condemning himself.

Significantly, when the Supreme Court first had an opportunity to discuss the legitimacy of plea bargaining as a tool of criminal justice in 1970, it approved the practice with the following cautionary disclaimer set out in a footnote:

> We here make no reference to the situation where the prosecutor or judge, or both, deliberately employ their charg-

ing and sentencing powers to induce a particular defendant to tender a plea of guilty.

Eight years later in the *Hayes* case, the Court pushed aside that significant concern in the name of expediency:

> It follows that, by tolerating and encouraging the negotia-
> tion of pleas, this Court has necessarily adopted as constitution-
> ally legitimate the simple reality that the prosecutor's interest
> at the bargaining table is to persuade the defendant to forego
> his right to plead not guilty.

As a trial judge in the trenches, so to speak, I can tell you that innocent defendants *are* falsely condemning themselves in the course of the "give and take" of plea bargaining. I offer the following examples.

The first time a defendant tried to plead guilty before me even though he thought he was innocent was when I was assigned to the juvenile division early in my judicial career. Sixteen years old, he was charged with carrying a concealed weapon. His lawyer told me that "they" wished to enter a guilty plea, and that, in return, the prosecutor would recommend probation. After advising the young man of his rights, I asked him what he had done.

He told me that he was sitting on his back stoop peeling an apple with a steak knife that he had just taken from the kitchen. A couple of his friends came by, and they decided to tussle. He put the knife in his boot so "nobody would get hurt." A neighbor didn't like the noise and called the cops. The officers came and searched everyone. They found the knife in the boot. The boy was charged with carrying a concealed weapon.

After examining the police report, which confirmed that the knife was part of the family's steak knife set, I asked the boy why he was pleading guilty. "My lawyer told me to," was his reply. The lawyer was less than helpful when I asked him why he advised a guilty plea, given his client's story. "C'mon, judge, they're recommending probation. Let's not take all day on this."

A charge of carrying a concealed weapon in Wisconsin requires that the prosecutor prove beyond a reasonable doubt that the person found with the weapon was "armed" with it, that is, that the implement or device was being carried as a weapon and not for some other purpose. If the boy's story were true, he was not guilty. I rejected the proffered guilty plea, and we went to trial. The evidence overwhelmingly supported the boy's story, and he was found not guilty. The boy's lawyer left the courtroom grumbling about my "waste" of "everyone's time."

Another time, a young man appeared before me charged with disorderly conduct. A crowd of youths had gathered in a school-yard on a summer evening to play in and watch a basketball game. Following a scuffle between some of the players and spectators, the police were called. The young man, then twenty-one, was accused first of spitting at a cop's shoes and then of struggling when the cop tried to arrest him. According to his lawyer, an earnest member of the state public defender's staff in his early thirties, he wanted to plead guilty because of the plea-bargaining deal they had been offered. "I explained to him the possible penalty," the lawyer told me, and "that if he doesn't believe he is guilty that you rarely accept those."

I told them that I never accept guilty pleas from persons maintaining their innocence, and I then asked the young man why he wanted to plead guilty. "Because I want to get it over with," he replied.

"I only accept guilty pleas from people who are guilty," I told them. "We will set it down for trial. You have a good lawyer who will give you a good defense. And you will be acquitted if you are not guilty."

At the trial, the police officer repeated the charge that the defendant had spit at him, hitting "the tip of my foot." When he tried to arrest the defendant, the officer testified, another young man in the crowd had grabbed him from behind, and they had struggled. Finally, reinforcements arrived, and both the defendant and the other young man were taken into custody.

When the defendant took the stand, he testified that by the time the officers had arrived, the fight to which they had been summoned was over. He said that when he saw one of the policemen struggling with another of the young men, he walked over to let them know that. The defendant testified that when the officer's partner approached, "I started talking to him, telling him everything was over." According to his testimony, the officer told him to "calm down, or I'd be under arrest."

"Were you excited?" his lawyer asked.

"Well, I was just telling them that they shouldn't do [his friend] like that. . . . They had thrown him to the ground and were stomping his head on the ground, scooting his head on the ground. . . . And another officer told me to calm down. Then he kicked my legs out from under me and threw me on the grass and put his knee in the back of my head and pulled my neck back." He denied having done anything to trigger the officer's response, and he specifically denied spitting at or toward him.

The jury didn't believe the police, and the defendant was acquitted. Later, the defense lawyer told me he had thought he would never be able to win because of "all those police officers on the other side." Interestingly, one of the officers later appeared before me in another case. When he and his partner showed up late for an afternoon trial session, having kept everyone waiting, including a jury of twelve citizens, I asked one of them to step out of the courtroom. "Where were you?" I asked the one who remained behind. He explained that they were at a fast-food place down the block but, for some reason, the service had been very slow. I then recalled the one who had stepped out and repeated my question. He replied that their squad car had had engine trouble.

Another example of the attempted "false self-condemnation" that the Supreme Court had said was "unlikely" happened when a defendant wanted to plead guilty despite her conscientious lawyer's advice to the contrary. She was charged with false imprisonment, a two-year felony that is committed by any person who "intentionally confines or restrains another without that person's consent and with knowledge that he or she has no lawful authority to do so." The woman was accused of taking an eleven-month-old baby from the home of her former lesbian lover. The assistant district attorney offered to recommend two years probation in return for her guilty plea.

When I asked the woman what she had done, she told of going to the mother's apartment at three in the morning and finding her in bed with another woman. The infant was stranded on the middle of the floor, diaperless, dirty, and crying. The defendant and her lover argued about both the baby and "the other woman." She then grabbed the baby and returned to her own home. When the police arrived, the baby was clean, fed, and happy. She told me she had persuaded her friend not to have an abortion and that she was the infant's godmother.

After hearing the woman's story, I reminded everyone that I did not accept guilty pleas from defendants unless they were ready to admit that they were, in fact, guilty. I also told them that if the defendant was telling the truth, she was not guilty. I repeated that I do not punish defendants who want to go to trial and that I do not reward defendants who plead guilty. She said she was pleading guilty because she was being held in jail in lieu of $5,000 bail and that since the prosecutor was going to recommend probation, a guilty plea would be her ticket to freedom. That was on a Friday. I told her that we would try her case the following Monday, even though some other matters, involving persons who were not being held in custody, would have to be delayed. The trial took one day, and the jury found her not guilty after deliberating less than an hour.

In 1982, a case came before me that was strikingly similar to *Hayes*. It concerned a woman in her early forties who we'll call Jane Doe. Mrs. Doe had been accused of stabbing her husband as he slept. Too poor to hire a private lawyer, Mrs. Doe was being represented by an extremely able and tenacious attorney on the public defender's staff, Victoria McCandless.

Like many other intrafamily criminal cases, the one involving Mrs. Doe and her husband was layered with complexity. McCandless hired a psychologist in an attempt to reach the core issue. Ultimately, the psychologist's report found its way into the public file, and it told of Mrs. Doe's turbulent life with her husband, a twenty-two-year period that, the psychologist noted, had "many elements of a classic battering relationship" which she described as one where the "partners report times of violence and abuse, but the good times are described in an almost idyllic fashion. . . . It is the honeymoon times that make it so hard for such couples to separate from one another despite violent conflicts." According to the psychologist, the night of the stabbing was described this way:

> Mrs. [Doe] reports that her husband had discovered that she had taped a phone conversation with a woman he had been seeing. She called him to come home to discuss the matter and he arrived home drunk. She went upstairs to watch television and he came into the room, called her names and hit her in the head with the remote control for the T.V. Her children, who had left the home when their father returned, had called

the police who refused to remove Mr. [Doe] from the home. Mrs. [Doe] said she wanted her husband to know what it was like to hurt and she did not want to be hit again.

When her husband fell asleep, she went back to the kitchen and got a large paring-type knife, went back upstairs and stabbed her husband. She says "I just couldn't handle him hitting me anymore. He gets away with it all the time." Mrs. [Doe] says that although she wanted to hurt her husband like he had hurt her, she has since regretted the actions because she still loves him.

Apparently, the stabbing was not too serious. Mr. Doe was taken to the hospital, but no stitches were required.

Mrs. Doe saw the psychologist on February 25, 1982, eleven days after the stabbing. Three days after the stabbing, on February 17, Mrs. Doe, together with her children and her lawyer, had kept an early-morning appointment with an assistant district attorney. According to a sworn written statement called an affidavit that McCandless filed with the court, the Doe children supported their mother's story of abuse. McCandless reported that the prosecutor had this reaction:

> He said "he was impressed by her children and how supportive they were, but that if he was in their place he would have said to hell with both defendant and her husband and would have left town and never had anything to do with either of them . . . he told defendant he couldn't understand why she hadn't left her husband and why she put up with his abuse, and that she was in his opinion a "dangerous person" because she had not removed herself from the situation earlier.

Mrs. Doe started to cry, according to McCandless, but she managed to respond "that she couldn't have left her husband previously because she didn't have a job or any money of her own, but that she did have a job now." The prosecutor ended the session by telling McCandless that he hadn't yet decided what charge, if any, to file against Mrs. Doe.

Five days later, Mrs. Doe and McCandless met with the assistant district attorney again. Mr. Doe and his lawyer were there also. According to McCandless's affidavit, Mr. Doe told the prosecutor that "his wounds were not serious," and that he didn't believe his wife had wanted "to kill him or seriously injure him because they have much larger knives in the house she could have used." "If she wanted to kill me, I'd be dead," McCandless quoted him as saying to the assistant district attorney. He denied hitting his wife the evening of the stabbing, and, as recalled by McCandless, he said he felt she "needs help and should see a doctor."

After that second meeting with the assistant district attorney, McCandless sent him copies of the psychologist's report and an evaluation of Mrs. Doe by a psychiatrist. Mrs. Doe had cervical cancer in 1973. She later had had a complete hysterectomy and, in 1979, a heart attack. Additionally, she had several "voluntary admissions for psychiatric care in 1980 as a result of marital stress."

There was another meeting between McCandless and the assistant district attorney on March 24. In the interim, according to McCandless's affidavit, Mrs. Doe told a social worker for victims and witnesses who was working with the district attorney's office that she had "lied" about being hit on the night of the stabbing.

The March 24 meeting did not go well for Mrs. Doe. According to McCandless's sworn statement, the prosecutor was harsh and unresponsive: he "demanded that defendant inform him why she had not resolved her problems with her previous counseling, and indicated he felt her failure to do so meant she really hadn't tried." He also "accused defendant of continuing to consume alcohol excessively, and of being a dangerous and self-destructive person because she drank, and because she hadn't divorced her husband previously." According to her lawyer, Mrs. Doe again broke down and began to cry.

The prosecutor asked Mrs. Doe to leave and started what the *Hayes* case called the "give and take" of plea bargaining. His offer, according to McCandless, was simple: he "said he would give defendant a 'big break' if she pled guilty to misdemeanor battery, otherwise he would charge her with a felony; and that . . . she had five minutes . . . to give him an answer."

McCandless discussed the offer with her client and then told the prosecutor that they needed more time to consider it. According to McCandless's sworn statement, the assistant district attorney "reacted in a belligerent fashion and demanded an answer immediately, stating he would charge defendant with a felony if defendant didn't agree to plead guilty to a misdemeanor battery and that she [McCandless] would end up getting defendant charged with a felony because of her representation of defendant."

Mrs. Doe ultimately decided to plead not guilty. On March 25, the prosecutor issued a criminal complaint charging Mrs. Doe with the five-year felony of "endangering safety by conduct regardless of life." The complaint recited Mr. Doe's version of the event as well as Mrs. Doe's admission to the police that "her husband beat her up so she waited for him to fall asleep and then stabbed him twice in the chest."

In Wisconsin, as in many other states that do not use grand juries to weigh the evidence prior to formally charging a person with a crime, no person may go to trial on a felony charge unless the prosecutor can persuade a judge that there is probable cause to believe that the defendant has committed a felony. The hearing in Wisconsin at which that is attempted is called a "preliminary examination," and if the prosecutor is successful, he or she can then charge the defendant with *any* felony, as long as the new charge is "not wholly unrelated" to the evidence adduced at the preliminary examination. Using that charging tool, the prosecutor—according to McCandless—now had a new deal: plead guilty to the five-year felony of endangering safety by conduct regardless of life or be charged with attempted first-degree murder. The maximum penalty for attempted first-degree murder had changed since the days of Jesse Lee White and the "Milwaukee Three"; it was now twenty years. Despite the new stakes, the defendant, like Hayes ten years earlier, stood firm and pled not guilty.

McCandless asked me to dismiss the attempted murder case, arguing that the prosecutor had overcharged her client in an attempt to extort a guilty plea. In light of *Hayes,* she had a very heavy burden. Since McCandless would have to testify at any hearing about her conversations with the assistant district attorney, she was forced to withdraw as Mrs. Doe's attorney by the lawyers' code of ethics. To replace her, the public defender appointed a private criminal defense lawyer with a superb national reputation, Milwaukee-based James Shellow.

Shellow formally appeared as Mrs. Doe's lawyer for the first time on July 7. He announced calmly that he looked forward to a thorough exploration of prosecutorial charging practices, and he indicated that he would subpoena the district attorney in connection with that inquiry. The next time all parties were in court, the assistant district attorney—who had charged Mrs. Doe first with the five-year felony of endangering safety by conduct regardless of life and then with the twenty-year felony of attempted first-degree murder and had, reportedly, initially offered a simple nine-month misdemeanor charge in exchange for an early guilty plea—asked me to dismiss the prosecution entirely. Mr. Doe, who was in court in support of the prosecutor's request, said he would refuse to testify even if it meant he would go to jail for contempt of court. I granted the request and Mrs. Doe walked out of the courtroom a free woman.

Although I will never know whether the district attorney's office would have continued the prosecution if Shellow had not been the defense lawyer, his entry into the case was the only really new element. Mr. Doe had declined to testify before and, indeed, the prosecutor had presented his case to the judge hearing the preliminary examination without his help.

Most of us are proud of our system of criminal justice because we believe it protects the innocent both from a potentially overzealous government on the one hand and all of us from predatory criminals on the other. Much of this pride is unwarranted, not only because we are too lenient with dangerous criminals and give short shrift to victims, but because even the innocent too often become enmeshed in a web from which there is no escape. Indeed, in the November 7, 1983, issue of *The National Law Journal*, one legal commentator argued that guilty pleas should not be used as evidence in civil lawsuits because of the tainting effects of plea bargaining: "Since a defendant may plead guilty for numerous reasons unrelated to actual guilt, convictions stemming from such pleas offer little assurance of reliability."

Those who plead guilty to "get the matter over with" even though they are innocent, regardless of whether "the matter" is a sexual solicitation charge or something more serious, have to live with the consequences of their decision. To an innocent person, even probation is a constant reminder of an unfair criminal justice system. To a guilty person, unjustified leniency is a spur to further criminal activity. Perhaps Charles Silberman and political scientist Jonathan Casper, whom he quotes, sum it all up best:

> They are disillusioned by the unfairness—apparent or real—that they experience in court. From a defendant's perspective, Casper writes, "outcomes do not seem to be determined by principles or careful consideration of persons, but by hustling, conning, manipulating, bargaining, luck, fortitude, waiting them out, and the like." Indeed, "the system has no real moral component in the eyes of the defendant." On the contrary, defense lawyers and judges, no less than prosecutors, policemen, and probation officers, seem to be operating on a moral level no different from the one on which criminals themselves operate.

Silberman cautions that "this can only encourage criminal behavior" because "respect for law and belief in its legitimacy are more effective instruments of social control than is fear of punishment." Whether Silberman's analysis of the respective efficacies of punishment versus respect is accurate or not, it is clear that both elements are necessary to preserve order. Plea bargaining weakens both. In short, it is a Janus-faced evil that doubly compromises our criminal justice system. The guilty smirk at its impotence; the innocent are rubbed raw by its haste.

FIVE

The Paml Shade

SEVERAL YEARS BEFORE I became a judge, I was a guest auctioneer for Milwaukee's public television station during a number of their annual fund-raising auctions.

Public television stations all over the country use these auctions to supplement the money they receive from the government and other contributors. For months prior to the auction, dozens of volunteers comb the community seeking contributions from local merchants. The auction usually lasts a week, and viewers bid on the various donated items. Several "celebrity" auctioneers take two-minute turns in selling five or six items by quickly describing the item and telling the "donor's value" as sort of a bidder's guide. As people call in their bids, a "board marker" writes the current high offers on a large tablet. The master of ceremonies moves from bid-board to bid-board, so that perhaps four or five of them are covered every fifteen minutes. This helps home viewers gauge their bidding strategies. After fifteen minutes or so, the high bidders for each board are announced.

One year, I was in the middle of my three-hour auctioneer's shift when I noticed a strange item listed for sale on the bid-board next to me. It was a "paml shade." I had never heard of a paml shade, so during a break, I went over to the people working that board and asked. "It's that shade over there," I was told, being directed to an average-looking table lamp. "It must be the material or something," they said.

I looked at the tag, and sure enough, it said "paml shade." There was no mention, however, of just what paml was. "The people at home must know what it is," a fellow auctioneer said. "We're getting some bids." It seemed a logical enough explanation. After all, I had never heard of the word *bubbler* (which is

85

what Midwesterners call a drinking fountain) until I had moved to Wisconsin. Perhaps, I thought, paml was a Midwestern lamp-shade style.

Suddenly, it struck me that *paml* was merely a transposition of *lamp*. Inertia had just carried it along as everyone had re-copied the transposition and, indeed, had announced it on tele-vision. Someone even purchased a paml shade.

The debate over plea bargaining is, in many respects, similar to that "paml" shade. Plea bargaining's defenders have per-suaded most observers that the practice is an ancient and neces-sary criminal justice tool. Despite the reality, that argument has reverberated with little contemporary protest or inquiry. At-tempts to retranspose the letters, as it were, have for the most part been futile.

One of the few who have inquired into the plea-bargaining myth is Professor Albert W. Alschuler. A legal historian, Profes-sor Alschuler has sifted through the dusty pages of the past in an effort to discern plea bargaining's origins. In a scholarly arti-cle published in the prestigious *Columbia Law Review*, he meticu-lously demonstrates that plea bargaining was basically unknown prior to the turn of the twentieth century. Rather, Alschuler con-cludes, the practice was born in the bowels of corruption that then permeated most big-city criminal courts, as petty thieves and low-level politicos scurried through their byzantine, dimly lit, and grimy corridors bartering justice. As Mark H. Haller, another legal scholar, has pointed out, "Many of the positions in the criminal justice system were bestowed as rewards for political service, while politically influential fixers, saloonkeepers, bail bondsmen, and others influenced the outcome of cases to reward political activity or provide favors to constituents."

Typical of the genre described by Alschuler and Haller was the New York County Courthouse in the early twentieth century, where, for a number of years, one of its bootblack stands was a combination throne and rostrum for ward boss George Washing-ton Plunkitt. A look at Plunkitt's operations sheds some light on plea bargaining's spiritual forebears.

George Washington Plunkitt made millions of dollars during the course of a long political career. He was, at various times, a police magistrate, a state senator, an assemblyman, a county su-pervisor, and an alderman. He left his voiceprint on the American scene when he explained, "I seen my opportunities, and I took 'em."

Plunkitt rationalized his many years of public (and private) "service" by making a distinction between "honest graft" and "dishonest graft." "Honest graft" was the use of inside information and connections to make a quick and often hefty buck. "Dishonest graft" was downright thievery. As he explained, "Ain't it perfectly honest to charge a good price and make a profit on my investment and foresight? Of course it is."

You don't, of course, make the right connections by being a homebody. You've got to go out and help people with, among other things, their legal troubles. Plunkitt was not a lawyer, but that didn't stop him. This is how his chronicler, William L. Riordon, described one of Plunkitt's mornings:

> 8:30 A.M.: Went to the police court to look after his constituents. Found six "drunks." Secured the discharge of four by a timely word with the judge, and paid the fines of two.

Clearly, there is bargaining, albeit primitive, at work here. Various quid pro quos are being passed among the three corners of the triangle: Plunkitt is getting a favor from the judge; the drunks are getting a favor from Plunkitt in return for their political services (past or future) to Plunkitt; Plunkitt has either helped the judge in the past or will help him in the future. It is bargaining with political influence as the currency. I am certain that few, if any, believed that there was anything wrong.

I don't know whether Plunkitt ever took any money for his "timely words" with judges; others clearly did. One of Plunkitt's contemporaries was a well-connected New York defense lawyer who was described as follows in a 1914 account located by Professor Alschuler:

> He would "stand on the street in front of the Night Court and dicker away sentences in this form: $300 for ten days, $200 for twenty days, $150 for thirty days."

No wonder serious people both in and out of the legal profession condemned this early plea bargaining at every opportunity. In 1877, well before the practice was permitted to take root, the Wisconsin Supreme Court characterized a deal between a prosecutor and a defense attorney to go easy on the defendant in

return for his testimony against alleged accomplices as "hardly
. . . distinguishable . . . from a direct sale of justice." A year
later, the Supreme Court of Michigan agreed: the "danger," it
wrote, is that "prosecuting attorneys, either to save themselves
trouble, to save money to the county, or to serve some other
improper purpose," would obtain guilty pleas with promises of
leniency.

Human nature being what it is, plea bargaining flourished
and deals teemed, hidden from view beneath the rotted logs of
corruption. As courthouse denizens increasingly took advantage
of what Plunkitt euphemistically referred to as "opportunities,"
more responsible elements in the legal community articulated their
opposition. In 1927, for example, the highly regarded New York
intermediate appellate court, the Appellate Division of the Supreme Court serving Manhattan and The Bronx, declared:

> It is a matter of common knowledge that district attorneys
> frequently bargain with those charged with crime, and either
> under a promise of immunity, or acceptance of a plea of lesser
> degree than that for which the defendant was indicted, those
> deserving of extreme punishment are permitted to escape with
> a suspended sentence. We deplore the tendency of some dis-
> trict attorneys, following the course of least resistance, thus to
> relax the rigid enforcement of our penal statutes.

In a 1928 report, the dean of the University of Illinois Law School
told how most guilty pleas were the results of "a session of bargaining with the State's Attorney" usually through the use of an
intermediary, to whom the dean referred as a "fixer." "This sort
of person," he wrote, "is an abomination, and it is a serious indictment against our system of criminal administration that such
a leech not only can exist but thrive." The president of the Chicago Crime Commission studying the problem agreed and condemned plea bargaining as "paltering with crime." The dean of
the Harvard Law School, Roscoe Pound, was equally critical in a
book published two years later.

> Prosecutors publish statements showing "convictions" run-
> ning to thousands each year. But more than ninety percent of
> these "convictions" are upon pleas of guilty, made on "bargain
> days," in the assured expectation of nominal punishment, as
> the cheapest way out, and amounting in effect to license to vi-
> olate the law.

More recently, in 1957, the respected federal Court of Appeals Judge Richard T. Rives wrote that "liberty and justice are not the subjects of bargaining or barter." Yet in 1970 and then again in 1971, the Supreme Court disagreed and gave the bazaar its imprimatur.

In 1959, Robert M. Brady was charged by a federal grand jury with kidnapping. Since his victim had not been released unharmed, he faced the death penalty if "the verdict of the jury shall so recommend." While he could, accordingly, avoid a possible death penalty by giving up his right to a jury trial, the judge refused to permit the jury waiver. The judge thus ruled that if Brady did not want to plead guilty, he would be tried before a jury. Brady would then face a possible death sentence if found guilty.

Brady first maintained his innocence. Then, after a codefendant confessed and agreed to testify against him, Brady changed his plea to guilty. The Federal Rules of Criminal Procedure required the judge to ascertain whether that decision to forgo a trial was "made voluntarily with understanding of the nature of the charge." The trial judge did this twice. This is how it went on the day Brady was sentenced, some eight days after he had changed his plea:

The Court: Having read the presentence report and the statement you made to the probation officer, I want to be certain that you know what you are doing and did know when you entered a plea of guilty the other day. Do you want to let that plea of guilty stand, or do you want to withdraw it and plead not guilty?

Defendant Brady: I want to let that plea stand, sir.

The Court: You understand that by doing that you are admitting and confessing the truth of the charge contained in the indictment and that you enter a plea of guilty voluntarily, without persuasion, coercion of any kind? Is that right?

Defendant Brady: Yes, Your Honor.

After the plea was accepted this second time, Brady was sentenced to fifty years imprisonment (later reduced to thirty).

Eight years later, Brady sought release from prison. He gave three reasons: (1) his guilty plea had not been voluntary because any trial would have exposed him to the death penalty; (2) his lawyer had unfairly pressured him into pleading guilty; and (3) he had been promised a more lenient sentence in return for his guilty plea. A different judge held a hearing on these allegations. He found that Brady's lawyer had not pressured him to plead guilty and that there had been no plea bargain. Additionally, the judge rejected Brady's contention that the death penalty threat had coerced his plea. Rather, he determined, as a matter of fact, that Brady's decision to plead guilty had been triggered by the codefendant's cooperation.

The United States Supreme Court does not decide issues of fact; it resolves legal disputes based on the facts found at the trial court level. The federal courts of appeal will occasionally reject a trial judge's factual determinations (or those made by a jury) because, in the appellate court's view, those determinations are not supported by any credible evidence; but the Supreme Court will rarely, if ever, review the facts when a court of appeals has upheld the trial court on that point. As we have seen, the trial judge who heard Brady's 1967 request to be released found that there had been no plea bargaining: Brady had been promised nothing in return for his guilty plea. The court of appeals reviewed this factual finding and affirmed. Although the Supreme Court therefore had no reason even to discuss plea bargaining when it decided Brady's case in 1970, it did.

The Supreme Court recognized that a guilty plea—a defendant's saying, in effect, "I committed the crime, and I want to give up my right to make the prosecutor try to prove me guilty beyond a reasonable doubt to the satisfaction of a jury of my fellow citizens, and I'm ready to take my punishment"—is a "grave and solemn act." The Court acknowledged that there are many reasons why a defendant might freely and voluntarily plead guilty at various stages in the criminal process:

> For some people, the breach of a State's law is alone suffi-
> cient reason for surrendering themselves and accepting pun-
> ishment. For others, apprehension and charge, both threaten-
> ing acts by the Government, jar them into admitting their guilt.
> In still other cases, the post-indictment accumulation of evi-
> dence may convince the defendant and his counsel that a trial

is not worth the agony and expense to the defendant and his family.

The Court then observed that some defendants plead guilty because they either believe they will get a more lenient sentence from a judge in return for a guilty plea, or they believe they will be punished with a stiffer sentence if they go through with a trial. Viewing this to be little different from Brady's alleged predicament vis-à-vis the possibility of receiving the death penalty following a jury trial, the Court ruled that guilty pleas were not invalid merely because they might be "motivated by the defendant's desire to accept the certainty or probability of a lesser penalty rather than face a wider range of possibilities extending from acquittal to conviction and a higher penalty authorized by law for the crime charged." Although the Court could have ended its analysis at that point and should have—our law prides itself on not having judges decide issues unless the particular case they are considering requires it—the justices went ahead to give plea bargaining their gratuitous blessing:

> For a defendant who sees slight possibility of acquittal, the advantages of pleading guilty and limiting the probable penalty are obvious—his exposure is reduced, the correctional processes can begin immediately and the practical burdens of a trial are eliminated. For the State there are also advantages— the more promptly imposed punishment after an admission of guilt may more effectively attain the objectives of punishment; and with the avoidance of trial, scarce judicial resources are conserved for those cases in which there is a substantial issue of the defendant's guilt or in which there is a substantial doubt that the State can sustain its burden of proof.

After noting that "at present well over three-fourths of the criminal convictions in this country rest on pleas of guilty, a great many of them no doubt motivated at least in part by the hope or assurance of a lesser penalty than might be imposed if there were a guilty verdict after a trial to judge or jury," the Court added somewhat disingenuously:

> Of course, that the prevalence of guilty pleas is explainable does not necessarily validate those pleas or the system which produces them. But we cannot hold that it is unconstitutional

for the State to extend a benefit to a defendant who in turn extends a substantial benefit to the State and who demonstrates by his plea that he is ready and willing to admit his crime and to enter the correctional system in a frame of mind that affords hope for success in rehabilitation over a shorter period of time than might otherwise be necessary.

The Court thus gave two major reasons for its support of plea bargaining: (1) barter. The defendant, by saving us all the time and trouble of a trial, has extended "a substantial benefit to the State" and deserves to be paid; and (2) repentance. The defendant's guilty plea—albeit in return for leniency—shows that he repents his evil ways and is ready to assume the burdens of good citizenship. Let's briefly examine these two foundational contentions.

Barter. Once barter becomes an acceptable method of resolving such criminal justice issues as guilt, innocence, and sentence, can there be any limitation on the nature of the *currency* used?

Normally, of course, a criminal either gets a light sentence or gets other charges dismissed in return for his guilty plea to, perhaps, a reduced charge. Other times, however, a criminal will receive consideration if he is able to, in Judas-goat fashion, lure others into the law enforcement corral. For example, in Milwaukee County, as elsewhere, young men and women who are picked up for dealing relatively small amounts of drugs are offered a chance to "work off" some or all of their charges by turning in other violators. Several years ago, as related to me by a lawyer familiar with the case, one young man who was apparently having trouble meeting his "quota" of six persons offered to turn in his attorney if that would count for two. Sure enough, a search of the lawyer's office revealed a packet of drugs in one of the filing cabinets; however, the chemical makeup of the saliva on the packet's flap matched the client, not the lawyer. If a young and fairly inexperienced lawyer is worth two street dealers, how much is an older, more established lawyer worth? How much a priest? How much a teacher? How much a newspaper editor? How much a judge?

Obviously, the more prominent the target, the more exciting the hunt *and* the greater the payoff for the prosecutor (prestige and political advancement) and the informer. In a January 1983 article in his publication *The American Lawyer,* author, publisher, and investigative journalist Steven Brill argues that the potential for abuse is enormous.

The incentives for erstwhile defendants-turned-agents-provocateur to produce new defendants for the prosecutor's grist—not only to preserve the bargain but to reap cash payments and bonuses as well—can result in the ensnaring of innocent victims in carefully orchestrated traps. The government used Melvin Weinberg in its so-called Abscam prosecutions after Weinberg, convicted of mail fraud in 1977, had gone to work for the FBI in return for probation. One of Weinberg's targets was former U.S. Senator Harrison Williams of New Jersey. Yet as Brill relates the story, Weinberg apparently had to coach Williams to sound like a convincing influence peddler for his scheduled conversation with an FBI agent, posing as an Arab sheik, which everyone but Williams knew was going to be videotaped. The coaching session was itself memorialized on tape. In one interesting excerpt, Weinberg tells Williams, "You tell him in no uncertain terms, 'Without me there is no deal. I'm the man who's gonna open the door. I'm the man who's gonna do this to use my influence.' " Later, Weinberg apparently tried to allay any concern the senator might have had: "It goes no further; it's all talk, all bullshit." Williams was convicted. His conviction was upheld on appeal. The senator went to prison.

Whatever the merits of the Abscam prosecutions, some argue that government prosecutors should not, in Brill's words, use "criminals-turned-informants" to lay "integrity-test traps" for citizens unsuspected of specific criminal activity. Chief Abscam Prosecutor Thomas Puccio apparently disagrees and told Brill that the "best safeguard is the honesty of the target. An honest man will not succumb." Perhaps; but just as we recognized long ago that it was improper to pay police officers or judges in proportion to the tickets they wrote or the fines they collected, it is inappropriate to permit one crook to buy his freedom by inciting other persons to violate the law. There are, of course, circumstances where you need a crook to catch a bigger crook; accordingly, it may be necessary sometimes to offer leniency in exchange for this help. However, as Brill forcefully suggests, the practice should be carefully monitored and infused with adequate protections. Where it is not, the whole enterprise may fail as jurors acquit in reaction to what they perceive to be serious abuses.

For example, John DeLorean's trial lawyers accused the prosecution of permitting an acknowledged criminal to trade his way out of his own difficulties with the law in exchange for "getting" the high-society automaker. The informer, called a "gun for hire" by the federal judge presiding at the trial, admitted he also wanted a share of any assets seized from DeLorean by the government. After DeLorean's acquittal, one juror criticized the government's operation and said that he hoped the jury's decision would have an "impact on the future."

If justice is to be bartered, are we limited to "in kind" trades? As Professor Alschuler has pointed out in one of his many scholarly articles on plea bargaining, courts in Florida and North Carolina recently permitted the ultimate quid pro quo. Defendants accused of violating drug laws were placed on probation following their "donations" to local governments of hundreds of thousands of dollars. The beneficiary of the Florida drug smugglers' philanthropy was the Fort Lauderdale Police Department.

The North Carolina deal was arranged by colorful criminal defense lawyer Joel Hirschhorn. Hirschhorn—known to colleagues as "Diamond Joel" both for the jewelry he wears and for the sparkle of his courtroom style—got his client five years probation even though he was busted with fourteen tons of marijuana, the biggest cache in Hyde County history (the runner-up: two *pounds*). The largesse of this "philanthropy" was the local school system, the county sheriff's department, and the State Bureau of Investigation. Fifteen days after he received probation, Hirschhorn's client was arrested in the Miami airport for possession of eleven grams of marijuana. In an interesting display of *chutzpah,* the man attempted to deduct the payments from his income taxes as charitable contributions. In November 1985, the Tax Court firmly said "no."

The contribution of money in exchange for leniency has not been limited to drug cases. In the fall of 1984, a Dade County, Florida, judge permitted a scofflaw with some seventy traffic citations—some of which were punishable by incarceration for three years each—to avoid jail altogether in exchange for a plea-bargained deal: a $5,000 fine and a $50,000 "gift" to a local YMCA and a Miami hospital.

Another instance of letting a defendant pay off the system in cash was thwarted when a sexual assault victim's natural father alerted the media. In July 1983, Upjohn Pharmaceutical heir Roger A. Gauntlet pled no contest to raping his then-sixteen-year-old stepdaughter two years earlier. According to a December 5, 1983, article in *The National Law Journal,* the forty-one-year-old Gauntlet's plea was in exchange for dropping four other sex charges involving the girl and her younger brother. Although Gauntlet's maximum possible sentence was life imprisonment and, according to *The National Law Journal,* a presentence report recommended a fifteen-year term, the Kalamazoo, Michigan, judge to whom the case was assigned apparently was going to place Gauntlet on five years probation with a one-year work-release term in the county jail on condition that he donate between one and two million dollars to a local rape counseling center. After a public outcry, the judge disqualified himself and blasted what he called "a frightening pattern" that he saw "developing in the area of criminal justice—the clamor for 'popular justice.' "

The new judge assigned to Gauntlet's case placed him on probation for five years, subject to three conditions: first, that he serve a year in the county jail; second, that he submit himself to reversible "chemical castration" by taking the drug Depo-Provera, ironically manufactured by Upjohn; and third, that he pay over $25,000 in court costs. At his sentencing, the judge unintentionally vindicated Judge Lois Forer's assessment of the way some in the criminal justice system view incest. He told Gauntlet that he was "not a violent rapist" but was rather "a man who had warm personal feelings for your stepchildren, but you let it get out of hand."

In Chapter 1, we saw how, in the early days of our jurisprudence, the wealthy were able to "pay" for their crimes with money and thereby avoid the severe punishment that awaited the less affluent. There appears to be no rush to emulate the few jurisdictions that have traded leniency for monetary contributions, but I see little substantive difference between a county accepting a payment of several hundred thousand dollars from a drug dealer in return for a light sentence and a county permitting its criminals to "cop" their pleas in order to save several hundred thousand dollars in court expenses. Of course, the former has the odor of bribery while the latter is defended as "efficient." But as we shall see, the abolition of plea bargaining will *not* appreciably increase the number of trials or the expenses after perhaps an initial spurt designed to test any ban's resolve.

Repentance. The other major reason behind the *Brady* decision's approval of plea bargaining was the Court's view that "an admission of guilt is the first step towards rehabilitation." The justices in *Brady* echoed a report prepared by a distinguished American Bar Association panel and approved by the association's House of Delegates in 1968, which sanctioned leniency in return for a defendant's guilty plea because of the belief that this aids "in ensuring the prompt and certain application of correctional measures." As they saw it, the defendant has thereby "acknowledged his guilt and has shown a willingness to assume responsibility for his conduct." Twelve years later, this naive view was modified in the ABA's revised and massive 1980 *Standards for Criminal Justice.* While still supporting plea bargaining, the group now recognizes that

> A defendant who pleads early in a criminal proceeding may do so for a variety of reasons (*e.g.,* to escape pre-trial confinement or to take advantage of an attractive offer). Such a defendant may be totally unreceptive to the "correctional measures" sought to be "promptly" and "certainly" imposed against the defendant.

A commission formed to study the causes of the infamous Attica prison rebellion discovered that most inmates, in addition to being "unreceptive" to the imposition of correctional measures, were—strangely enough—"bitter" at the end result of what the Supreme Court has called the "give and take" of plea bargaining. Many of them believed they did not receive effective legal representation and that the judge "did not keep the state's promise of a sentence which had induced them to enter guilty pleas." This bitterness, of course, tends to undercut rehabilitative efforts.

It may very well be that some "courthouse conversions" are genuine, but it has been my experience that almost every defendant who pleads guilty, regardless of his or her intelligence, education, or prior record, is highly skilled at making the *mea culpa* drip with seemingly unalloyed sincerity. Indeed, this real-life variation of method acting is part of the plea-bargaining game. As sociologist Abraham S. Blumberg put it in "The Practice of Law as Confidence Game," discussed earlier, the guilty plea is often "a charade, during the course of which an accused must project an appropriate amount of guilt, penitence, and remorse. Having adequately feigned the role of the 'guilty person,' his hearers will engage in the fantasy that he is contrite" and that he merits leniency. "It is one of the essential functions of the criminal lawyer that he coach and direct his accused-client in that role performance." Indeed, every day thousands of cries of "I'm sorry" echo through the corridors of justice—drowning out the moans of crime victims.

As we saw in Chapter 4, there is another side to plea bargaining's dilution of the law's sense of justice: its encouragement of false self-condemnation by those who are unable to withstand the double-edged sword of prosecutorial blandishments and threats. Significantly, Justices William Brennan, William O. Douglas, and Thurgood Marshall recognized this and criticized the *Brady* majority's "discourse on plea bargaining," which they felt was "at best, only marginally relevant" to the case. They were afraid that guilty pleas would be extorted from defendants by prosecutors eager to avoid trials. As already discussed, the majority also resonated this concern:

> We would have serious doubts if the encouragement of guilty pleas by the offers of leniency substantially increased the likelihood that defendants advised by competent counsel, would falsely condemn themselves.

The simple fact is that plea bargaining *does* increase the likelihood of false self-condemnation, even though a defendant may be represented by competent counsel. Indeed, a couple of months after *Brady* was decided, the Supreme Court implicitly made false self-condemnation less psychologically onerous by permitting a plea bargain to stand even though the defendant steadfastly maintained his innocence *at the time he pled guilty*!

Henry C. Alford was accused of killing a man in Forsyth County, North Carolina. He was charged with the capital crime of first-degree murder. Although protesting his innocence, he pled guilty to second-degree murder, a charge for which the death penalty was not authorized, as part of a plea bargain. He later explained his reasons:

> I pleaded guilty on second degree murder because they said there is too much evidence, but I ain't shot no man, but I take the fault for the other man. We never had an argument in our life and I just pleaded guilty because they said that if I didn't they would gas me for it, and that is all.

The trial judge accepted his guilty plea and sentenced him to a thirty-year prison term.

After stewing about it for a number of years, Alford tried to get out. He complained that his guilty plea had been coerced by the death penalty threat and that, in any event, he never *did* admit his guilt. Not surprisingly, a number of judges agreed with him that, at the very least, it was unseemly for a civilized society to send self-proclaimed innocent people to prison without a trial. The Supreme Court disagreed, noting that the prosecutor "had a strong case of first-degree murder against Alford," and if Alford had wanted to plead guilty to a charge he said he did not commit in order to avoid a possible death penalty, that was his privilege.

Significantly, whatever merits the particular decision might have had in Alford's case—where he was seeking to avoid the death penalty—it has been used by judges, prosecutors, and defense lawyers all over this country in noncapital cases as an excuse to accept guilty pleas from defendants who maintain their innocence. At the very least, this charade lets the defendant who is in fact guilty avoid coming to grips with his or her crime.

Although *Brady* put the Supreme Court behind the plea-bargaining concept, its comments on that issue were, after all, what lawyers and judges call *dicta:* statements of policy not essential to the case's result. An extreme example of *dictum* would be a court's discourse on the relative merits of forced busing to foster school integration in the course of a decision involving an antitrust dispute between a major brewery and one of its distributors. A year and a half after *Brady,* however, the Supreme Court was faced squarely with the plea-bargaining issue in a case whose result turned on that issue.

Rudolph Santobello came to a New York court charged with two felony gambling counts. His lawyer and an assistant district attorney from The Bronx reached a deal: Santobello would plead guilty to one misdemeanor charge, and, in return, the prosecutor would "stand silent" at sentencing—that is, he would make no recommendation. When the day of sentencing finally arrived, Santobello was before a different judge, and there was a different prosecutor. The new assistant district attorney had not been told of the agreement, and when he recommended the maximum one-year term in light of Santobello's extensive criminal record, the defense lawyer objected. The trial judge responded that he was not bound by any prosecutor's recommendation and that he would accordingly impose the penalty he believed was appropriate: "I am not at all influenced by what the District Attorney says, so that there is no need to adjourn the sentence. . . . It doesn't make a particle of difference what the District Attorney will do, or what he doesn't do." The judge then referred to the presentence report and its recitation of what the judge characterized as Santobello's "history of a long, long serious criminal record." The report noted that Santobello "is unresponsive to supervision in the community. He is a professional criminal." The judge sentenced Santobello to the New York City Correctional Institution for one year. Santobello, seizing the prosecutor's innocent mistake as a ground for appeal, challenged his sentence.

Rudolph Santobello's sentence was affirmed by New York's intermediate appellate court; New York's highest court, the Court of Appeals, denied review. When the United States Supreme Court got the case, it removed any doubt that it was accepting plea bargaining as both "essential and desirable." It ruled that Santobello was entitled to the benefit of his plea bargain, and it did not matter that the "breach" was inadvertent or that it did not affect the judge's sentencing decision. The Court sent the case back to New York "in the interests of justice" for a determination as to the more appropriate remedy: either specific performance of the plea bargain at resentencing before a different judge, or permitting Santobello to withdraw his guilty plea, which would in effect return the case to square one. On remand, New York's intermediate appellate court chose the first alternative over a stinging dissent by Justice Aaron Steuer, who saw the whole dispute as a tempest unworthy even of the teapot in which it raged. Steuer blasted the original plea bargain as "giving away the court house" and noted that Santobello had "an unbroken record of vicious criminality" and was "among the last persons to be a legitimate object of leniency." He would have preferred allowing Santobello to withdraw his guilty plea "and let his fate depend on the outcome" of a trial on the original charges. That was not to be, however. The Santobello case took *Brady* one step further: judges were not only passive bystanders who had to permit plea bargaining; they now had to enforce the deals as they would any commercial contract.

Santobello is directed against prosecutors—they must live up to the letter of their bargains with the defendant. But the Supreme Court has gone even further in its role as the principal author of the *Rules of Criminal Procedure* for the federal courts. The Rules—which are reviewed and, where it thinks appropriate, modified by Congress—recognize three types of payoffs in return for a guilty (or no contest) plea:

• the prosecutor's agreement to dismiss other charges then pending against the defendant;
• the prosecutor's agreement either to recommend, or not to oppose the defendant's request for, a specific sentence, with the understanding that the judge is not bound either by the recommendation or by the request;
• the agreement of the prosecution and the defense that "a specific sentence is the appropriate disposition of the case."

Since the second type of agreement recognizes that the judge is not bound by any recommendation or request, the prosecutor need merely say the words agreed upon (as the prosecutor in Santobello's case did not), and the judge may nevertheless do what he or she believes to be appropriate. If the judge is unexpectedly harsh, the defendant does not get to change his mind and withdraw his guilty plea. On the other hand, the judge's sentencing discretion is substantially circumscribed by the first and third types of agreement. In either case, the agreement may be accepted or rejected by the judge, but if it is accepted, he or she *must* abide by its terms. If the judge does not accept the plea bargain, the defendant is permitted to withdraw the guilty plea. While the committee that helped to write the *Rules* emphasized that no federal trial judge was forced to give effect to plea negotiations, one United States court of appeals has prohibited the trial judges within its territory from categorically rejecting all plea bargains where the prosecutor seeks to dismiss one or more counts in a multicount indictment in return for a guilty plea to only one of the charges.

Treating plea-bargained deals as enforceable contracts can, under some circumstances, lead to some pretty bizarre results. As we have seen in Santobello's case, it can lead to enforcement of a prosecutor's ritualistic "Your Honor, the People have no recommendation" in the face of a judge's comment that he would shoulder the sentencing burden (which, after all, is the judge's and the judge's alone) unswayed by *any* recommendation. In Michigan, it prohibits the prosecution from retrying a defendant on the original charges should he successfully challenge his plea-bargained guilty plea to a lesser offense. And when intervening events change basic premises, it can gut even the minimal protections afforded by the original deal. Consider, for example, the California case of *People* v. *Collins.*

In November 1974, Michael Jay Collins was charged with one count of armed robbery, six counts of burglary, two counts of forceable rape, three counts of assault with intent to commit rape, and three counts of forceable oral copulation. As part of a plea bargain, he agreed to plead guilty to a reduced charge of *consensual* oral copulation in return for a dismissal of *all* the other charges. Prior to sentencing, a judge committed him to a state hospital as a "disordered sex offender," where he stayed for just over a year and a half. During that time, however, the California legislature repealed the law that made fellatio and cunnilingus between consenting adults a criminal offense. When Collins appeared for sentencing, his attorney argued that the act to which he had pled guilty was no longer a crime, and therefore any sentence would be unlawful. The trial judge rejected that argument as specious and sentenced Collins to a one-to-fifteen-year term of imprisonment. The California Supreme Court reversed.

Although it rejected Collins's argument that none of the fourteen dismissed counts could be revived as a "bounty in excess of that to which he is entitled," it did limit any reinstatement of the counts to one, with the proviso that any resulting sentence of incarceration be no greater than three years.

The United States Supreme Court's sanction of plea bargaining has come relatively late, after almost a century of condemnation by many responsible members of the legal profession. Before *Brady* said plea bargaining was okay, defendants would solemnly state that they were pleading guilty simply because they were guilty and that no one had promised them leniency in return. This "ritual of denial," which everyone in the courtroom knew was false, only added to the hypocrisy. Although what the *Hayes* Court has called "this previously clandestine practice" is now exposed to public scrutiny, it is still wrong. The justices knew this and uneasily apologized for its many infirmities: "Whatever might be the situation in an ideal world, the fact is that the guilty plea and the often concomitant plea bargain are important components of this country's criminal justice system."

It might very well be that if plea bargaining *were* essential to the functioning of our criminal justice system, it would have to be tolerated as the lesser of two evils. As we recall from Chapter 2, David L. Bazelon, the former chief judge for the United States Court of Appeals in Washington, D.C., in a decision written several years before *Brady,* recognized that plea bargaining was not the imperative all seemed to assume:

> The arguments that the criminal process would collapse unless substantial inducements are offered to elicit guilty pleas have tended to rely on assumption rather than empirical evidence. In many jurisdictions lacking sophisticated resources for criminal investigations, a large proportion of suspects apprehended are caught red-handed. The arguments "But what if everyone did not plead guilty?" has force only to the extent that a sizeable proportion of defendants have some motivation to plead innocent. If the defendant does have some hope of acquittal, the right to a trial assumes overarching importance. If he does not, there is some presumption that most men will not indulge in a meaningless act.

Some six years after Judge Bazelon wrote those words, his prediction was tested when Alaska's attorney general, Avrum M. Gross, abolished plea bargaining statewide. Appointed attorney general in December of 1973, Gross took control of all of the state's district attorneys in Alaska's unique centralized criminal justice system. His new policy was announced in a memorandum dated July 3, 1975, addressed to "all district attorneys." With the exceptions for unusual circumstances, permission for which "will be given sparingly," there were to be no sentence concessions or charge reductions in exchange for guilty pleas. Sentencing recommendations and charge reductions could still be made, but only if they were warranted by the facts and were not used "simply to obtain a plea of guilty."

Prior to issuing the memo, Gross had already discussed abolition with his district attorney staff. There had been much opposition, and the old canards were repeated. He was told that every defendant would demand a trial and that Alaska's criminal justice system would grind to a halt. He thought otherwise, and in a portion of the memorandum reminiscent of Columbus's reassurances to his crew as they sailed off into the unknown, Gross held the rudder firm:

> It is entirely possible that immediately after implementation of the policy the Public Defender's office or private counsel may simply balk at pleading anyone, with the result that we will have a temporary pile-up of cases. I think if we make it clear that we will not back off the policy, the situation will be temporary and after awhile things should return to something like normal.

Two and a half weeks later, Gross told his district attorneys that the key to abolishing plea bargaining was the careful screening of cases *before* defendants were charged. "Again I stress," he wrote, "charge what you can prove and then do not deviate from it unless subsequent facts convince you that you were erroneous in your initial conclusion." He reminded them that "you will have more chance of obtaining a guilty plea if you make the charge realistic in the first instance." He also recognized that plea bargaining rests on expediency and attempted to deflect a major worry:

I told the judges that while I knew of their hesitancy about doing away with plea bargaining, I hoped they would give the system a fair try. I know that it will require them to try more criminal cases, and I sympathize with their concerns about that. Nonetheless they have a responsibility to try criminal cases if necessary and I have confidence that they will do whatever is necessary to perform that responsibility.

Gross also made sure his prosecutors recognized that much of the time previously taken up by haggling with defense lawyers could be better spent "devoted to preparing for and trying cases."

Before Gross's 1975 ban on plea bargaining, the practice had been as rampant in Alaska as anywhere else. As one Alaskan judge related, it was part of the defense lawyer's job to go to the district attorney "to see what could be worked out." Often, a lot "could be worked out." An assistant district attorney told how one of his colleagues had eleven cases set for trial in one week:

He hadn't even looked at one of the files. He dealt them all out on the last day, and he was proud of himself. I'm afraid we were giving away the farm too often. It was a little difficult to sleep at night.

This same prosecutor then put it all in context:

The whole system became ridiculous. We were giving away cases we plainly should have tried. We often said to ourselves, "Hell, I don't want to go to trial with this turkey; I want to go on vacation next week." We learned that a prosecutor can get rid of everything if he just goes low enough.

This jibes with the advice that noted criminal defense lawyers F. Lee Bailey and Henry B. Rothblatt give their colleagues in a book on how to defend cases involving rape and other violent crimes: "You will find the closer the trial date comes, the more inclined the prosecutor will be to agree to a plea for the defendant."

Change wasn't easy, however. Gross recently recalled that at first he "received almost no cooperation." Almost every segment of the criminal justice system was against abolishing plea bargaining, each for its own reasons. The prosecutors and judges were concerned that the system would be backlogged with cases awaiting trial as well as with the potential extra work. Defense lawyers worried about stiffer sentences for their clients and, for the private defense bar, their ability to make a buck. The police were also opposed because, according to Gross, plea bargaining makes their life easier:

> Once I did it, however, the police realized very quickly that the trade-off for doing away with plea bargaining was increased screening of the cases that they brought to the DA's offices. This meant that the police were no longer able to do a poor investigation and then wait for the DA to bail them out through acceptance of a plea to a meaningless charge.

Since Gross had appointed all of the district attorneys, he was able to make his program stick. To everyone's surprise, it worked!

In 1980, the National Institute of Justice sponsored a study of the Alaskan experiment. It concluded that, despite all the dire predictions by the nay-sayers, the plea-bargaining ban was successful: "Guilty pleas continued to flow in at nearly undiminished rates. Most defendants pled guilty even when the state offered them nothing in exchange for their cooperation." Additionally, contrary to all expectations, the cases moved more quickly without plea bargaining than they had before abolition. According to the National Institute of Justice report,

> Supporters and detractors of plea bargaining have both shared the assumption that, regardless of the merits of the practice, it is probably necessary to the efficient administration of justice. The findings of this study suggest that, at least in Alaska, both sides were wrong.

Indeed, the disposition times for felonies in Anchorage fell from 192 days to just under 90. In Fairbanks, the drop was from 164 days to 120, and in Juneau, from 105 to 85. The study also concluded that sentences were more severe in those categories of crimes that had been most often the subject of plea bargaining before the ban, that is, those in which prosecutors had been making significant concessions to get guilty pleas.

Avrum Gross is no longer Alaska's attorney general. Yet his reform of that state's criminal justice system survives. It survives because, as he put it in a recent letter to me, he doubts that "the public would tolerate a return to the old system." It also survives because those professionals working in the system realize that things are better now. An Alaskan prosecutor probably said it best:

> Much less time is spent haggling with defense attorneys.
> . . . I was spending probably one third of my time arguing
> with defense attorneys. Now we have a smarter use of our time.
> I'm a trial attorney, and that's what I'm supposed to do.

Another one was even more upbeat: "My job is fun now, and I can sleep nights."

Can other states emulate the Alaskan experience? In my view they can if everyone in the criminal justice system is willing to hunker down and do some work. Indeed, two other jurisdictions have also successfully kicked the plea-bargaining habit. In the early 1970s, two candidates for district attorney—Harry Connick in New Orleans, Louisiana, and L. Brooks Patterson in Pontiac, Michigan—campaigned on a no-plea-bargain pledge. Both won and both have kept their promises.

The New Orleans jurisdiction has a population of a little over a half million. With sixty assistant district attorneys, it doesn't skimp on law enforcement. The plea-bargaining ban runs the whole gamut, from misdemeanors to felonies. According to Eric Dubelier, chief of Connick's twelve-person screening unit, they process between eight and nine thousand felony arrests and four to five thousand misdemeanor arrests every year. The key to their success is careful screening of the cases referred to them by the police. Approximately half these cases are "refused," that is, no charges are filed. To Connick and his staff, this is better than either taking weak cases to trial or attempting to wring guilty pleas from defendants when the evidence is not there.

Louisiana is a tough state. For example, the minimum mandatory penalty for armed robbery is five years. If the armed robbery is the defendant's second felony and is within five years after he completes the sentence for the first felony, the minimum jumps to thirty-three years. There is no parole for serious crimes. Nevertheless, cases move swiftly through Connick's office. Dubelier tells me that a defendant can be expected to go to trial within ninety days of arrest in many cases. The prosecutors in New Orleans are young lawyers seeking trials and, according to Dubelier, they try more cases per assistant district attorney than in almost any other prosecutor's office in the country. This willingness to go to trial, of course, actually *encourages* guilty pleas, because defense lawyers know that the threat to force the state to trial won't win any concessions.

Oakland County, Michigan, adjoins Detroit's Wayne County and has about a million people. In 1972, Brooks Patterson ousted the incumbent district attorney with a promise not to plea bargain any cases that involved either the sale of narcotics or the possession of drugs with the intent to sell. The plea-bargaining ban at first only affected suspected drug dealers, but Patterson has gradually broadened its scope to include, as of this writing, drunk driving cases in which the victim was killed, armed robbery, any felony committed with a gun, burglary (called breaking and entering in Michigan), crimes against the elderly, and offenses committed while the criminal is either on probation or parole. Patterson tells me that, unlike neighboring Wayne County (Detroit), he strictly enforces the Michigan's law that adds two years to a sentence if the felony was committed while the criminal was armed with a gun. He says his firm policy is working well and has not resulted in the backlog of cases that some people predicted. He notes that although there was an initial spurt of not-guilty pleas, the surge subsided as soon as defense lawyers knew he was serious.

While the plea-bargaining bans instituted by Connick and Patterson have not been subjected to the microscopic analysis given to Alaska's, the experiences there confirm that plea bargaining is not essential to the efficient functioning of our criminal justice system. Everything I have seen supports that view and corroborates what Avrum Gross in Alaska, Brooks Patterson in Pontiac, and Harry Connick in New Orleans have demonstrated: guilty defendants will, by and large, plead guilty whether they expect a deal or not. Typical is the following exchange in a theft-from-person case. I had earlier refused a deal in which the lawyers wanted me to let the defendant plead guilty to a lesser charge. Now, on the day of trial, the defense lawyer proposed what he called an "alternative":

> The court was reluctant to accept an amendment of the charge from a Class D [five-year] Felony of Theft From Person to a Class A [nine-month] misdemeanor. I've discussed this with my client and with [the prosecutor] and he is prepared to enter

a plea of guilty to the amended charge of theft, a Class E [two-year] felony theft. So it would be a reduction from a Class D to a Class E.

The Court: Well, either he took it from the person of the [victim] or he didn't?

The prosecutor then remarked that the stolen item (a radio, I believe) had been snatched from the victim's hands. I replied that if that was true, it was a theft-from-person case. "Let's get the jury in here," I told my bailiff. The defense lawyer interrupted, "Your Honor, he is prepared to enter a plea of guilty to the charge of theft from person."

The Court: Only if he's guilty of that. I don't accept guilty pleas from innocent people.

"He's guilty, Your Honor," the defense lawyer assured me. "He's prepared to advise the court of that."

In another case, a defendant was accused of raping a number of women and young girls while masked and armed with a gun. He had spread terror throughout the community and was popularly referred to in the media as "the ski mask rapist." I rejected a proposed deal in which the defendant would plead guilty to seven counts of reduced charges in return for a dismissal of the others and told the defendant and both lawyers that I was prepared to try each and every charge.

The defendant went to trial on the first two charges and was convicted. Moments before we were scheduled to select a jury in the second trial, the defendant said he would plead guilty to all the charges that the prosecutor believed he could take before a jury. As a result, not only was the defendant convicted at the trial of two counts of rape while armed with a gun, he pled guilty to two additional counts of rape while armed with a gun, to six counts of rape while masked and armed with a gun, to four counts of armed and masked robbery, and to two counts of attempted armed and masked robbery. In light of his serious criminal record, including an earlier rape, I sentenced him to the maximum term of 360 years. As I said in passing sentence,

> Now there comes a point when a responsible judge has to say "enough!" There comes a time when a responsible judge

has to say to a criminal that there are no more chances left. Justice demands it. The sense of what is right demands it.

Wisconsin is one of the few states that permit a criminal defendant to change judges if he doesn't like the judge to whom his case is assigned. The defendant bumps a judge by filing a document known as a "request for substitution of judge," and as a result of my stand against plea bargaining, I received many such requests, even though lawyers knew that their clients would always get a fair trial in my court. Indeed, the acquittal rate in felony jury trials over which I have presided has fluctuated between a low of 33 percent and a high of 40 percent. As one particularly candid defense lawyer put it,

> The district attorney recommended the minimum penalties. My client discussed the matter with me and is aware of the fact that the court has not been following the district attorney's recommendations in these cases and consequently he is asking me to see if I can find a different judge for him.

Another lawyer was equally blunt: "I'm filing a substitution of judge against the Honorable Ralph Adam Fine because you won't accept this great plea bargain that we've got worked out."

When I asked what kind of plea bargain, the defense lawyer replied, "I don't even want to tell you. You'd be so grossed out." Incredibly, the Milwaukee County district attorney once actually suggested letting the defendant *pick* his or her judge (as opposed to the statutory right to "bump" one judge) in return for a quick guilty plea. The public was outraged, and the suggestion faded like mist on a clear, cold winter day.

We should all be properly "grossed out" by the plea bargaining as it is practiced throughout the country. In New York, for example, a person described by *The Wall Street Journal*'s Stanley Penn as a senior criminal justice official characterized the process as "a kind of preordained dance" in which everyone plays a part:

> The Legal Aid guy asks the assistant DA, "What kind of sentence can I get for my client?" Then the Legal Aid guy goes to his client and says, "I got a deal that'll make your mouth water." The client takes it. The judge, who's passive in all this, goes along with it.

A Washington, D.C., prosecutor told Professor Alschuler that in his jurisdiction "even a burglar with a bad record often pleads guilty to a misdemeanor with the assurance of a six-month sentence or, perhaps, a year's probation."

Federal Judge Herbert J. Stern has compared plea bargaining to a "fish market" that "ought to be hosed down." The practice is so obviously immoral, so obviously unfair, and so obviously unjust that expediency is the *only* excuse contemporary defenders have for it. To get a firm handle on the debate, Professor Kenneth Kipnis has compared the practice to a hypothetical system of "grade bargaining" in school, which would involve "give and take" barter between students and overworked teachers. The instructors might not want to read term papers, for example, and would be willing to give a B to avoid the task. Many students would know that they would have but a slim chance for an A and that their papers would most likely pull C's or below if graded fairly. The B compromise provides a number of "benefits." It gives more certainty to the students who accept the deal, and it saves the teachers work. Since teachers do not have to read as many term papers, they can "process" students more efficiently, and the school can trim the size of its faculty. Indeed, to encourage grade-bargaining deals, the school's controlling body could even permit teachers to grade more harshly those papers they *did* have to read. With the possible exception of a few students who thought they deserved an A and therefore "gambled with the conscience" of the instructor but lost, all the participants would be happy with the deal: students would get good grades, teachers' jobs would be easier, and the taxpayers would save money. Nevertheless, bargaining is as deeply flawed an approach to academics as it is to criminal justice: the practice would weaken incentive in school just as it weakens credibility in court. As Professor Kipnis, a critic of both grade- and plea bargaining has written, "grades, like punishments, should be deserved."

Alaska, Pontiac, and New Orleans have debunked the expediency argument: the criminal justice system simply does not need plea bargaining. Given all the bad things plea bargaining brings with it, if we don't need it, we shouldn't tolerate it. However, abolition will require work and dedication. As Robert C. Erwin, then an associate justice of the Alaska Supreme Court, told Professor Alschuler in a June 1976 interview,

A no plea-bargaining policy forces the police to investigate their cases more thoroughly. It forces prosecutors to screen their cases more rigorously and to prepare them more carefully. It forces the courts to face the problem of the lazy judge who comes to court late and leaves early, to search out a good presiding judge, and to adopt a sensible calendaring system. All of these things have happened here.

They can happen everywhere, if we only try. As Judge Stern told me, recalling his days as a federal prosecutor without plea bargaining, "It worked for me, and I tell you, it would work for anybody."

SIX

The Urge To Confess

ALTHOUGH TRIALS ARE usually described as searches for the truth, the quests are often beset with many detours, hazards, and, indeed, outright barriers. Some of the barriers and detours, such as the rules of evidence, which govern all trials, are necessary. They help, rather than hinder, the pursuit. Others, however, have been placed along the way for reasons unrelated to the search for truth; they permit criminals to escape conviction because, in the late Supreme Court Justice Benjamin N. Cardozo's famous phrase (written when he was the chief judge of New York), a "constable" may have "blundered."

The modern-day trial is a forum for persuasion. Each side presents evidence in an attempt to convince a neutral and disinterested fact-finder (usually a jury, but occasionally a judge sitting alone) that something is true. In a civil case, for example, the dispute may be over which car ran the red light at the corner of Elm and Maple. In a criminal case, the dispute may be whether the defendant robbed Jim's liquor store.

There are essentially two types of evidence: the testimony of witnesses who tell what they have seen, heard, or otherwise personally experienced, and tangible items (called *exhibits*) that have some bearing on the dispute. The rules of evidence operate much like a complex valve. They govern the flow of testimony and exhibits so that the jury hears and sees only those things that are most probative of the issues it has to decide. In the liquor store robbery trial, for example, testimony about Marilyn Monroe and her movies might be interesting to those curious about the actress, but obviously it would have absolutely nothing to do with the case; it would be *irrelevant*.

The rule requiring that evidence be relevant to the issues

112

keeps the trial on track. There are myriad other rules whose rationales are less clear and whose application can be frustrating to lawyers and laymen alike. Nevertheless, these rules also keep the search for the truth uncluttered by inconsequential and potentially misleading facts. Consider, for example, the rule against hearsay, which prevents one person from relating another person's version of an event:

Q: Mrs. Jones, which car went through the red light?

A: Well, I wasn't there, but my husband Sam was passing by that very moment and he tells me that it was definitely the black Chevy.

If the other side objects, the judge won't let the well-intentioned Mrs. Jones tell the jury what her husband had to say because that party's lawyer can't effectively test the accuracy of *Mr. Jones*'s observations by asking *Mrs. Jones* questions: What was *he* doing at the time of the accident? Did *he* have a clear view of the scene? Was *he* distracted? Could *he* actually see the traffic light, or is he relying on what someone else might have told him?

The running-the-red-light example is a fairly straightforward application of the rule against hearsay. The rule itself, however, is exceedingly complex, and not all hearsay is excluded. Rather, in some rough way, the law balances the need for certain evidence, the difficulty in getting eyewitness testimony, and the reliability of the hearsay statement. Thousands of books and articles have analyzed the rule against hearsay and its numerous permutations and exceptions. Two quick examples before we move on: The question "Sir, when were you born?" obviously calls for a hearsay response. The witness does not remember when he was born—he remembers what others have told him. But just think how cumbersome—and often impossible—it would be to require eyewitness testimony on this issue. Similarly, a dying murder victim's accusation against the alleged killer is admissible into evidence as long as the victim knew he was dying because the law considers such statements to be reliable (on the theory that no one will go to his Maker with a lie on his lips) and, since the victim may be the only witness to the murder, his or her last words are often necessary for any prosecution.

*   *   *

The rules of evidence, as they have evolved over the course of centuries, are an attempt to isolate for the jury information that is both relevant and reliable. On the other hand, the rules of *exclusion*—fashioned by some judges to keep the police from overstepping the bounds of their authority—prevent the jury from learning things even though they may be pertinent and trustworthy.

Daniel Webster once observed that "the guilty soul cannot keep its own secret." Confession is the voice of conscience, and, as any police officer will tell you, men and women generally have a natural compulsion to confess: to tell of their misdeeds, to take their punishment, and to move on, *even though they may realize it is not in their interest to do so.* Dr. Theodor Reik, in a series of lectures given to the Vienna Psychoanalytic Association first published in 1925 and fittingly called *The Compulsion to Confess,* discusses this special dilemma:

> There is the endeavor to deflect any suspicion from himself, to efface all traces of the crime, and an impulse growing more and more intense suddenly to cry out his secret in the street before all people, or in milder cases, to confide it at least to one person, to free himself from the terrible burden.

Of course, there are exceptions to this inner urge. There are persons without consciences to whom an armed robbery is no more significant than a sneeze or a cough. Hardened criminals and those schooled in the ways of the criminal justice system will usually successfully resist the temptation to bare all to the police although they often relieve their urge to confess by confiding in friends, casual acquaintances they meet in taverns, and cellmates. Indeed, law enforcement investigators are frequently able to solve crimes because they learn of these informal confessions.

Many influential judges and law professors have sought to stifle the wrongdoer's natural urge to confess. As a result, they have not only hindered effective and efficient law enforcement, they have—in the area of confession and elsewhere—turned the quest for criminal justice into a boardgame chase in which one false move by the police can result in freedom for the guilty. The seminal Supreme Court decision concerning confessions is, of course, *Miranda* v. *Arizona.* We will examine *Miranda* in the context of history. Since the decision was designed to prevent what the majority thought was improper police conduct, we must start with those dark days when torture was an accepted law enforcement tool for obtaining confessions.

Apart from its obvious immorality, we reject torture as a crime-solving tool because statements extracted by the forceps of pain are not trustworthy. Throughout history, men and women have confessed to incredible things to spare themselves the rack's agony or the whip's lash. As the late Supreme Court Justice Hugo Black wrote in 1940,

> The testimony of centuries, in governments of varying kinds over populations of different races and beliefs, stood as proof that physical and mental torture and coercion had brought about the tragically unjust sacrifices of some who were the noblest and most useful of their generations. The rack, the thumb-screw, the wheel, solitary confinement, protracted questioning and cross questioning, and other ingenious forms of entrapment of the helpless or unpopular had left in their wake of mutilated bodies and shattered minds along the way to the cross, the guillotine, the stake, and the hangman's noose.

Nevertheless, in ages when investigative techniques were fairly rudimentary, torture was extensively used; it was a fairly easy way of resolving disputed issues. As a British civil servant in India of the 1870s commented, "There is a great deal of laziness in it. It is far pleasanter to sit comfortably in the shade rubbing red pepper in some poor devil's eyes than to go about in the sun hunting up evidence."

Interestingly, torture was once used because it was thought to *enhance* testimonial validity. In ancient Greece, for example, slaves who were witnesses in either civil or criminal cases were routinely tortured because, as one scholar explained, a slave was believed to be so "absolutely at the mercy of his master" that he "would naturally testify in accordance with the master's wishes unless some stronger incentive to speak the truth were brought to bear."

The "judicial" use of torture got its impetus once thirteenth-century Europe had weaned itself from the methods of proof—oath taking and the ordeal—that we discussed earlier. Officially sanctioned torture occurred mainly on the Continent, where the roles of prosecutor and judge merged into one man and where the burden of proof for serious offenses was extraordinarily high:

there had to be two unimpeachable witnesses who actually saw the crime. This high burden—"clearer than the noonday sun"— was established in order to instill as much certainty into the verdicts that were to be rendered by man as was thought to have previously been previously in the verdicts rendered by God.

Since very few persons commit crimes in front of two unimpeachable witnesses, convictions would have been very rare if suspects did not confess. Theoretically, an inquisitor could only use torture to get a confession if he had independent evidence of guilt and its application was strictly regulated in accordance with complex guidelines. Needless to say, these niceties were often ignored in the haste to bring suspected malefactors and heretics to book.

Torture was less pervasive in England. The fulcrum of English procedure was the jury trial, and it remained unhampered by impossible standards of proof. But even there, torture had its moments of prominence, primarily during the sixteenth and seventeenth centuries when inquisition displaced prosecution for certain crimes, especially under the aegis of the infamous Star Chamber. Nevertheless, English procedure eschewed the Continent's extensive reliance on torture, especially after the Star Chamber was abolished in 1641. As one historian explained,

> The torture could not very well take place in the presence of the jury. Such a thing would have been too shocking to men who were, after all, the neighbors of the prisoner; and if it was inflicted upon him in secret beforehand, he would be certain to recant at the trial, and tell how his confession had been wrung from him by suffering, with a strong probability of arousing violent prejudice in his favor; for a jury would be very differently affected by such a scene than a body of magistrates hardened by constantly dealing with criminals.

That ideal, although not completely accurate, explains why torture was never officially part of our Anglo-American system of justice, with the exception of that one dark period in England.

As discussed in earlier chapters, criminal law serves society by protecting order and property and by preserving each person's right to live unmolested. Law, in essence, should be no more than a codification of the Golden Rule. Of course, in a perfect world, in which everyone's inner gyroscope was attuned to that Golden Rule, we would need no laws. Unfortunately, our world is far from perfect: laws are needed to protect us not only from predators who rob and rape but also from those whose law-enforcement zeal or, tragically, sadistic malevolence override the bounds of humanity. Simply put, both lawmen and the lawless are subject to the law. Confessions compelled by torment are rightfully beyond the law's pale.

Raymond Stewart's bludgeoned body was found in his simple Mississippi farmhouse on the afternoon of March 30, 1934. That night, the local deputy sheriff took a suspect, a young black man by the name of Yank Ellington, to the murdered man's home, where a lynch mob had already gathered. When Ellington denied any part in the murder, the mob tried to force a confession. Two times they hung him from a tree and then cut him down. They then tied him to the tree and scourged him until his blood soaked their whips. Still Ellington refused to confess. The mob, now apparently exhausted by its frenzy, permitted the tortured man to limp home. It was a mere respite from his agony. The next day, he was arrested by the deputy sheriff. Ellington was whipped again. Finally, when he could withstand no more, he confessed.

Two other suspects, Ed Brown and Henry Shields, were arrested and tortured until they, too, confessed. This is how two justices of the Mississippi Supreme Court described the whole sorry episode in their opinion dissenting from their colleagues' hands-off refusal to interfere with local justice:

> [T]he same deputy, accompanied by a number of white men, one of whom was also an officer, and by the jailer, came to the jail, and the two last named defendants were made to strip and they were laid over chairs and their backs were cut to pieces with a leather strap with buckles on it, and they were likewise made by the said deputy definitely to understand that the whipping would be continued unless and until they confessed, and not only confessed, but confessed in every matter of detail as demanded by those present; and in this manner the defendants confessed the crime, and as the whippings progressed and were repeated, they changed or adjusted their confession in all particulars of detail so as to conform to the demands of their torturers.

Those responsible for the outrage freely admitted it. Indeed, when he was later asked about the beatings' severity, the deputy sheriff replied, "Not too much for a Negro; not so much as I would have done if it were left for me."

The defendants repeated their confessions the next morning, and two days later, they were charged by the local grand jury. That afternoon, they were arraigned. Although some of them offered to plead guilty, the trial judge refused to accept any guilty pleas. Rather, he appointed lawyers to represent them and set the trial to start the following morning. The confessions were used and, not surprisingly, the defendants were convicted. The sentence was death. Everyone—the trial judge, the prosecutor, the local constabulary—was aware that there had been torture. To the dissenting justices of the Mississippi Supreme Court, the events read "more like pages torn from some medieval account, than a record made within the confines of a modern civilization which aspires to an enlightened constitutional government." Nevertheless, the conviction was affirmed. Later, the United States Supreme Court reversed and recognized that the fundamental principle of due process prevented the use of torture-extorted confessions.

The use of torture to force confessions was not, of course, limited to the South. The so-called third degree was commonplace all over this nation, but courts, to their credit, generally stood firm in striking down criminal convictions based on such patent violations of human rights. Indeed, a decade before the case involving Ellington, Brown, and Shields reached Washington, the Mississippi Supreme Court also condemned the practice with stirring eloquence:

> We know there are times when atrocious crimes arouse people to a high sense of indignation. And this is true especially in cases where an upright citizen is murdered without cause. But the deep damnation of the defendant's crime ought not cause those intrusted with the enforcement of the law to swerve from the calm and faithful performance of duty. Coercing the supposed state's criminals into confessions and using such confessions so coerced from them against them in trials has been the curse of all countries.

The object of these justices' obloquy was the use of "the water cure"—holding a man down and pouring water up his nose until he confessed—which the court described as "a specie of torture well known to the bench and bar of this country." Prodded by this barbaric practice, one John Fisher had confessed to a murder. He and a codefendant were separately tried. It was Fisher's conviction that the Mississippi Supreme Court reversed on due process grounds. The other fellow was not so fortunate. Although acquitted in his trial, he was lynched immediately thereafter. The local sheriff, who was supposed to protect prisoners in his custody, was later fined $500 for "dereliction of duty."

Rejecting coerced confessions is an "exclusionary rule" founded in history, common sense, and humanity. It was also fair to both the accused *and* the victim: if voluntary, the confession could be used; if not voluntary, it was excluded. Unfortunately, this rational approach has been abandoned. As we shall see, the new rules of exclusion are mined with elaborate and often artificial barriers to the truth. They have twisted the criminal law into a series of byzantine mazes, traps that ensnare even the most knowledgeable policemen, lawyers, and judges.

On June 13, 1966, five men—justices of the United States Supreme Court—decreed in *Miranda* v. *Arizona* that perfectly *voluntary* statements made by a person suspected of criminal activity in response to questions while in police custody would no longer be admissible into evidence unless the police told him four things *before* asking any questions:

• He has a right to remain silent. If he does decide to answer any questions, he can stop whenever he wants and can pick and choose among the questions he wishes to answer without his silence being used against him.
• Anything he does say may be used against him in court.
• He has an immediate right to a lawyer.
• He will get a free lawyer if he cannot afford to hire one.

Additionally, the suspect would have to acknowledge that he had these rights and that he was expressly giving them up (or "waiving" them).

The decision was "written" by the then-Chief Justice Earl Warren, although Bob Woodward and Scott Armstrong report in their book *The Brethren* that Warren rarely wrote the opinions to which he attached his name. Rather, he told his law clerks— recent law school graduates—how he wanted the cases to turn out. They dug up research to support his view and drafted the opinions. As explained by Warren's biographer, respected law professor Bernard Schwartz, the clerks were given "a great deal of discretion, particularly on the reasoning and research supporting the decision." This decision-first, reasoning-afterward methodology is a *legislative* approach to judging. It breaks with, rather than builds upon, the past of prior legal precedent.

The late Justice Felix Frankfurter—a liberal law professor but a judicial conservative—once observed that "the vagueness of a constitutional command" does not warrant judges' infusing it with their own "private notions" of social policy. Francis Bacon also warned that "judges ought to remember that their office is *jus dicere,* not *jus dare;* to interpret law and not to make law, or give law."

Legislators are elected to make policy decisions and will be replaced by those more in tune with what the people want if they choose wrongly. On the other hand, all federal judges have lifetime appointments and many state court judges, especially those on the appellate level, are also given protected tenures.

Judges are, appropriately, largely immune from the pressures that govern the legislative and executive branches. Alexander Hamilton called the judiciary the "least dangerous branch" precisely because its powers were limited. Without those limitations of self-restraint, however, it becomes the *most* dangerous branch and subjects the nation to the will, and whims, of men and women who are answerable to no one. The *Miranda* decision highlights this danger of law-making by judges. Significantly, it prevailed by the slimmest of margins: the four other justices violently disagreed. Prior to *Miranda,* the law refused to chill a criminal's desire to clear his conscience: the confessions were admissible as long as improper means were not used. The decree was a cataclysmic change in the law.

The *Miranda* case actually involved the appeals of four men who were separately convicted of various crimes. Michael Vignera was arrested for the robbery of a dress shop in Brooklyn, New York. He admitted committing the crime and was identified by the store owner and a saleslady. However, he had not been told that he had a right to a lawyer or that he had a right not to say anything. Convicted, he was sentenced as a third-felony offender to a term of thirty to sixty years.

Roy Allen Stewart was arrested when Los Angeles police discovered that he had endorsed some dividend checks taken in a series of purse-snatch robberies in which one of the women was killed. When asked if they could search his house, Stewart told the arresting officers, "Go ahead." They discovered various things taken from five of the robbery victims. Over the next five days, Stewart was questioned nine different times, and, during the last session, he admitted to robbing the dead woman but contended that he had not meant to hurt her. He was convicted of first-degree murder and robbery. The jury fixed the penalty as death. The California Supreme Court threw out the convictions because he had not been told that he could have a lawyer and that he could refuse to tell the police anything.

Carl Alvin Westover was arrested by the Kansas City police for two local robberies. He was also wanted by federal officials in California for two bank robberies. The Kansas City officers questioned Westover the night of his arrest and the next morning. They did not tell him that he had a right to a lawyer or that he could remain silent. Nevertheless, Westover maintained his innocence. The Kansas City authorities then let the FBI ask him about the California holdups. The federal agents warned Westover that he didn't have to say anything, that whatever he did say could be used against him in court, and that he had a right to a lawyer. After two and a half hours, Westover confessed. He was convicted of two counts of robbery and sentenced to two consecutive fifteen-year prison terms.

Ernesto Miranda was arrested by Arizona authorities for the kidnapping and forceable rape of an eighteen-year-old girl. He was taken to a Phoenix police station, where he was identified by the victim (to whom Chief Justice Earl Warren's decision later artfully referred in euphemistically aseptic legalese as "the complaining witness"). After two hours of questioning, Miranda gave a detailed oral confession and then wrote out and signed a brief summary, which recited that it had been voluntarily made and "with full knowledge of my legal rights, understanding that any statement I make may be used against me." He was not, however, told that he had a right to have a lawyer present during the questioning. Miranda was convicted of kidnapping and rape and sentenced to concurrent terms of twenty and thirty years.

The Supreme Court reversed the convictions of Vignera, Westover, and Miranda and affirmed the California Supreme Court's reversal of Stewart's conviction. From then on, the United States Supreme Court commanded, police officers who question suspects in custody first have to tell them that they needn't say anything, that what they do say will be used against them if they do say anything, and that they can have a lawyer (retained or appointed) present during the questioning. If these "*Miranda* warnings*" are not given, and the rights encompassed by them clearly and expressly waived, any statements, either admitting or denying guilt, cannot be used at trial even though they were freely made. In the course of the lengthy opinion, the five justices recognized that the statements given by Stewart, Vignera, Westover, and Miranda were not "involuntary in traditional terms." Nevertheless, the majority's concern was "not lessened in the slightest" because

> In each of the cases, the defendant was thrust into an unfamiliar atmosphere and run through menacing police interrogation procedures. The potentiality for compulsion is forcefully apparent, for example, in *Miranda*, where the indigent Mexican defendant was a seriously disturbed individual with pronounced sexual fantasies, and in *Stewart*, in which the defendant was an indigent Los Angeles Negro who had dropped out of school in the sixth grade. *To be sure, the records do not evince overt physical coercion or patent psychological ploys. The fact remains that in none of these cases did the officers undertake to afford appropriate safeguards at the outset of the interrogation to insure that the statements were truly the product of a free choice.*

I have italicized the last two sentences because I think they emphasize the essential thrust of the decision: criminal investigation was no longer to be an absolute pursuit of the truth (with appropriate due process safeguards to prevent extortion of confessions). It was now to be a contest in which one player, the police, would have to alert the other player, the suspect, if and when he was about to make a bad move and, if so, to make certain he understood the consequences.

One of the significant policy points upon which the majority relied and which has been cited ever since as a measure of the decree's reasonableness was that the FBI had routinely been giving the warnings they were now imposing on state and local law enforcement. Indeed, Bernard Schwartz's highly acclaimed biography of Earl Warren, *Super Chief*, reports that one of the justices present at the March 6, 1966, conference where the *Miranda* case was discussed and voted upon recalled that the FBI argument was "perhaps the critical factor" in persuading some of the fence-sitting justices over to Warren's side. Yet as Justice John Marshall Harlan noted in his dissent, the FBI warning procedures fell "sensibly short of the Court's formalistic rules," which were now being dictated for the entire country. Thus, Harlan wrote, "there is no indication that FBI agents must obtain an affirmative 'waiver' before they pursue their questioning. Nor is it clear that one invoking his right to silence may not be prevailed to change his mind."

The five-to-four decision requiring that suspects be warned of their Fifth Amendment rights against compulsory self-incrimination during pretrial investigations went well beyond its original scope as framed by the provision's language ("No person . . . shall be compelled in any criminal case to be a witness against himself") as well as beyond its history. The dissenting justices were outraged both by the majority's fast and loose interpretation of history and by what they saw as the imposition of unrealistic and totally unwarranted restrictions on police questioning:

> What the Court largely ignores is that its rules impair, if they will not eventually serve wholly to frustrate, an instrument of law enforcement that has long and quite reasonably been thought worth the price paid for it. There can be little doubt that the Court's new code would markedly decrease the number of confessions. To warn the suspect that he may remain silent and remind him that his confession may be used in court are minor obstructions. To require an express waiver by the suspect and an end to questioning whenever he demurs must heavily handicap questioning. And to suggest or provide counsel for the suspect simply invites the end of the interrogation.

Dissenting Justice John Marshall Harlan bitterly called the historical edifice erected by his five brethren a *trompe l'oeil*—an illusion—and pointed out that, despite a common misconception fostered by the majority's opinion, the new judge-imposed rules were not aimed at police brutality:

Those who use third-degree tactics and deny them in court are equally able and destined to lie as skillfully about warnings and waivers. Rather, the thrust of the new rules is to negate all pressures, to reinforce the nervous or ignorant suspect, and ultimately to discourage any confession at all. The aim, in short, is toward "voluntariness" in a utopian sense, or to view it from a different angle, voluntariness with a vengeance.

Harlan noted that the conviction of the bank robber Westover (whom he described as "a seasoned criminal") was overturned even though he was "practically given the Court's full complement of warnings" but "did not heed them." The situation involving the rapist Ernesto Miranda was even more frustrating. This is how Justice Harlan told the story:

On March 3, 1963, an 18-year-old girl was kidnapped and forcibly raped near Phoenix, Arizona. Ten days later, on the morning of March 13, petitioner Miranda was arrested and taken to the police station. At this time Miranda was 23 years old, indigent, and educated to the extent of completing half of the ninth grade. He had an "emotional illness" of the schizophrenic type, according to the doctor who eventually examined him; the doctors' report also stated that Miranda was "alert and oriented as to time, place, and person," intelligent within normal limits, competent to stand trial, and sane within the legal definition. At the police station, the victim picked Miranda out of a lineup, and two officers then took him into a separate room to interrogate him, starting at about 11:30 a.m. Though at first denying his guilt, within a short time Miranda gave a detailed oral confession and then wrote out in his own hand and signed a brief statement admitting and describing the crime. All this was accomplished in two hours or less without any force, threats or promises and—I will assume this though the record is uncertain—without any effective warnings at all.

Miranda's oral and written confessions are now held inadmissible under the Court's new rules. One is entitled to feel astonished that the Constitution can be read to produce this result. These confessions were obtained during brief, daytime questioning conducted by two officers and unmarked by any of the traditional indicia of coercion. They assured a conviction for a brutal and unsettling crime, for which the police had and quite possibly could obtain little evidence other than the victim's identifications, evidence which is frequently unreliable.

There was, in sum, a legitimate purpose, no perceptible unfairness, and certainly little risk of injustice in the interrogation. Yet, the resulting confessions, and the responsible course of police practice they represent, are to be sacrificed to the Court's own finespun conception of fairness which I seriously doubt is shared by many thinking citizens in this country.

The keystone of the *Miranda* majority's logic was, as we have seen, that "the unfamiliar atmosphere" into which an arrested person is thrust is so inherently coercive that the warnings are required to guarantee that any statements made in response to questioning are "truly the product of a free choice." If no questions are asked, of course, the suspect is free to say anything he or she wishes. The majority explained:

> The fundamental import of the privilege while an individual is in custody is not whether he is allowed to talk to the police without the benefit of warnings and counsel, but whether he can be interrogated.

With this critical issue in mind, Justice Byron R. White's dissenting opinion illumined the inherent flaw in the Court's "bright line" test (either the warnings are given and the rights waived or they are not):

> Although in the Court's view in-custody interrogation is inherently coercive, the Court says that the spontaneous product of the coercion of arrest and detention is still to be deemed to be voluntary. An accused, arrested on probable cause, may blurt out a confession which will be admissible despite the fact that he is alone and in custody, without any showing that he had any notion of his right to remain silent or of the consequences of his admission. Yet, under the Court's rule, if the police ask him a single question such as "Do you have anything to say?" or "Did you kill your wife?" his response, if there is one, has somehow been compelled.

There was nothing wrong, the dissenters argued, with the former standards, which required the pretrial statements to pass the due process muster of voluntariness. As Harlan pointed out, the Supreme Court, over the years, had "devised an elaborate, sophisticated, and sensitive approach" for assessing whether confessions met that standard. By contrast, under *Miranda*, if no warnings were given or if the rights were not clearly waived, no response by a suspect can be used as evidence of guilt *even though the response was clearly voluntary.* Application of this mechanistic approach has led to the escape—or near escape—of many guilty persons from the clutches of justice.

On the afternoon of Christmas Eve, 1968, ten-year-old Pamela Powers was with her family at the Des Moines, Iowa, YMCA watching her brother compete in a wrestling tournament. She went to the restroom but never returned.

A recent mental hospital escapee by the name of Robert Williams had been living at the Y. Soon after Pamela's disappearance, Williams was seen carrying a bundle through the Y's lobby. A fourteen-year-old boy who helped him open his car door later told authorities that Williams's bundle had two skinny white legs sticking from it. Williams drove off; the car was found, abandoned, 160 miles away in Davenport. Though the authorities suspected Pamela had been killed, they had no direct proof that she was dead. Williams was charged with abduction, and a warrant was issued for his arrest.

A day and a half later, on December 26, a lawyer told the Des Moines police that he had just received a call from Williams and had made arrangements for Williams to turn himself in to the Davenport authorities. When Williams surrendered in Davenport, he was arrested, advised of his *Miranda* rights, and booked.

Williams was brought before a judge in Davenport for his arraignment. The judge again told him of his rights under the *Miranda* decision. After the brief court session, Williams consulted with a Davenport lawyer who also told him not to talk to the police until he was able to discuss his case with the lawyer in Des Moines.

Two police officers from Des Moines picked Williams up for the return trip. Before they left, one of them reminded Williams that he had a right to have a lawyer present at any questioning. The officer also told Williams that he wanted to make sure that Williams understood that he did not have to say anything because it would be a long trip to Des Moines and they would "be visiting" along the way. Williams again consulted with his Davenport lawyer, who repeated that he was not to say anything to the police during the trip. The lawyer also told the officers not to ask Williams any questions.

The weather was bad, and, before they had been on the road very long, Captain Cletus Leaming, the officer in the back seat with Williams, began to "visit" with him. Leaming knew Williams considered himself to be a very religious person. Among the things Leaming told Williams was that he thought the girl's body had been left near Mitchellville, a town between Des Moines and Davenport. This was his testimony at a pretrial hearing in response to interrogation by Williams's lawyer:

Q: You didn't ask Williams any questions?
A: No sir, I told him some things.
Q: You told him some things?
A: Yes, sir. Would you like to hear it?
Q: Yes.
A: All right. I said to Mr. Williams, I said, "Reverend, I'm going to tell you something. I don't want you to answer me, but I want you to think about it when we're driving down the road." I said, "I want you to observe the weather. It's raining and it's sleeting and it's freezing. Visibility is very poor. They are predicting snow for tonight. I think we're going to be going right past where that body is, and if we should stop and find out where it is on the way in, her parents are going to be able to have a good Christian burial for their daughter. If we don't and it does snow and if you're the only person that knows where this is and if you have only been there once, it's very possible that with snow on the ground you might not be able to find it. Now I just want you to think about that when we're driving down the road." That's all I said.

Q: About where were you when you said that?
A: Well, not very far out of Davenport. This is on the freeway.

Q: And now when you got to Mitchellville, did you ask him if he thought about it?
A: No. As we were coming towards Mitchellville, we'd still be east of Mitchellville a ways, he said to me, "How do you know that would be at Mitchellville?" And I said, "Well, I'm an investigator. This is my job, and I just figured it out." I said, "I don't

know exactly where, but I do know it's somewhere in that area."
He said, "You're right, and I'm going to show you where it is."

They found the body. The little girl had been raped and murdered.

At his trial, Williams sought to exclude all his statements as well as the evidence gathered as a result of those statements. The trial judge denied the motion on the ground that by voluntarily taking the officers to the body, he had given up his right not to talk without his lawyer being present.

Williams was convicted of murder, and the Supreme Court of Iowa affirmed the conviction. Williams then sought release from a United States district court judge via the ancient remedy of *habeas corpus*, alleging that his constitutional rights had been violated.

Habeas corpus is Latin for "thou have the body." Although it began as a device to bring a reluctant defendant to court to answer *civil* charges by a plaintiff seeking damages or the return of property, it was frequently used by our early English forebears to compel the many lords who exercised private criminal jurisdiction to produce their prisoners at the King's court so that the prisoners could find out why they were being locked up. Soon expanded to permit a challenge to any detention claimed to be unlawful, *habeas corpus* is such an important predicate of liberty that our Constitution prohibits its suspension except when "in cases of rebellion or invasion the public safety may require it," and then only by the Congress.

The federal judge agreed with Williams that his rights had been violated and granted the writ of *habeas corpus*. A federal appeals court agreed. The United States Supreme Court, on a five to four vote, affirmed and remanded the case back to the Iowa trial court for a retrial.

Writing for the slim majority, Justice Potter Stewart believed that what Williams's appellate lawyers derisively called the "Christian burial" speech had been a ruse to overcome the multiple warnings. In effect, he believed it denied Williams his right to have a lawyer's help. He quoted Leaming's trial testimony:

Q: In fact, Captain, whether he was a mental patient or not, you were trying to get all the information you could before he got to his lawyer, weren't you?

A: I was sure hoping to find out where that little girl was, yes, sir.

Years later, Leaming told a Des Moines newspaper reporter that he "was just being a good old-fashioned cop" and didn't see anything wrong in what he had done. Five Supreme Court justices disagreed. Even the majority recognized that that crime "was senseless and brutal, calling for swift and energetic action by the police to apprehend the perpetrator and gather evidence." Nevertheless, they tossed out the conviction so as not to condone what they called a "clear violation" of Williams's constitutional rights.

Chief Justice Warren Burger's angry dissent called what the majority had done "intolerable" and condemned the way the Court "mechanically and blindly keeps reliable evidence from juries." One can almost taste the venom in the Chief Justice's words:

> Williams is guilty of the savage murder of a small child; no member of the Court contends that he is not. While in custody, and after no fewer than *five* warnings of his rights to silence and counsel, he led police to the concealed body of his victim. The Court concedes that Williams was not threatened or coerced and that he spoke and acted voluntarily and with full awareness of his constitutional rights. In the face of all this, the Court now holds that because Williams was prompted by the detective's statement—not interrogation but a statement—the jury must not be told how the police found the body.

The other dissenting justices criticized the majority's opinion in equally strong language and concluded, in the words of Justice White, that the officers "did nothing 'wrong,' let alone 'unconstitutional.' "

Williams was retried for the murder of Pamela Powers. Although the prosecution was forbidden to use his statements or tell the jury how they found Pamela's body, they did persuade the trial judge to let the jury know where, and in what condition, the body had been found on the theory that a large search party combing the area would have discovered it anyway. Williams was convicted and sentenced to a life term in the penitentiary.

The case later returned to the Supreme Court, and on June 11, 1984, fifteen and a half years after Pamela had been raped and murdered, it was finally put to rest. This time, on a seven-to-two vote, the Court agreed with the state trial judge and upheld Williams's second conviction, thereby affirming the "inevitable discovery" exception to the exclusionary rule.

The divergence of judicial thought in *Williams* highlights the essential artificiality of the *Miranda* rules. Nowhere was this made more clear than in an angry exchange between Justices John Paul Stevens and Byron R. White in the second appeal. Stevens wrote that he agreed that Williams's conviction should be affirmed, but he criticized Captain Leaming for deciding to "dispense with the requirements of law." "Thanks to" him, wrote Stevens, "the State of Iowa has expended vast sums of money and countless hours of professional labor in his defense. That expenditure surely provides an adequate deterrent to similar violations; the responsibility for that expenditure lies not with the Constitution, but rather with the constable."

Justice White disagreed. Captain Leaming, he explained, was "no doubt acting as many competent police officers would have acted under similar circumstances and in light of then-existing law. That five Justices later thought he was mistaken does not call for making him out to be a villain or for a lecture on deliberate police misconduct and its resulting costs to society." Neither does it make the police officer "wrong" or, for that matter, the state courts of Iowa "wrong" in upholding Williams's original conviction. Rather, as the late Supreme Court Justice Robert H. Jackson (who also served as this nation's chief prosecutor at the Nuremberg war crimes trial) observed in the early 1950s, the varying views reflect "a difference in outlook found between personnel comprising different courts" and that "reversal by a higher court is not proof that justice is thereby better done."

> There is no doubt that if there were a super Supreme Court, a substantial proportion of our reversals of state courts would also be reversed. We are not final because we are infallible, but we are infallible because we are final.

Williams was ultimately brought to justice—a claim that cannot be made in many of the cases in which the prosecution is forbidden to use an accused's statements. But the question of whether his first conviction should have been overturned and, indeed, whether the exclusionary rule's application to voluntary confessions should be modified persists. Any analysis of this issue must be made in the light of *Miranda*'s underlying rationale: that it is improper for the police to elicit perfectly voluntary statements unless they first do all they can to discourage the statements from being made.

As we have seen, most people voluntarily confess because they *want* to, just as most people who smoke first started because they wanted to. The late Chief Justice Earl Warren's implicit intent in fashioning rules to prevent juries from hearing defendants' statements that are not "involuntary in traditional terms" was to place all criminals on an equal level in dealing with law enforcement:

- The hardened recidivist offender whose experience with the system gives him a "cops get nothing for nothing" attitude. He won't tell the police anything unless he gets a deal in return.
- The socially secure person (wealthy or knowledgeable) who is already aware of his rights to remain silent and to have a lawyer and is able to claim those rights without prompting.
- The socially insecure person (poor or unknowledgeable) who, ignorant of his rights, will *voluntarily* confess for all of the reasons we have already discussed.

Since the first two categories of criminals may be able to avoid the siren lure of confession unassisted, Warren contended that the third category of criminals must be prevented from doing what they instinctively want to do (short, perhaps, of taping their mouths shut). The *Miranda* warnings must therefore be given, and once a suspect indicates in the least way that he doesn't want to talk or that he wants a lawyer, all questioning must stop. Although the suspect may waive or relinquish any of the *Miranda* rights even after they have been invoked, the prosecution has a heavy burden of showing that any waiver was voluntary and untainted by police conduct. To return to the smoking analogy, it would be as if the government required an affirmation by everyone seeking to buy a pack of cigarettes that he or she has read the surgeon general's warning, has understood that warning, and has nevertheless decided to make the purchase. Furthermore, before he could make the sale, the merchant would have to demonstrate that the customer's decision was unaffected by tobacco company advertising or by any other form of persuasion. (To those who think that this analogy makes trivial the important issues at stake, I ask, Why do you elevate the right of a smoker to harm his own body over the right of a criminal to voluntarily confess his crime?) To see how heavy some judges would make the "waiver" burden, we look to the Supreme Court of North Carolina.

Willie Butler was convicted of kidnapping, armed robbery, and felonious assault for the holdup of a Goldsboro, North Carolina, gas station, which left the attendant paralyzed. Arrested by the FBI in New York on a fugitive warrant, Butler was orally advised of his *Miranda* rights and then, while at the FBI office, was given an "advice of rights" form to read and sign. Butler told the agents that he understood his rights but would not sign; he said, "I will talk to you but I am not signing any form." He did not ask for a lawyer, and he freely told the agents about the robbery. Nevertheless, the North Carolina Supreme Court reversed his conviction because he had never *specifically* waived his right to counsel by saying, for example, "I hereby don't want a lawyer," or words of similar import.

The United States Supreme Court, on a close five to three vote (one justice did not participate in the decision), reversed and reinstated Butler's convictions. The Court held that Butler's actions clearly indicated a knowing and voluntary waiver and that an *explicit* statement of waiver was not needed. However, the dissenting justices strongly criticized the majority for permitting trial courts in similar circumstances "to construct inferences from ambiguous words and gestures." They argued that *"Miranda* requires that ambiguity be interpreted against" law enforcement. Again, the law enforcement officer was criticized by the dissenters not only for not doing everything he could to discourage the defendant from talking but apparently also for his failure to read the entrails of judicial precedent: "Had agent Martinez simply elicited a clear answer from Willie Butler to the question, 'Do you waive your right to a lawyer?' this journey through three courts would not have been necessary."

Of course, had the FBI agent used those words, Butler might have finally gotten the hint that he should not talk even though he wanted to, and perhaps another serious crime would have gone unpunished. On the other hand, had Butler still confessed in the face of the words suggested by dissenting Justice William Brennan, there might have been a dispute as to whether Butler—who went through the eleventh grade—understood what *waive* meant. Indeed, there are some who argue that since very few criminals of the third type discussed above—the socially insecure person ignorant of his rights—can understand the full import of the *Miranda* rights even when they *are* explained, *no confessions should be taken at all.* For example, a study conducted under the aegis of the *California Law Review* shows that only some 42 percent of adults tested "adequately" understood the warnings. Thus, highly respected liberal law professor Yale Kamisar has suggested that public defender lawyers be placed at every police station to advise all suspects upon arrest and to keep police from questioning them.

Willie Butler almost escaped justice because some appellate judges thought his decision to talk without first consulting a lawyer was not articulated with sufficient specificity. Thomas J. Innis also almost escaped justice, despite waivers that were clear and unambiguous, because some judges thought the police had made an unfair appeal to his conscience.

Innis was arrested for murder and armed robbery. His arrest was triggered by the complaint of Gerald Aubin, a Providence, Rhode Island, taxi driver. Aubin told the police that he had just been held up by a man with a sawed-off shotgun, and that he had let him off in an area near a school for handicapped children. The police were especially interested in Aubin's report because the body of another cab driver, killed by a shotgun blast to the back of the head earlier that week, had been found in a shallow grave the day before. While he was at the police station, Aubin saw the robber's picture on a bulletin board. He later fingered the same man from a different picture he picked out of a group of photographs presented to him.

Police searched the area where Innis had been let off. At 4:30 A.M., they saw him. He was unarmed. Innis was arrested and advised of his *Miranda* rights. In a few minutes, a police sergeant arrived. He too gave Innis the required warnings. A police captain showed up just after the sergeant, and he also repeated the

Miranda litany. In response to this third set of warnings, Innis finally got the hint and said he wanted to speak to a lawyer. The captain told the other officers to take Innis to police headquarters, and he instructed them not to question or intimidate him.

During the ride downtown, two of the officers talked. This is how one of them, Joseph Gleckman, related it later in court:

> At this point, I was talking back and forth with Patrolman McKenna stating that I frequent this area while on patrol and there's a lot of handicapped children running around in this area, and God forbid one of them might find a weapon with shells and they might hurt themselves.

Q: Who were you talking to?
A: Patrolman McKenna.
Q: Did you say anything to the suspect Innis?
A: No, I didn't.

Innis overheard the conversation. "Turn around," he told them. "I'll show you where the weapon is." One of the officers radioed the captain, who met them where Innis had told them to stop. The captain *again* reminded Innis of his *Miranda* rights. Innis replied that he understood but that he "wanted to get the gun out of the way" because of the children. The shotgun was found under some rocks in a nearby field.

At his trial, Innis sought to have his statements and the shotgun excluded. The trial judge refused, noting that the officers' concern was "entirely understandable" and that Innis had voluntarily agreed to show them the gun. Innis was convicted. The Rhode Island Supreme Court, voting three to two, reversed. They reasoned that by telling the officers he wanted to speak to a lawyer, Innis had exercised his right to be left alone. The dialogue concerning the shotgun and the children, they contended (drawing an analogy from the so-called "Christian burial" speech in *Williams*), was merely a subtle attempt to coerce a confession. Recognizing that "most of the other evidence against the defendant was circumstantial in nature," they ruled that the prosecution should not benefit from "the improper remarks of Officer Gleckman."

Although the United States Supreme Court later reinstated Innis's conviction, the vote was again close, six to three. In a decision written by Justice Potter Stewart, the Court recognized that *Miranda*'s prohibition of custodial interrogation applied to comments "reasonably likely to elicit an incriminating response" as well as to direct questioning, but that since there was nothing "to suggest that the officers were aware" that Innis "was peculiarly susceptible to an appeal to his conscience concerning the safety of handicapped children," there had been no violation.

Justice Thurgood Marshall, joined by Justice William Brennan, bitterly dissented:

> One can scarcely imagine a stronger appeal to the conscience of a suspect—*any* suspect—than the assertion that if the weapon is not found an innocent person will be hurt or killed. And not just any innocent person, but an innocent child—a little girl—a helpless, handicapped little girl on her way to school. The notion that such an appeal could not be expected to have any effect unless the suspect were known to have some special interest in the handicapped verges on the ludicrous. As a matter of fact, the appeal to a suspect to confess for the sake of others, to "display some evidence of decency and honor," is a classic interrogation technique.

In a separate opinion, Justice Stevens also objected to the reinstatement of Innis's conviction. He argued that the distinctions drawn by the majority were disingenuous:

> The difference between the approach required by a faithful adherence to *Miranda* and the stinted test applied by the Court today can be illustrated by comparing three different ways in which Officer Gleckman could have communicated his fears about the possible dangers posed by the shotgun to handicapped children. He could have:
>
> (1) directly asked Innis:
>
>> Will you please tell me where the shotgun is so we can protect handicapped schoolchildren from danger?
>
> (2) announced to the other officers in the wagon:
>
>> If the man sitting in the back seat with me should decide to tell us where the gun is, we can protect handicapped children from danger.
>
> or (3) stated to the other officers:
>
>> It would be too bad if a little handicapped girl would pick up the gun that this man left in the area and maybe kill herself.

In my opinion, all three of these statements should be considered interrogation because all three appear to be designed to elicit a response from anyone who in fact knew where the gun was located.

The comments of Justices Marshall and Stevens are instructive on two levels. First, was the murdered cab driver not *innocent*? Was *he* not entitled to life, and was *his* family not entitled to *his* love and companionship? And what about the safety, lives, and families of those who might be *future victims* if Innis were permitted to escape justice? It is interesting that the rights of victims or potential victims are rarely discussed by those who would tie the police to an etiquette well beyond the Marquis of Queensberry as a precondition to the admission of perfectly reliable evidence.

Second, I fail to see the harm in permitting the police to provide an avenue for voluntary confessions. In this regard, I agree with Justice Stevens that there is little difference between the three hypothetical statements. The appeals to "decency and honor" which Justice Marshall so decried are appropriate methods to "catch the conscience" of a suspect. Indeed, such appeals might even generate conscience formation in a person otherwise bereft of feeling. Dr. Theodor Reik has passionately described the underlying dynamics:

> To the criminal, confession means that his conscience has acquired its voice. He becomes, through the spoken repetition, conscious of the significance of his deed. . . .
> In his confession, the criminal has admitted his misdeed to the community, as the child once admitted his naughtiness to his real father or to his substitute. As the confession of the child unconsciously represents a new wooing for love, an attempt at regaining the lost object, the criminal shows in his confession his intention to reenter society by declaring himself deserving of punishment. The outsider is on his painful detour back to the family of man.

The *Miranda* exclusionary rule often blocks that return. In many instances, it and the search and seizure exclusionary rule permit those who are clearly guilty to avoid their rendezvous with justice, as we will see in the next chapter.

SEVEN

Boardgames

At 1 A.M. ON Thursday, August 26, 1976, sheriff's deputies in Alameda County, California, got a call from Barry Floyd Braeseke. Then twenty years old, Braeseke told them that someone had killed his parents and his grandfather. When they arrived at Braeseke's home, the deputies found the three bodies. Each had died from multiple wounds inflicted by a .22-caliber rifle. Braeseke told the deputies that he had last seen the three alive at 9 P.M., when he and a friend had gone to the movies. Noticing that there was no sign of a forced entry and, despite some evidence of ransacking, that many things that normally would have been taken in a burglary were left untouched, the deputies asked Braeseke to come with them to the station for further questioning. They talked to him for a little more than an hour.

There were discrepancies in Braeseke's story and, seeing splattered blood on his trousers, the deputies read him his *Miranda* rights. Braeseke agreed to talk. He explained that he must have gotten the blood on his clothing when he was checking the bodies. When the officers replied that one could not get a splatter pattern that way and that they believed he killed his parents and grandfather, Braeseke said he did not want to talk without a lawyer present. The deputies stopped asking him questions, placed him under arrest, and began to book him.

In the course of the routine booking process, a police sergeant asked Braeseke for his name, address, and date of birth. When the sergeant asked him for his next of kin, Braeseke fell silent and asked the sergeant if he could speak to him in private and off the record. The sergeant agreed, and Braeseke asked him, hypothetically, what would happen to him if, in fact, he had committed the murders, and "What if I tell you the rifle was somewhere where some kids may find it?" The sergeant replied that although he would appreciate any information Braeseke could give him, the young man would still have to go to jail. He then asked Braeseke whether he could "turn the tape recorder on and can we get a statement from you to that effect?" Braeseke said yes. The following is a transcription of part of that taped conversation with the sergeant asking the questions:

Q: Barry, we have talked previously regarding the fatal shooting of your parents last night, uh, and we actually got to the point where you said you wanted to have a lawyer before you went any further. Then during the routine booking and filling out of the arrest form, you asked if you could speak to me, is that correct?

A: Yeah.

Q: And you—what I'm saying is that you came forward to me and asked if—asked to talk to me regarding the incident, is that correct?

A: Yes.

Q: And you're doing this of your own free will . . .

A: Hell yeah, yes.

Q: . . . being well aware of the fact that you still have the right to have a lawyer present.

A: Yes, yes.

Q: To have him present for any and all questioning, and that if you . . .

A: I understand that.

Q: And if you cannot afford to hire one, the courts will appoint one for you.

A: Yeah, yes.

Q: Okay, keeping all of this in mind, Barry, would you like to run down to me what did happen at your house tonight?

A: I don't know how I can start.

Q: Let's start with dinner.

Braeseke then confessed to the killings. He was convicted of three counts of first-degree murder. The Supreme Court of California reversed on a four-to-three vote, ruling that the prosecution did not prove that Braeseke's decision to talk to the sergeant was a "knowing and intelligent waiver of his *Miranda* rights." Justice

William P. Clark, Jr., bitterly dissented in an opinion in which two of his colleagues joined:

How did the constable blunder? What did the officers do that they should not have done? What should have been done that was left undone?

The conduct of the police was irreproachable. Therefore, the lesson ("prophylactic effect") derived from today's decision can only be that this court no longer accepts convictions based on voluntary confessions. This despite the fact that many convicted criminals (few criminals, of course, are convicted) would go free but for confessions. Worse, recognition that some desire to tell the truth—and should be permitted to do so—escapes the majority of our court.

There can be no doubt but that this twenty-year-old defendant knowingly and intelligently waived his *Miranda* protections. . . .

It would be difficult to imagine more compelling evidence of waiver of one's privilege to sit silent. Conversely, defendant's desire to describe his conduct to those charged with its solution is clear and should not be frustrated by our court.

The prosecution tried to get the United States Supreme Court to hear its appeal (the Supreme Court can pick the cases it wishes to review), but was turned down. Justice William Rehnquist attacked the California Supreme Court's decision as coming "extraordinarily close to the adoption of a rule that in *no* cases can waiver be inferred from the actions and words of the person being interrogated."

Hayward, California attorney James Leonard Crew represented Braeseke at his trial; he had unsuccessfully attempted to have the inculpatory statements excluded. Yet when Braeseke's convictions were overturned and the United States Supreme Court refused to review the case and Braeseke repeated the chilling details of the triple murder for Mike Wallace on CBS's "60 Minutes," Crew, able to separate his responsibilities as a defense lawyer from his feelings as a citizen, decried the illogic of it all in the following letter to the justices of the United States Supreme Court:

Gentlemen:

Your recent decision in the case of People vs. Barry Braeseke was predictable. On the other hand, it is difficult to

understand how a system of laws conceived to protect innocent people can become twisted to give freedom to a
person who deliberately kills three innocent human
beings, thereafter confesses four times to these killings,
(the last confession being on national television) and with
all of this somehow finds that freedom awaits him.

I write in this case with special interest, as I was the trial
attorney appointed by the courts of Alameda County to represent the above-referenced defendant. I also happen to be
a responsible citizen in my community and shudder to
think that my family has now been given less protection by
our courts. No wonder the citizens in this country refer to
attorneys in a disrespectful fashion and to many of our
courts with comparable lack of respect.

Very truly yours,

James Leonard Crew

Crew, described by *Time* magazine as "a tough, able defender," was criticized by attorneys for writing the letter. Nevertheless, he has stuck firmly to his belief that the criminal justice
system needs an infusion of common sense. Ironically, Braeseke
was convicted again on his retrial when the prosecution, barred
from using the statements given to the officers, played his "60
Minutes" confession, for which no *Miranda* warnings were required. In all likelihood, Braeseke would have walked away from
the murders had he not succumbed to what Reik characterized
as the impulse "to free himself from the terrible burden" via the
airwaves.

Braeseke's urge to confess, and the police officers' careful
attention to what they thought the law required, reminds me of
a sad case over which I presided involving a young man accused
first of sodomizing a little boy and then of tossing him from a
high bridge to his death in the Milwaukee River below. Before
the boy's killer was found, tried, and convicted, the lad's disappearance was extensively publicized and caused a panic among
Milwaukee parents; the panic was fanned by the child murders
then taking place in Atlanta, Georgia.

James Blockman, a young black man, first came to the attention of law enforcement when, during the early-morning hours of March 31, 1981, he went to a Milwaukee television station, ostensibly looking for work. However, he told the assistant news manager that he had seen a black male push a black child into the Milwaukee River near Milwaukee's Locust Street bridge. The assistant news manager called the police, and an officer asked Blockman if he would voluntarily tell his story to detectives downtown. Blockman agreed.

He repeated his story for the detectives and then took them to the place where he said he had seen the assault. Later that morning, however, he changed his story, telling the detectives he had been lying. They arrested him for obstructing the police and advised him of his *Miranda* rights, which he said he understood. They then asked him more questions and placed him in a lineup to determine whether he was the person a witness had seen with the little boy the day he disappeared. When the witness failed to pick him out of the lineup, Blockman was released.

Two weeks afterward, on April 13, the little boy's body was found in the Milwaukee River. Later that day, Milwaukee police detectives asked Blockman to return with them to headquarters for additional questioning. He agreed and was again advised of his *Miranda* rights, which he again said he understood. He repeated his initial version of having been a witness to, rather than an actor in, the little boy's murder; he agreed to take a lie detector test the following day. When he expressed some concern about being able to make it down to the detective bureau because he did not have bus fare, they assured him that they would give him a ride. They did not arrest him but let him return to his home.

The next day, when the officers were late, Blockman anxiously called police headquarters to find out where they were. When the detectives finally arrived, they asked him to retrace the route he said he had seen the man and the boy take before the murder. Blockman agreed. They again advised him of his *Miranda* rights, which he said he understood. There were sufficient discrepancies in his story that one of the detectives, as he later testified, felt that an arrest for the young boy's murder would be warranted. However, Blockman was not arrested at that point; rather, he was permitted to take the lie detector test.

Blockman was taken to the polygraph examiner's office just

before noon. The examiner again advised him of his *Miranda* rights, which Blockman said he understood. He then willingly took the test. He was asked several questions concerning the little boy's death. After the end of the formal questioning, the polygraph examiner, a detective lieutenant, asked Blockman whether there was anything he wanted to say "about this matter." Blockman replied, according to the polygraph operator's testimony, that he "didn't know any more about it." On cross-examination by Blockman's lawyer, the polygraph operator phrased it this way: "I said 'there must be something you want to tell us,' and he said 'no.' "

The polygraph operator did not stop his interrogation there. Rather, according to his testimony, he asked Blockman whether he had been sexually abused as a child, because this might have caused him to want to sexually abuse little children. He also mentioned to Blockman that it was as if Blockman were sitting in a dentist's office waiting for a painful tooth to come out and that many children were imprisoned inside their own homes by the fear that a child-killer—some big "hairy beast," as he put it— was stalking the streets of Milwaukee. In apparent response to these comments, Blockman started to tell the polygraph operator how he had met the little boy and had gone with him to the Milwaukee River. The polygraph operator stopped the conversation, placed Blockman in a locked interrogation room, and located the detectives in charge of the case. The detectives readvised Blockman of his *Miranda* rights, which he again said he understood, and obtained a full confession, which they later had him repeat on tape.

Blockman's lawyer sought to have the statements to the polygraph operator and the confession excluded from the trial. He claimed that when Blockman told the polygraph operator that he didn't want to say anything more about the murder, he had invoked his right to silence. The legal analysis initially focused on whether Blockman was "in custody" at the time. If he was, his statements to the polygraph operator—as well as those to the detectives, even though they readvised him of his *Miranda* rights— might, under prevailing appellate decisions, have to be excluded.

As we have seen, the *Miranda* rights are precipitated by what the five justices termed the "inherently coercive" aspects of being in police "custody." Blockman's lawyer wanted me to find that his client was "in custody" during the polygraph examination because the police admittedly would not have let him leave had he wished to do so. In an extensive written decision, I rejected that approach as one that would "erect an artificial barrier to the receipt of confessions freely and voluntarily made." Instead, I adopted the approach of the Supreme Court of Alaska among other authorities, which required that there be either "an actual arrest or other *overt* restraint" on a person's freedom that would lead a reasonable person *with an innocent mind* to believe that he or she was not free to leave. Only then, in my view, would there be sufficient "custody" for *Miranda* purposes. Stated another way, there could only be "coercion" stemming from "custody" if an innocent person in the position of the suspect would have been aware that he or she was in custody. To permit, however, a purely subjective custody analysis from the vantage point of a suspect's guilty mind would set too low a threshold of police action: a guilty person might construe even innocuous police contact as a significant restraint. As I wrote at the time,

> A rule of "custody" which triggers *Miranda* restrictions on the mere station house interrogation of those individuals who initiate contact with law enforcement officers or who voluntarily comply with their requests—absent arrest or overt restraint—would only thwart effective law enforcement without any concomitant benefit.

Blockman's initial voluntary contact, of course, was not with law enforcement but with a local network television affiliate. However, as I explained in the decision, those "volunteered statements in connection with such a widely publicized disappearance could have reasonably been foreseen . . . to invite the attention of law enforcement." A jury convicted Blockman of first-degree sexual assault and second-degree murder. I sentenced him to the maximum period of incarceration permitted in Wisconsin for those crimes: two consecutive twenty-year terms.

My analysis in the *Blockman* case, while consistent with the *Miranda* strictures, is also in key with a sensible approach to the law of confessions: voluntary statements should not be excluded from evidence. Simply put, we should return to the law as it was prior to the five-to-four *Miranda* decision when, as Justice Harlan noted in his dissent, "the role of the Constitution has been only to sift out *undue* pressure" and to exclude those confessions that were coerced. A fairly good rule of thumb was suggested by longtime Northwestern University law and criminal justice professor Fred E. Inbau, who recommended that the law enforcement officer first ask himself or herself, "Is what I am about to do or say apt to make an innocent person confess?" Inbau calls this the "only understandable test of confession admissibility."

A return to a voluntariness analysis should be more palatable now to those who believed that the *Miranda* decision was necessary at the time. Law enforcement throughout this country has changed. We are generations away from the age when, in some jurisdictions, the "third degree" was tolerated or even encouraged. Police officers today have been schooled in the *Miranda* requirements and are sensitive to the rights of suspects. But they are also sensitive to society's right to be free of predation, and they rightfully see a continued strict *per se* application of *Miranda* as a hindrance to effective and fair law enforcement, especially in those unwitnessed crimes of violence in which there is usually little evidence other than a confession. As Miami, Florida, Police Detective John Spears told Thomas E. Ricks of *The Wall Street Journal* in the fall of 1985, in 40 percent of all homicides, "if you don't have a confession you don't have a case." Accordingly, as Ricks reports, police officers have to walk a tightrope of literal compliance with *Miranda* while, at the same time, attempting to do their job effectively. For example, Ricks writes of Spears's tactic of placing a suspect arrested at a murder scene "in a car alongside a silent officer" because, as Spears puts it (referring to the compulsion to confess we have already discussed), "Nine times out of ten, he'll initiate a conversation—'I shot the dirty S.O.B. because of this'—and that's admissible evidence."

Of course, whether Spears is correct or whether some judge will say that the psychological pressure was the equivalent of "interrogation" under the *Miranda* rule remains to be seen. Clearly, however, there should be nothing wrong with keeping avenues for voluntary confessions open. This is precisely what the Omnibus Crime Control and Safe Streets Act of 1968 attempted to achieve for criminal trials in federal courts.

In the wake of the outrage generated by *Miranda* (and other decisions that erected hurdles to effective law enforcement) a subcommittee of the Senate's Judiciary Committee held extensive hearings on the problem. After reviewing the testimony and the other material presented during the course of its investigation, the committee drafted comprehensive legislation designed to correct some of the more serious problems. It concluded:

> The committee is convinced from the mass of evidence heard by the subcommittee, much of which is printed in the transcript of hearings, that the rigid and inflexible requirements of the majority opinion in the *Miranda* case are unreasonable, unrealistic, and extremely harmful in law enforcement. Instance after instance are documented in the transcript where the most vicious criminals have gone unpunished, even though they had voluntarily confessed their guilt.

Since the *Miranda* decision "encourage[d] Congress and the States to continue their laudable search for increasingly effective ways of protecting the rights of the individual while promoting efficient enforcement of our criminal laws," the committee believed that its return to standards of voluntariness would be constitutional.

The law applies to all federal court criminal trials. It provides that any confession "shall be admissible in evidence if it is voluntarily given." The judge is given the responsibility of determining, out of the jury's presence, whether the confession was in fact voluntary; if it was, the jury would be instructed "to give such weight to the confession as the jury feels it deserves under all the circumstances." In assessing voluntariness, the federal trial judge was directed to consider

> all of the circumstances surrounding the giving of the confession, including (1) the time elapsing between arrest and arraignment of the defendant making the confession, if it was made after arrest and before arraignment, (2) whether such defendant knew the nature of the offense with which he was charged or of which he was suspected at the time of making the confession, (3) whether or not such defendant was advised or knew that he was not required to make any statement and that any such statement could be used against him, (4) whether

or not such defendant had been advised prior to questioning of his right to assistance of counsel; and (5) whether or not such defendant was without the assistance of counsel when questioned and when giving such confession.

None of the factors is "conclusive" on whether the confession was or was not voluntary.

A minority of the Senate Judiciary Committee believed not only that the legislation was unnecessary but that it was unconstitutional as well. They pointed out that the *Miranda* Court had specifically warned that "[w]here rights secured by the Constitution are involved, there can be no rule making or legislation which would abrogate them."

Unfortunately, this issue has not yet been resolved, even though the law has been on the books for almost two decades. As contemporaneously predicted by Columbia law professor Herbert Wechsler, who was unsympathetic with the *Miranda* decision, the law has become a "dead letter." Doubts about its constitutionality have prevented its use.

In fact, even some critics of the *Miranda* rules seem reconciled to their continued use. For example, Chief Justice Warren E. Burger wrote, in a concurring opinion in the *Innis* case that we discussed earlier, "The meaning of *Miranda* has become reasonably clear and law enforcement practices have adjusted to its strictures; I would neither overrule *Miranda,* disparage it, nor extend it at this late date."

Whether or not wholesale revision of *Miranda* is now possible, the Supreme Court should infuse a sense of moderation into the rule of exclusion so that law enforcement actions that do not unfairly chill a suspect's freedom to claim his or her constitutional rights will not prevent the admission into evidence of a perfectly voluntary confession. As of this writing, the Court— tentatively, at least—seems to be doing precisely that.

In the early-morning hours of September 11, 1980, two Queens, New York, police officers on routine patrol were told by a young woman that she had just been raped by a six-foot-tall black man wearing a jacket with "Big Ben" emblazoned on the back. She told them the man was armed with a gun and had entered a nearby supermarket. The officers drove to the market, and one of them, Frank Kraft, went in while his partner radioed for help. Officer Kraft saw the suspect, a young man later identified as Benjamin Quarles. Quarles saw Kraft and ran toward the rear of the store. Kraft followed with his gun drawn and, after losing sight of Quarles for a few seconds, was finally able to corner him.

By this time, at least three other policemen had arrived. As he frisked Quarles, Kraft noticed that he was wearing an empty shoulder holster. Kraft handcuffed Quarles and asked where the gun was. "The gun is over there," Quarles said, nodding toward some empty cartons. After he found a loaded .38-caliber revolver in one of the boxes, Kraft formally arrested Quarles and then, for the first time, advised him of his *Miranda* rights. Quarles said he understood his rights, agreed to talk, and admitted that the gun was his.

Quarles was charged with illegal possession of a weapon (the woman who said she was raped disappeared), but the trial judge excluded his statements to Officer Kraft: the "the gun is over there" comment because it was in response to a question while Quarles was in custody but before he had been given his *Miranda* warnings, and the admission of ownership because it naturally flowed from his earlier—and, in the judge's view, tainted—statement. The prosecution appealed the judge's ruling, and the New York appellate courts affirmed. On June 12, 1984, the Supreme Court, in a decision written by Justice William H. Rehnquist, reversed and carved out an "exigency exception" to *Miranda*'s exclusionary rule:

> The police in this case, in the very act of apprehending a suspect, were confronted with the immediate necessity of ascertaining the whereabouts of a gun which they had every reason to believe the suspect had just removed from his empty holster and discarded in the supermarket. So long as the gun was concealed somewhere in the supermarket, with its actual whereabouts unknown, it obviously posed more than one danger to the public safety: an accomplice might make use of it, a customer or employee might later come upon it.
>
> In such a situation, if the police are required to recite the familiar *Miranda* warnings before asking the whereabouts of the gun, suspects in Quarles' position might well be deterred from responding. Procedural safeguards which deter a suspect from

responding were deemed acceptable in *Miranda* in order to protect the Fifth Amendment privilege; when the primary social cost of those added protections is the possibility of fewer convictions, the *Miranda* majority was willing to bear that cost. Here, had the *Miranda* warnings deterred Quarles from responding to Officer Kraft's question about the whereabouts of the gun, the cost would have been something more than merely failing to obtain the evidence useful in convicting Quarles. Officer Kraft needed an answer to his question not simply to make his case against Quarles but to insure that further danger to the public did not result from the concealment of the gun in a public area.

The Court recognized that a contrary ruling would put the police in an often impossible quandary:

> We decline to place officers such as Officer Kraft in the untenable position of having to consider, often in a matter of seconds, whether it best serves society for them to ask the necessary questions without the *Miranda* warnings and render whatever probative evidence they recover inadmissible, or for them to give the warnings in order to preserve the admissibility of evidence they might uncover but possibly damage or destroy their ability to obtain that evidence and neutralize the volatile situation confronting them.

Justices Marshall, Brennan, and Stevens dissented and condemned the majority for endorsing "the introduction of coerced self-incriminating statements in criminal prosecutions."

The *Quarles* case is, in my view, an appropriate narrowing of *Miranda*. As we saw, the decision to require that police give *Miranda* warnings to suspects in custody was a policy determination by five justices based on their cursory analysis of legislative-type information; that is, information studied by legislative bodies in their analysis of whether new laws are needed. It thus violated a basic principle of our tripartite system of government, which entrusts the legislature to legislate, the executive to enforce, and the judiciary to interpret. Difficulty ensues when these distinctions become blurred, because judges simply do not have the resources to engage in the type of wide-ranging investigation coupled with full and open debate that are essential to a rational law-*making* process.

The great strength of sound judicial analysis is that each case is decided on the narrowest possible grounds. Each new decision thus rests on the accretion of hundreds of years of precedental wisdom. To paraphrase Sir Isaac Newton, who once observed that if he saw farther it was because he stood "on the shoulders of giants," our judges see more clearly when their field of examination is lit by the insight of those who have already considered similar problems. Unfortunately, some judges have eschewed this approach in favor of issuing sweeping, legislative-type directions and mandates that rest not on the collective wisdom of the past but on the social concerns of a few judges. As we have seen, the application of such sweeping and inflexible mandates can, when applied to uniquely different individual cases, bruise common sense.

A particularly clear example of "legislating" by judges was the *Mapp* v. *Ohio* exclusionary rule mandate in search and seizure cases.

The Fourth Amendment to the United States Constitution provides:

> The right of the people to be secure in their persons, houses, papers, and effects, against unreasonable searches and seizures, shall not be violated, and no Warrants shall issue but upon probable cause, supported by Oath or affirmation, and particularly describing the place to be searched, and the persons or things to be seized.

This great protection of individual liberty, like most of the Bill of Rights, was a child of this nation's break with England. It emerged from the womb of our Revolution with strength and vigor because the two outrages against which it was addressed were particularly fresh in the minds and memories of those great men who founded this Republic. The first outrage, the *general warrant,* permitted the British government to ruthlessly suppress all dissent. Most prominent during the Star Chamber's tenure, general warrants were used by Crown officers to root out "offensive" activity. Valid for the life of the King in whose name they were issued, general warrants permitted roving bands of government agents to search for and seize anything or anyone they thought was inimical to the King's interests. Unlike the Fourth

Amendment's "probable cause" command, general warrants were issued on suspicion, speculation, or for reasons only tangentially linked to their ostensible purpose. Indeed, from 1557 to 1640, general warrants issued to a private printing guild permitted it to destroy the equipment of unlicensed printers.

The ultimate demise of the general warrant in England started with the case of John Wilkes, a member of Parliament. In 1763, Wilkes published an anonymous pamphlet critical of the British Crown. Lord Halifax, then the British secretary of state, issued a general warrant to four officials that directed them to swoop up anyone who had had anything to do with the pamphlet. In the course of three days, forty-nine persons were arrested. Ultimately, they learned Wilkes's identity and sought to arrest him on the warrant's authority. Since the warrant did not bear his name, he refused to submit and called it a "ridiculous warrant against the whole English nation." Taken into custody, Wilkes and the others who were arrested sued Halifax and his subalterns. They won and were awarded substantial damages. Lord Chief Justice Pratt, in a courageous decision, characterized the general warrant as "totally subversive of liberty."

The Fourth Amendment's second seed was the hated *writ of assistance*, which so bedeviled the colonists in their continuing dispute with England over taxation. The writs were a special form of general warrant and permitted British customs inspectors to search for proof of smuggling and, in so doing, suspected tax avoidance. Again, the writs were issued without any showing of probable cause. They were valid for the life of the King. They were condemned in a famous speech by James Otis as "the worst instrument of arbitrary power . . . that was ever found in an English law book." John Adams, for one, reckoned that the "Child Independence" was born when, after the death of George II in 1760 and over the strenuous objections of the colonists, new writs of assistance were issued.

Until 1914, the fact that evidence may have been seized in violation of the Fourth Amendment did not affect its use in a subsequent criminal trial. But decisions issued by the United States Supreme Court in that year and in 1920 held that property that could be lawfully owned (for example, business records, as opposed to contraband such as illicit drugs) was not admissible into evidence against the owner if it had been illegally seized by government agents. By 1925, the exclusionary rule was extended to contraband (a can of cocaine) as well. This Fourth Amendment–based search and seizure exclusionary rule, however, only applied in federal courts: the states were free to accept or reject the Supreme Court's logic.

One of the states that rejected the exclusionary rule's logic was New York. In a 1926 opinion written by the state's then Chief Judge (and later a justice of the United States Supreme Court) Benjamin Nathan Cardozo, New York's highest court weighed the benefits of adopting an exclusionary rule against its burdens: "On the one side is the social need that crime be repressed. On the other, the social need that law shall not be flouted by the insolence of office. There are dangers in any choice."

Cardozo concluded that, on balance, victims of unlawful government activities should be compensated in other ways: with money damages or by levying penal or disciplinary sanctions against the offending officers. Absent a change in the law by the legislature, Cardozo viewed the alternative as beyond the appropriate bounds of judicial action:

> We are confirmed in this conclusion when we reflect how far-reaching in its effect upon society the new consequences would be. The pettiest peace officer would have it in his power through overzeal or indiscretion to confer immunity upon an offender for crimes the most flagitious. A room is searched against the law, and the body of a murdered man is found. If the place of discovery may not be proved, the other circumstances may be insufficient to connect the defendant with the crime. The privacy of the home has been infringed, and the murderer goes free.

In Cardozo's immortal phrase, "The criminal is to go free because the constable has blundered."

The right of the states to apply their own standards was affirmed by the United States Supreme Court in 1949, when it held that although the Fourth Amendment's protection against unlawful police intrusion was binding on the states, the states were not bound by the exclusionary rule attending in the federal courts. All this changed a decade later when the Court reversed itself and decided that evidence seized in violation of the Fourth Amendment was no longer admissible in state courts, either. The case was *Mapp* v. *Ohio*.

Dollree Mapp lived alone with her teenage daughter on the second story of a two-family house in Cleveland. Three policemen came to her house one early afternoon seeking a person they wanted to talk to about a recent bombing; they had heard he was hiding out there. Mapp called a lawyer who was representing her at the time in a civil matter, and he advised her that she did not have to let the officers in unless they had a warrant. For the next two and a half hours, the police—in the words of Justice William O. Douglas—"laid siege to the house." More police arrived, and when Mapp's lawyer showed up, they told him that they had a warrant; however, they refused to show it to him. A police officer then broke in through the back door. When confronted by Mapp on the steps leading to her apartment, the officer waved a piece of paper, which he described as a warrant. She grabbed the "warrant" and stuffed it down the front of her blouse. After a brief scuffle, the officer retrieved the paper and had her handcuffed. She was taken upstairs and made to sit on a bed while the police rummaged through her house. Although the man for whom they were looking was not found, they did come across some booklets, pictures, and a drawing, all of which the officers thought were obscene. Mapp was arrested, tried, and convicted for possession of pornographic material.

Mapp's case came to the Supreme Court on the obscenity issue: namely, whether under the First Amendment—in the words of her lawyer's brief—Ohio law could "dictate to the mature adult what books he may have in his own private library." The only place the exclusionary rule issue was mentioned was in a perfunctory comment in a "friend of the court" brief submitted by the American Civil Liberties Union on Mapp's behalf. The ACLU asked, without argument, that the Court reconsider its 1949 ruling permitting the states to devise their own methods to protect Fourth Amendment rights: "It is our purpose by this paragraph to respectfully request that this Court re-examine this issue and conclude . . . that evidence illegally obtained . . . not be admissible in state criminal proceedings."

As Bernard Schwartz tells us in his book *Super Chief,* when the justices met in conference to discuss Mapp's case, it was their general consensus that her conviction should be vacated on First Amendment grounds, that is, because they believed Ohio's anti-obscenity statute was clearly unconstitutional. Justice Douglas, however, thought it would be a good case through which to extend the search and seizure exclusionary rule to state courts. Justices Warren and Brennan quickly agreed, but the plan was dropped because none of the others would go along.

Justice Tom C. Clark was assigned to write the decision reversing the obscenity conviction on First Amendment grounds. Then, a little later, as they were riding on the elevator, Clark, who had been thinking about the issue in the meantime, turned to Justices Black and Brennan and asked, "Wouldn't this be a good case" to overturn that 1949 decision, as Douglas had wanted? They agreed, and Clark set about his task but with this different direction in mind.

The justices outside the liberal coterie were not privy to the change. In a 1983 article, Justice Potter Stewart says he was "shocked when Justice Clark's proposed Court opinion reached my desk," and he wrote his colleague a note telling him so. Stewart warned against such a precipitous ruling: "In all honesty, I seriously question the wisdom of using this case as a vehicle to overrule an important doctrine so recently established and so consistently adhered to." He complained that the question of imposing the exclusionary rule on the states "was not even discussed at the Conference, where we all agreed, as I recollect it, that the judgment should be reversed on First Amendment grounds." The justice then cautioned that if the 1949 case were to be reconsidered, "I myself would much prefer to do so only in a case which required it, and only after argument of the case by competent counsel and a full Conference discussion."

Stewart's request for restraint was brushed aside. Although the Court voted six to three to overturn Mapp's conviction, only five justices voted to impose the exclusionary rule on the states. Stewart voted to reverse the conviction for the First Amendment reasons the justices had agreed to in their conference.

The basic policy point of Clark's majority opinion was that alternative measures of protecting Fourth Amendment rights simply had not worked and that the Amendment had, in essence, become a mere "form of words." In commenting on Cardozo's warning that the exclusionary rule would set the criminal free merely "because the constable has blundered," Clark grasped the nettle of his convictions:

> In some cases that will undoubtedly be the result. . . . The criminal goes free, if he must, because the law sets him free.

Nothing can destroy government more quickly than its failure to observe its own laws, or worse, its disregard of the charter of its existence.

Justice Harlan and the other dissenters, on the other hand, believed that the short-circuiting of the orderly judicial process and the heavy-handed mandate to the states was the endangerment. The states, they argued, should be permitted the freedom to cope "with their own peculiar problems in criminal law enforcement." Justice Harlan, whose counsel of caution was rejected in the rush, ended his dissent with a touch of sadness:

> I regret that I find so unwise in principle and so inexpedient in policy a decision motivated by the high purpose of increasing respect for Constitutional rights. But in the last analysis I think this Court can increase respect for the Constitution only if it rigidly respects the limitations which the Constitution places upon it, and respects as well the principles inherent in its own processes. In the present case I think we exceed both, and that our voice becomes only a voice of power, not of reason.

The harsh consequences that flowed from *Mapp* can be seen in a case involving the brutal murder of Pamela Mason. Then fourteen, Pamela lived with her mother and younger brother in Manchester, New Hampshire. On the evening of January 13, 1964, she left her home for a babysitting job. Eight days later, her frozen body was discovered on a snowdrift a few miles from her home, her throat slashed and a bullet in her head. Police suspicion quickly focused on Edward Coolidge, and when the police discovered that the bullet in Pamela's head had come from one of his rifles, they sought and obtained a search warrant for Coolidge's car. They presented their evidence to the state's attorney general, who was authorized to issue arrest and search warrants under the then-existing New Hampshire law. He issued a warrant permitting the search, and additional incriminating evidence was found. Coolidge was tried and convicted of murder and was sentenced to a life term of imprisonment. Some seven years later, the United States Supreme Court overturned the conviction because the attorney general, as New Hampshire's chief law enforcement officer and the person who was in charge of Coolidge's prosecution, was not the neutral, disinterested judicial officer the Fourth Amendment envisioned. Since the warrant he issued was, therefore, invalid, the incriminating evidence found as a result of that warrant would have to be kept out of evidence.

Believing that Coolidge's conviction should have been affirmed, Justice Black condemned the majority for treating "the exclusionary rule as a judge-made rule of evidence" in order to "enforce" their "own notions of proper police conduct." He pointed out that there was "no language in the Fourth Amendment which provides any basis for the disqualification of the state attorney general" to issue search warrants. After reviewing the facts that were presented under oath to the attorney general, Justice Black concluded that it was "difficult to imagine a clearer showing of probable cause." At most, the dissenters argued to no avail, the law enforcement officers had made a harmless mistake in good-faith reliance on then-existing law. No wonder Chief Justice Warren E. Burger characterized the case as one that "illustrates graphically the monstrous price we pay for the exclusionary rule in which we seem to have imprisoned ourselves." Thirteen years later, the Court would finally grant itself parole from that imprisonment.

Significantly, Woodward and Armstrong's *The Brethren* reports that *Coolidge* was almost the case by which the Court overruled the *Mapp* decision. The sticking point was, apparently, Justice Black. He wanted to bend *Mapp,* not break it, and thereby fashion a good-faith exception. Justice Harlan, on the other hand, wanted the whole cake: if *Mapp* was not to be overturned, he believed he was bound by its strict requirements. Since the exclusionary rule's opponents could not agree on an approach, the liberals prevailed and Coolidge's conviction was vacated. Later, Black would write of his continuing frustration over cases that seem "calculated to make many good people believe our Court actually enjoys frustrating justice by unnecessarily turning professional criminals loose to prey upon society with impunity."

The "good-faith" exception to the search and seizure exclusionary rule was finally born, in 1984, when the Supreme Court decided that evidence obtained by law enforcement officers acting in good-faith reliance on a search warrant would no longer be excluded merely because a reviewing court decided that it had been issued on insufficient probable cause or because of some technical defect in the warrant itself. One of the cases that was midwife to this exception shows how far the "boardgame" mentality has infected some of my colleagues.

Sandra Boulware's badly burned body was found in a vacant lot in the Roxbury section of Boston in the early-morning hours of Saturday, May 5, 1979. An investigation led the police to one of her former boyfriends, Osborne Sheppard. He told them that he was at a local gambling house from 9 P.M. Friday until the time Boulware's body was discovered at 5 A.M. The alibi, however, did not check out. One of the gamblers told the police that Sheppard had borrowed a car at 3 A.M. to give some men a ride home and, although the trip should have taken only fifteen minutes, Sheppard did not return until five.

The police talked to the man whose car Sheppard had borrowed and found that there was fresh blood and clumps of hair on the rear bumper and in the trunk. Armed with this information, Detective Peter O'Malley, in accordance with the Fourth Amendment, wrote out and signed under oath an application for a warrant to search Sheppard's home. The affidavit recited the results of the investigation as probable cause to believe that specific items of evidence relating to the murder would be found. As required by the Fourth Amendment, Detective O'Malley's sworn statement listed the items with particularity.

After the district attorney, the first assistant district attorney, and a police sergeant checked his affidavit to make sure it was adequate, O'Malley took a warrant form to a judge. Since it was Sunday, however, the only form he was able to find was one that was used in drug cases. O'Malley made some changes on the warrant and mentioned this to the judge. The judge, who was at home, also tried to find a more suitable form. When he couldn't, he modified O'Malley's form and signed it. The judge assured Detective O'Malley that the warrant was okay. Unfortunately, he was not as careful as he should have been; the printed form warrant authorized the police to "search for any controlled substances" and drug paraphernalia.

The police found bloodstained clothing and Boulware's hairpiece at Sheppard's residence. He was tried and convicted of murder. The Supreme Judicial Court of Massachusetts, however, reversed. The court held that "although the police conducted the search in a good faith belief, reasonably held, that the search was lawful and authorized," the typographical mistakes required enforcement of *Mapp*'s exclusionary rule. When the prosecution sought review by the United States Supreme Court, Sheppard's lawyers admitted that if the judge issuing the warrant had merely crossed out the controlled substances language, had attached O'Malley's sworn statement to the form, and had written "see attached affidavit," they would have no case. That was not done, however, and they sought to hold the prosecution to the form's literal language, language that did not meet Fourth Amendment standards because it authorized a search for drugs and drug paraphernalia based on an affidavit seeking evidence of a murder.

The Supreme Court, in a seven-to-two decision, reversed and reinstated Sheppard's conviction. Justices Brennan and Marshall dissented and argued that although "the affidavit submitted by the police set forth with particularity those items that they sought authority to search for, it is nevertheless clear that the warrant itself—the document which actually gave the officers legal authority to invade [Sheppard]'s privacy—made no mention of those items" and that accordingly the search was unlawful. They called the majority's good-faith exception a "crabbed reading of the Fourth Amendment" and a "grave mistake."

The issues presented by the rule excluding evidence gathered as a result of a Fourth Amendment violation are not simple. Despite a General Accounting Office study, which shows that the rule has had little impact in the *federal* courts, there is no doubt that many *state* court criminals—especially in drug cases—are escaping conviction and punishment because some constable may have blundered. Thus, for example, a 1976 to 1980 study by the U.S. Department of Justice's National Institute of Justice reported that over 4,000 felony arrests in California (4.8 percent) were rejected for prosecution because of *Mapp* problems; over 70 percent of those involved drugs. The figures were even higher for the counties of San Diego (8.5 percent) and Los Angeles (11.7 percent and 14.6 percent in two offices). Tragically, almost half of those not prosecuted were rearrested almost three times each, on the average, during a two-year follow-up period. Significantly, most crime (especially crime that terrorizes the community, such as murder, rape, robbery, and burglary) is prosecuted in state, not federal, courts.

Over the years, the rationale behind the exclusionary rule has been one of deterrence: in the words of Justice Stewart, to "compel respect" for the Fourth Amendment "in the only effectively available way—by reducing the incentive to disregard it." Yet the empirical evidence on whether the exclusionary rule significantly deters unlawful police activity is less than clear. However, *no one* wants the police to be able to break into people's homes and rummage through their personal things whenever they choose. That would be a return to the hated general warrants and writs of assistance. *Something*, therefore, must be done to prevent Fourth Amendment violations. But the exclusionary rule is simply the wrong remedy, even if it is within the constitutional power of the federal judiciary to impose it on the states. This is how Utah Supreme Court Justice and former University of Chicago Law Professor Dallin H. Oakes set the argument in a seminal article he wrote in 1970:

> Only a system with limitless patience with irrationality could tolerate the fact that where there has been one wrong, the defendant's, he will be punished, but where there have been two wrongs, the defendant's and the officer's, both will go free.

The officer who transgresses, acting in bad faith, should be punished. Freeing the criminal because of the blunder, however, merely punishes society. Indeed, those who resist even the good-faith exception to the exclusionary rule would, as Justice White reminds us, suppress perfectly reliable evidence even "where the constable has *not* blundered."

There are mechanisms already in place to bring rogue cops to book. Those whose rights have been violated by law enforcement can sue for money damages in state or federal courts. Additionally, many communities have police review boards, which can discipline officers who overstep the legitimate bounds of law enforcement. These remedies should be strengthened, fine-tuned, and expanded. Ultimately, they should be able to replace the exclusionary rule, which, as federal appeals Judge Malcom Richard Wilkey has noted, is "a complete distortion of the truth."

I agree with Chief Justice Burger that outright abandonment

of *Miranda* and *Mapp* may not be appropriate now: "Obviously the public interest would be poorly served if law enforcement officials were suddenly to gain the impression, however erroneous, that all constitutional restraints on police had somehow been removed." Indeed, there is some evidence that *Mapp* has made the police more careful—at least in cases where prosecution is envisioned (as opposed to where mere police harassment of petty criminals is the goal). A former deputy police commissioner in New York told *The New York Times* in a 1965 interview:

> The *Mapp* case was a shock to us. We had to reorganize our thinking, frankly. Before this, nobody bothered to take out a search warrant. Although the U.S. Constitution requires warrants in most cases, the U.S. Supreme Court had ruled that evidence obtained without a warrant—illegally if you will—was admissible in state courts. So the feeling was, why bother?

Until the legislatures fashion workable alternatives to exclusion so that illegal police activity will be effectively deterred without the courts' having to hide their eyes from the truth, the rules of exclusion should be applied with common sense and restraint. Reasonable law enforcement action taken in good faith should never result in a criminal's escape from justice. Our freedom from the imprisoning terrors of crime is too important to have that goal treated as a boardgame prize.

EIGHT

Playing With Fire

WE'VE SEEN HOW plea bargaining weakens the credibility of our criminal justice system and deterrence by, at the very least, making the criminal *think* he or she has avoided just punishment. Often, the criminal's perception is accurate.

As discussed earlier, we learn to avoid the flickering and alluring light at the candle's tip because the first time we touched fire, it hurt. Pain is nature's way of protecting us from injury. If some well-meaning genie wanted to spare us suffering and temporarily numbed our pain sensors, we would come to believe we were immune from fire's scorching power. As our limbs charred, however, we would sadly realize that the genie's kindhearted intervention was no favor.

Our juvenile justice system is like that misguided genie. Its leniency permits many youngsters to believe they are immune from sanction as they terrorize their peers and the community. When its protective cloak is finally removed, the newly turned adult is bewildered. Society, mourning its dead and maimed, also ponders, "What has gone wrong?"

In November 1981, a young man just three weeks past his nineteenth birthday sat quietly behind one of the big wooden tables in my court waiting to be sentenced. Six months earlier, he had killed a man who had befriended him and who had given him a job when no one else would.

Since the age of fourteen, the defendant—even now, no more than a youth—had been permitted a string of crimes before he was finally sent to Wisconsin's state reformatory: four burglaries, three thefts, one carrying a concealed weapon, one forgery, and

160

one auto theft. Sitting in adult court for the first time, he sounded contrite:

> All I can say is that I'm sorry for what I have done. I know I can't bring Sam back. I have to pay for my mistake, probably the biggest one I will ever make in my life. All I can do from here is start over and better myself and take whatever the court gives me.

However, I perceived that the anesthesia induced by a system that had coddled him for so long had not worn off entirely. This is how I put it that day:

> We have a record which has not taught him that the law deters criminal activity, but has taught him that the law, in essence, rewards criminal activity because nothing happens. The nerve transmitting pain has been cut by the criminal justice system and the lesson that was learned is that you can put your hand in the fire and nothing happens.

This young man's story is not unique. Young people everywhere pass through the juvenile justice system daily, shedding serious crimes—robbery, burglary, even homicide—as moulting birds shed their feathers. For example, in early 1985, one seventeen-year-old Wisconsin youth was accused of going on a five-day "holiday spree" with the $30,000 life savings that he had burglarized from an elderly couple who did not trust banks. According to a *Milwaukee Sentinel* article by John Fauber, he admitted to committing some twenty burglaries in a two-month period and had been placed on an "intensive" probation program twice. Undoubtedly, he had been repeatedly warned "this is your last break." But true sanctions, like the place on the horizon where railroad tracks meet, never seemed to come. I was reminded of the perhaps-apocryphal young delinquent who, when the judge told him he was going to give him "another chance," replied, "No, you're not, judge. You're giving me the same chance I had before."

The records of juveniles who keep getting "another chance" are replete with dismissals and deals as they learn the wrong lesson from well-meaning people who are just trying to be "kind and understanding." Thus, an author of a book on how to defend youngsters accused of crime notes:

Most juvenile justice professionals agree that the official recognition or acknowledgement of serious or vicious misconduct, whether through a trial or admission, has a devastating effect on the categorization of the individual's personality. . . . They will, therefore, strive for the least serious formal description of the misconduct.

During my year as a juvenile court judge, I saw the often-vicious actions of many young men and women described and charged euphemistically. Three examples come to mind. The first concerns a sixteen-year-old girl accused of attacking a twelve-year-old girl and her fourteen-year-old sister with a butcher knife. The dispute involved a mutual boyfriend. "I'll use this," she reportedly told the younger girl, holding the knife to her chest. "If you don't watch out, I'm going to kill you." The sixteen-year-old then, according to the police reports, turned the knife on the sister, warning her, "I'll stab you if you start anything." The district attorney's office charged the crimes as disorderly conduct, a charge that prevented my sending the girl to reform school.

The second example involves a seventeen-year-old boy who was stopped by two teachers from stabbing another student with a two-and-a-half-inch-bladed Boy Scout knife. That case, too, was charged as disorderly conduct. In the third case, the prosecutor first charged a fifteen-year-old boy with disorderly conduct for going after his brother with a three-foot ax, but then he wanted me to dismiss the case in exchange for the boy's promise to be good. I refused. Although none of the victims in any of these incidents was *physically* injured, the attackers got the wrong message by the "least formal description" of their serious crimes.

Disturbed by the almost routine use of the disorderly conduct veneer, I sent the following memorandum to the district attorney:

> As you know, a serious problem plaguing our school system is that juveniles feel they can take weapons to school with impunity. Attached is a copy of a juvenile petition alleging that a West Division student not only carried a concealed weapon to school but attempted to use it. Nevertheless, the student was charged with Disorderly Conduct (a Class B misdemeanor which precluded—by virtue of the charge alone—commitment to the boy's school).
>
> I accepted the student's guilty plea because, in reality, I had

no choice although I was uncomfortable in having my hands tied with respect to disposition. While prosecutors obviously have discretion with respect to the charges they issue, that discretion should be exercised in a manner which assists deterrence rather than hinders it.

Although the juvenile in this case evidently had no prior contacts with the Children's Court Center, that factor is a factor properly considered on disposition. Undercharging and thereby, in my view, usurping the court's role with respect to disposition, destroys the credibility of our criminal justice system.

He never responded.

Despite all the attempts to minimize lawbreaking by juveniles, millions of this nation's crime victims are victims of those whom the law calls "children." According to the latest government statistics, youngsters under the age of eighteen account for almost 10 percent of all arrests for murder; 15 percent of all arrests for forceable rape; 26 percent of all arrests for robbery; 36 percent of all arrests for auto theft; and 40 percent of all arrests for burglary. If you expand the age group to include all those twenty-one or younger, even these startling arrest percentages jump with alarming ferocity: murder, 23 percent; forceable rape, 31 percent; robbery, 49 percent; auto theft, 57 percent; burglary, 61 percent.

In Milwaukee, hardly a high-crime community, 63 percent of all juveniles arrested in 1984 were first arrested before they were fourteen. Children barely in their teens are being arrested for rape and robbery. Our schools have become a particularly nasty battleground. All over this nation, teachers and serious students are terrorized by thugs who make us all nostalgic for the days when the movie *The Blackboard Jungle* gave us a picture of a *tough* school. Today, that Hollywood-set school would undoubtedly receive accolades for its relatively calm learning environment.

Society seems paralyzed in the face of a tragic onslaught of juvenile crime. Some juvenile justice professionals blame most of the terror on the baby boom and general social unrest. In the words of a former commissioner of the New York City Department of Juvenile Justice, they urge that we "hold fast to civilizing values [leniency, that is] while we ride out the wave." Yet as political scientist Charles Murray points out in his carefully documented book *Losing Ground,* the late-1960s jump in arrests for serious crimes—a crest that has persisted to the present day—"was too sudden, too large, and lasted too long to be dismissed as just an anomaly of a turbulent decade." Indeed, between 1960 and 1975, the number of serious crimes rose 200 percent, while the number of young males (who are responsible for most crime) grew only some 50 percent.

The 1960s were the great watershed of criminal justice—and social—leniency. During that decade, two elements of what Murray calls "the risk equation" changed: there was a smaller chance of getting caught and, for those caught, a smaller chance of serious punishment. Thus, as he tells us, the absolute number of prisoners in the federal and state systems declined each year from 1961 to 1969, although crime *doubled* during that period. He calculates that in 1960 the odds of not being caught after five robberies was only one in fifteen. By 1980 the spree-robber's odds of escaping arrest had improved significantly, to twenty percent.

The risk equation changed for juveniles as well. Murray determined that in 1966, 1,200 juveniles from Cook County—Chicago—Illinois had been committed to state reform schools. In 1976, despite a significant increase in juvenile crime, less than 400 were committed. The typical Cook County juvenile sent to a state reform school for the first time had, according to Murray, an average of more than thirteen prior arrests. The message, in Murray's words, was clear:

> A youth hanging out on a tough street corner in 1960 was unlikely to know many (if any) people who could credibly claim to have gotten away with a string of robberies; in 1970, a youth hanging out on the same street corner might easily know several. When he considered his own chances, it would be only human nature for him to identify with the "successes."

Simply put, juveniles are committing more violent crimes at an earlier age, and few if any of the programs stressing leniency and rehabilitation have helped. Indeed, the Cambridge-Somerville Youth Project, started in the late 1930s, indicates that social welfare intervention may actually be *counterproductive.*

The Cambridge-Somerville Youth Project program divided

youngsters from run-down neighborhoods in Cambridge and Somerville, Massachusetts, into two groups. The first group received the kind of intensive counseling, tutoring, and recreational activities that we all like to think of as turning youth away from crime. The other group was left alone. A *New York Times* article appearing in March 1982 reported the bad news:

> In the late 1970s, a study of the program yielded depressing results: The treatment was judged harmful. Those who had been given the special attention had a higher rate of criminal convictions, alcoholism and mental illness than those who had been ignored. And the longer and more intense the treatment, the worse the outcome in later life.

One study of juvenile delinquents, however, did show some results. In the late 1970s, the American Institutes for Research concluded that locking up delinquents deterred at least some of them from further criminal activity.

Despite the clear evidence that increased criminal activity is the fruit of leniency, my colleagues and I who recommend a swift and stern response to crime are called "hanging judges" and are chastised for not recognizing crime's "root causes." Unfortunately, while the professionals "ride out the waves," as they put it, victims are *drowning* in the turbulent waters.

This country's juvenile justice systems are predicated upon leniency and understanding—for the criminal. As in the adult system, the victim is often looked upon as a nuisance.* Almost everywhere, punishment is an impermissible consideration. The focus is on what is "best" for the juvenile, and any disposition must be the "least-restrictive" alternative. This mindset is exemplified by the following—albeit extreme—position taken by one juvenile probation officer in response to my hypothetical question about what he would do about a fictional fifteen-year-old youth who might have machine-gunned more than a dozen people in downtown Milwaukee if that incident were the youth's first "contact" with the juvenile justice system and there were no other relevant factors to be considered. He said that he would proba-

---

*Recently, Milwaukee County remodeled and air conditioned the place where criminal suspects are interviewed for bail purposes. The room where victims and witnesses wait to see a prosecutor, however, was left stark and without air conditioning.

bly recommend "formalized probation" but would not rule out an informal disposition without conviction. This is how he explained it: "We think in terms of rehabilitation, and I would think that the juvenile would probably have an adequate chance of being rehabilitated given the least restrictive terms under the Code itself."

In December 1984, this "you get a couple of them free" attitude was applied to a seventeen-year-old who, along with a nineteen-year-old friend, stole a car, robbed a gas station with a sawed-off shotgun, invaded a home, and terrorized the family. The nineteen-year-old said they had also committed four other armed robberies which, together with two attempted armed robberies, had been dismissed as the result of a plea bargain. The seventeen-year-old was given a one-year commitment to Wisconsin's reform school, while his crime-spree companion was sentenced to forty-two years in prison. The juvenile court judge refused to order the seventeen-year-old to be tried as an adult because "that would be contrary to the best interests of the juvenile [and] the community" since the youth did not have a prior juvenile record. He called the spree an "aberration" that did not "reflect something so deep-seated that one would know by clear and convincing evidence that one year and nine months is not sufficient time to provide [him] with the supervision that would be needed."

One year and nine months was the maximum period the young man could be held in custody in the juvenile system. The judge felt that "the appropriate substantial individualized services" would be provided by the juvenile authorities, and although he recognized that rehabilitation might take longer than the twenty-one months, he felt that that was insufficient reason to send the youth to adult court, where he faced maximum penalties in excess of one hundred years. "You're very fortunate," he told the young man.

After seven months, the youth was released from the reformatory. Three months later, he and a friend were arrested for beating an eighty-five-year-old woman to death. The young men ultimately pleaded guilty to second-degree murder. According to their confessions, they were in the yard of the "very fortunate" youth when they saw the woman outside her home. The beneficiary of "another chance" yelled to his friend, "Let's get the old lady." They then jumped a fence and pummeled her to death. They left but later returned with two buddies. The four of them then burglarized and ransacked her home.

At sentencing, the young man who had earlier avoided waiver into adult court with expressions of contrition told the judge that he was "very sorry" and that he did not know "what got into me that night." The judge was unmoved. He called the woman's death "the final step in the tragedy" of a whole series of crimes the youth had committed against "elderly and vulnerable people" and sentenced him to the the maximum consecutive terms of twenty years for second-degree murder and ten years for burglary. The young man's major accomplice also received a thirty-year sentence. Their two friends, who had helped in the burglary, received lesser sentences.

The major problem with the juvenile justice system is that many young men and women who commit serious crimes are able to successfully manipulate the system. They are represented by a cadre of tax-supported attorneys who use all the tricks of the adult criminal courts, including plea bargaining. Young criminals know they will usually not get caught and that, when they do, very little will happen to them.

It wasn't always like this, however. For some sixty-odd years, young men and women who broke the law wound up in special courts. These courts were not bound by the limiting rules and procedures that governed the trial and disposition of adult criminals.

The first court specifically designed to deal with delinquent children opened in Chicago on July 1, 1899. Soon the specialized court concept spread throughout the country. It was a welcome change from the old common law under which children as young as seven would be arrested, jailed, tried, convicted, and imprisoned as if they were but little adults. What happened to twelve-year-old James Guild in the New Jersey of the 1820s is illustrative of the way it was before the early twentieth-century reforms.

James was accused of killing a sixty-year-old woman by the name of Catharine Beakes. The only thing we know about Catharine is that she lived with her son and a ten-year-old grandson. On the day of her death, her son was off working, and her grandson was in school. She was found lying in a mass of blood. Her skull had been bashed.

James, a servant of Beakes's neighbor, was arrested because he had been in the area. At first, he denied the murder. The next day, however, he confessed, apparently as the result of a promise of leniency. The trial judge struck the confession from the record because, in the patterned early-nineteenth-century prose of Chief Justice Charles Ewing, writing for the New Jersey Supreme Court, it had been lured "by delusive hopes of impunity excited" by "persons innocently misled by a common, and perhaps natural, but mistaken zeal to discover the perpetrator of a cruel and shocking outrage."

Five months after the first confession, James, who had been continuously kept in the town's "gaol," confessed again. This confession was used to convict him.

On appeal, James's lawyers contended that the second confession had been merely a natural consequence of the first—involuntary—admission, and that, to use modern parlance, it was therefore the tainted fruit of a poisoned tree. The New Jersey Supreme Court disagreed. It found that the first confession's taint had sufficiently attenuated so that the second confession was a product of the youth's free will. The Court pointed out that shortly before he had confessed again, the boy was told that he would die for his crime and that there was no hope of reprieve. Thus, there was no reason to confess falsely.

The conviction upheld, the chief justice, quoting Blackstone, addressed punishment: "Sparing this boy merely on account of his tender years, might be of dangerous consequence to the public by propagating a notion that children might commit such atrocious crimes, with impunity." James Guild, age twelve, was executed.

Reading the lengthy decision involving James Guild, I was struck by two things. First, both the trial court and the New Jersey Supreme Court were extremely conscientious in their attempt to do justice as they saw it. Second, despite an acute awareness of James's relative youth, they accepted without discussion or doubt, treating miscreant children as if they were but another species—albeit immature—of adult. It was this concept that the reformers tried to change.

Change came slowly. Gradually, the state stepped into the shoes of parents unable to provide their children with a proper and sound upbringing. This is how the Pennsylvania Supreme Court put it in 1839, when it upheld the commitment of a girl to a public institution known as the House of Refuge, over her father's objection:

> The House of Refuge is not a prison, but a school. . . . The object of the charity is reformation, by training its inmates to industry; by imbuing their minds with principles of morality and religion; by furnishing them with means to earn a living; and, above all, by separating them from the corrupting influence of improper associates. To this end, may not the natural parents, when unequal to the task of education, or unworthy of it, be superseded by the *parens patriae*, or common guardian of the community? . . . The infant has been snatched from a course which must have ended in confirmed depravity; and, not only is the restraint of her person lawful, but it would be an extreme act of cruelty to release her from it.

While we know nothing about the girl's age (an "infant" in the law is anyone who is not an adult) or her circumstances, the case expresses tenets of a doctrine that was going to play a seminal role in the development and ultimate demise of the juvenile courts as they existed prior to May 15, 1967.

The doctrine known as *parens patriae*—Latin for "father of the country"—was derived from the British view that the King was the guardian of all those who were unable to fend for themselves, either because they were minors without legal guardians or because they were under some other form of disability. It made the juvenile judge a substitute father, applying stern but caring discipline. The concept was expressed by a contemporary legal observer in a 1909 issue of *The Harvard Law Review:*

> The problem for determination by the judge is not, Has this boy or girl committed a specific wrong, but What is he, how has he become what he is, and what had best be done in his interest and in the interest of the state to save him from a downward career.

Emphasis was on informal, but thorough, investigation by a juvenile probation officer into the child's physical, mental, and environmental conditions so the judge could fashion an appropriate remedy. In short, the judge, unrestrained by traditional notions of due process, would act "as a wise and merciful father handles his own child." This was the ideal, again as described in *The Harvard Law Review* of 1909:

> The child who must be brought into court should, of course, be made to know that he is face to face with the power of the state, but he should at the same time, and more emphatically, be made to feel that he is the object of its care and solicitude. The ordinary trappings of the court-room are out of place in such hearings. The judge on a bench, looking down at the boy standing at the bar, can never evoke a proper sympathetic spirit. Seated at a desk, with the child at his side, where he can on occasion put his arm around his shoulder and draw the lad to him, the judge, while losing none of his judicial dignity, will gain immensely in the effectiveness of his work.

Of course, this system, which obviously worked best when the judges and other personnel were caring and dedicated, had flaws, most notably the general lack of accountability of those administering it. Petty tyrants could go unchecked as they imposed their own sadistic discipline on the helpless. By the same token, lax enforcement or a "business as usual" approach could let the dangerous slip through unchecked. Nevertheless, it seems that the road generally taken lay in the middle, where, in the words of one of the early juvenile judges, the court workers were not "sentimentalists any more than brutalists."

All this changed on May 15, 1967, when, with one justice dissenting, the United States Supreme Court decided that there was too much informality in the juvenile justice system and that "kindly" judges had too much discretion. In my view, the decision was an example of a "hard case" which makes "bad law," to use an old legal cliché.

The seeds of this change had been planted some three years earlier when Gerald Francis Gault, then fifteen, got into trouble again. Six months after he had been placed on probation for being with a boy who had stolen a wallet from a woman's purse, a next-door neighbor accused him and a friend of making a phone call that the Court described as of "the irritatingly offensive, adolescent, sex variety." On a June 1964 morning when both his mother and father were at work, Gerald and the friend were taken into custody by the local sheriff. Gerald's parents were not told, and when his mother returned from work at 6 P.M., she sent an older brother to look for him. They finally learned that Gerald was locked up. When they went to the juvenile detention home, the superintendent, who was also Gerald's probation officer, told them that a hearing would be held the next morning. He refused to release the boy.

The next day, an informal hearing was held in the judge's chambers. Gerald's mother and older brother were there, as was the detention home superintendent/probation officer. A second probation officer was also present. The next-door neighbor was not there and, indeed, never appeared at any of the proceedings. No transcript was kept of the meeting with the judge.

According to the juvenile judge's later recollection, Gerald's mother told him that while Gerald had admitted dialing the neighbor's phone number, he had claimed the other youth did the actual talking. However, the judge and one of the probation officers said Gerald admitted making some of the lewd remarks himself.

After the hearing, the judge said he would "think about it," and Gerald was returned to the detention home. A couple of days later, he was released. Another hearing was scheduled for a few days later.

All the people who were at the earlier meeting were at the next hearing. Gerald's father, who had been working out of town, was also there. Although Mrs. Gault asked that the next-door neighbor be summoned "so she could see which boy that done the talking, the dirty talking over the phone," her request was rebuffed by the judge, who said that that was not necessary. At the end of the hearing, fifteen-year-old Gerald Gault was committed to Arizona's State Industrial School until he was twenty-one, "unless sooner discharged by due process of law." If Gerald had been an adult, the severest penalty he could have received was incarceration for two months and a $50 fine.

Since no appeals were permitted from juvenile court commitment orders, Gerald sought release via *habeas corpus*. An Arizona trial judge declined to order Gerald released from custody; that decision was appealed to the Arizona Supreme Court, which affirmed. The United States Supreme Court reversed and, in the process, nullified over sixty years of juvenile court law. It decreed that henceforth every juvenile accused of criminal activity must be given certain procedural protections already afforded to adult defendants: the right to know, and to have one's parents or guardian know, what the charges are; the right to have a reasonable time to prepare a defense; the right to have the assistance of legal counsel and, if too poor to hire a lawyer, one paid for by the community; the right to see and hear accusers and ask them questions; the right to remain silent; the right to have appellate review and, concomitantly, the right to have a transcript of the proceedings. Most significantly, the Supreme Court also made legitimate the suppression of a child's most natural instinct when caught in a criminal act: to confess, to get it off his or her chest and take whatever punishment is due.

Punishment is a great cathartic, whether it be a harsh word to a youngster who has been rude or a spanking administered to one more mischievous. It resets the scales of right and wrong. Indeed, the study conducted by the American Institutes for Research in the late 1970s referred to earlier concluded that punishment of juveniles inhibits recidivism in direct proportion to its severity. In the words of a March 5, 1982, *New York Times* article, "Supervision of youths in their own homes resulted in a small reduction in criminal activity; placing them in group homes in the community produced a greater reduction, and sending youths to out-of-town group homes or locking them up in a small unit or a large reformatory resulted in the greatest reduction."

Yet contrary to what we all know from our own experiences as children and as parents, Justice Abe Fortas's opinion in the *Gault* case tells us that confession lured by a sense of duty or responsibility should, incredibly, *immunize* the confessor from punishment:

> It seems probable that where children are induced to confess by "paternal" urgings on the part of officials and the confession is then followed by disciplinary action, the child's reaction is likely to be hostile and adverse—the child may well feel that he has been led or tricked into confession and that despite his confession, he is being punished.

Purposeful punishment—feedback from bad behavior—is essential to the civilizing of our children. Those who would ignore this truism should "stop to consider," in the words of noted psychiatrist Manfred S. Guttmacher, "that the child born in the

modern aseptic delivery room is as savagely amoral as that produced by our neolithic progenitors." As William Golding percep-
tively shows us in his *Lord of the Flies*, children, left to their own
devices, quickly degenerate into manipulative savages. They, like
all of us, need an externally imposed structure of credible laws.

In an outstanding chronicle of his own pre-*Gault* rise from
the depths of juvenile delinquency, entitled *The Other Side of Delinquency*, Pennsylvania social worker Waln Brown credits his own
fairly lengthy stay at a "boys school" for his salvation, even though
he resisted the placement at the time and viewed the judge and
social workers as villains who were punishing him oppressively.
First, as Brown relates, it removed him from the environment
that had nurtured his rebelliousness. Second, he was "given a
chance to mature" because the school enforced a "well-defined,
though harsh, disciplinary code" that "put restrictions on my behavior." Third, the placement was long enough to permit the
maturation process to take root.

Gault has changed all of this. Its ethos imposes a "least restrictive alternative" rule on any juvenile disposition and thus
postpones meaningful action until it is often too late to be of
much good. As Brown has told me, delinquent youngsters are
now permitted to get away "with a whole lot of things" until the
situation has festered for a number of years and they have a
"real nasty record." Brown warns that once the pattern has been
cut, it is difficult to change.

While the consequences of *Gault* may cheer those who still
view the juvenile delinquent as nothing more than the apple-
stealer or obscene phone-caller he used to be rather than the
armed robber or rapist he has become, the absence of strictures
has eliminated incentives to conform to law. As Charles Murray
put it, "A youngster who found criminal acts fun or rewarding
and had been arrested only once or twice could have chosen to
continue committing crimes through the simplest of logics: There
was no reason not to." No wonder Justice Stewart, dissenting,
characterized the *Gault* decision as "wholly unsound as a matter
of constitutional law, and sadly unwise as a matter of judicial
policy."

Gault was an admittedly tough case on its facts—Gerald Gault's
penalty was more severe than the sentences many armed robbers
and some killers receive; and some of the reforms were un-

doubtedly necessary. But the decision has removed the lid from Pandora's box. Rather than fine-tuning a system that, despite some faults, generally impressed structure and a sense of credibility upon often emotionally immature children, the Supreme Court made them enemies of those who seek to help them. All of the rules that have made the adult criminal justice system less a pursuit of justice than a game to be won are now part of juvenile justice. As Alan Dershowitz has written in a book recounting his courtroom exploits, appropriately titled *The Best Defense,* "When a criminal lawyer represents a guilty defendant—and the vast majority of criminal defendants are guilty—his only realistic alternative may sometimes be to put the government on trial." Whatever merits trial by gambit may have in the adult criminal justice system, and whatever the merits of bartered justice, we do a disservice to our youth if we teach them at the very beginning of their lives that you can get away with crime if you can stonewall or have a smart enough lawyer.

Not long ago a woman told me how her younger brother, fifteen or sixteen years old, went along on a burglary with some friends. It was his first brush with the law, and when caught, he was frightened, ashamed, and genuinely repentant. The first thing he wanted to do was to admit his guilt, take whatever punishment was due, and get on with his life as a law-abiding teenager. Yet all this changed after Wisconsin's juvenile justice system got through with him. At his initial conference with his public-defender-appointed lawyer, he was told, "Don't worry, we'll bargain this down to a misdemeanor receiving stolen property and nothing will happen." When the boy protested that he *was* guilty and wanted to get it off his chest, the young lawyer told him not to be "a sucker."

The plea bargain, of course, involved two lies: first, he was involved in a *burglary;* second, the value of property taken was clearly more than the misdemeanor charge indicated. According to the woman, when her brother saw the charade, he walked away persuaded he had nothing to fear from the law after all. Many others his age share this view. These are the fruits of *Gault.*

NINE

Conflagration

I CAME TO the juvenile justice system as a neophyte judge. Elected to the bench in April 1979, I learned via the newspapers that the chief judge of our district had assigned me to the Children's Court. I was a civil, not a criminal, lawyer. The Children's Court tour required knowledge in two areas in which I had never practiced: I had never handled either a criminal or a juvenile case in my fourteen years as a lawyer. Accordingly, I spent the entire summer studying my new areas of responsibility. When I walked through the doors on August 1, 1979, I was ready to hit the ground running—and a good thing it was. Almost immediately, I was confronted with an unyielding bureaucracy and with the "one more chance" syndrome.

It is natural to want to believe that everyone is good, that everyone is honest. Thus, when J. G., who was convicted of burglary, pleaded with me not to send him to Wisconsin's secure juvenile institution for boys and promised to turn over a new leaf, I gave him "one more chance." Of course, I should have known by looking at his record and its dismal tale of unjustified leniency that he had made those promises to others as well. Yet he had never made those promises to *me*. Trustingly, I took him at his word. Although I sentenced him to the maximum one-year commitment to the Ethan Allen School for Boys in Wales, Wisconsin, I stayed the commitment on the condition that he adhere to a strict curfew and keep out of trouble. That very night—or, more accurately, in the early-morning hours of the next day (well past the curfew)—he was arrested for another burglary! As luck would have it, he drew me as the judge for this new crime. I ordered him held in secure detention pending not only the new charge but also a determination of whether the stay order in the

175

old case should be vacated. That was Friday, August 31, 1979.

On Tuesday, September 4, J. G.'s lawyer, an earnest and extremely capable young public defender, sought to have his client released from secure detention "so he may be given a chance to resume or, at least, you know, become or continue to be growing to be a useful citizen of the community." Wisconsin's statute provided that a juvenile could be kept locked up pending a hearing if the court found that he or she had "committed a delinquent act" after having been placed in "nonsecure custody" and "no other suitable alternative exists." Although the boy had not only clearly violated my curfew order the very day he promised to be good and might have committed the burglary as well, his probation officer advised that she "would have no objection to his release." I declined. The system's credibility, already tardy, would be delayed no longer and I told them:

> I could accept the probation officer's recommendation and place this youngster in the custody of his mother and send him home on conditions that he attend school, on conditions that he obey a curfew, on conditions that he just go to and from school and not deviate, but such an order would be a whisper into the wind. . . .
>
> So, it would be a sorry state of affairs if juvenile court justice were to become a revolving door; if the word were to go out from this building that conditions of probation mean nothing, that placement of trust in a juvenile by the Court is something to be toyed with and not taken seriously, and for that reason, the Court feels that the intent of the entire Chapter, which is structured on rehabilitation, founded upon rehabilitation, would be violated if this youngster were not to be held in secure detention.

The boy's lawyer immediately sought his release from another circuit judge via *habeas corpus.*

As previously discussed, *habeas corpus* is a fundamental right. Nevertheless, the legislature has always had the power to determine how and under what circumstances somebody may get the writ. In this case, the Wisconsin legislature specifically and unambiguously provided that while other circuit judges could issue writs of *habeas corpus* to "determine the legal custody of children" if that question was "incidental to the determination of causes pending" before them, circuit judges assigned to the Children's

Court had "paramount" jurisdiction over children alleged to be delinquent. Stated another way, if a writ of *habeas corpus* were to be sought, it would have to be sought either from an appellate judge or from one assigned to the Children's Court (there were three of us). Nevertheless, one of my colleagues who was then assigned to the adult criminal division ordered the boy released. That night, the boy committed yet *another* burglary!

As the boy's lawyer later told me with remarkable understatement, the youth was totally "unimpressed with the legal system." And for good reason. When the boy reached eighteen, he was permitted to start all over: he received two years probation for three burglaries in one night (two of the burglaries were dismissed in a plea bargain) and then, just over a year later and while he was still on probation, he got two years probation for a strong-arm robbery, which was reduced, again pursuant to a plea bargain, to theft from person.

Unjustified leniency is pervasive throughout the system. Earlier, I mentioned the seventeen-year-old boy who had gone on a spree with an elderly couple's life savings. Although the youth had admitted to twenty burglaries in a two-month period and had an extensive arrest record that included arson, forgery, and carrying a concealed weapon in addition to the burglaries, and although the juvenile justice system would soon lose jurisdiction over him, the juvenile judge who ordered him tried as an adult—apparently moved by the youth's long history of drug use—called that decision one of the toughest he had ever had to make. The prosecutor was less moved, noting that the youth was extremely manipulative and "engages in criminal activities to satisfy immediate gratification." The court commissioner in the adult system who ordered the seventeen-year-old held in lieu of $5,000 cash bail was also not impressed with the "it's society's fault" argument, noting that the youth's criminal record "would rival a fifty-year-old career criminal." Nevertheless, the prosecutor in the adult system, as the result of a plea bargain, decided to charge only *two* of the burglaries.

There are other examples that, sadly, are not unique; they are among those that have been reported in the Milwaukee press during the year and a half I have worked on this book. They mirror, I am afraid, problems throughout the country.

For example, in a chilling article, *Milwaukee Journal* reporter

Nina Bernstein related the sordid history of a young man who, during the course of his brief life, has sown nothing but misery. At fourteen he was accused of grabbing and exposing a breast of a junior high school classmate. Although unconsented sexual contact with someone between the ages of twelve and eighteen is a ten-year felony charge, second-degree sexual assault, if committed by an adult, the boy was permitted to plead guilty to the nine-month misdemeanor charge, fourth-degree sexual assault. Additionally, even though he had sexually assaulted another girl two years earlier, the case was "held open" for six months. This meant that if he got into no further difficulties, the case would be dismissed outright. Within the six-month period, the boy was back before the same judge—this time on a shoplifting charge. He was placed on probation for six months. "The very next day," Bernstein reported, "he attacked a 27-year old woman in an alley . . . grabbing her from behind, throwing her to the concrete, striking her when she struggled, and running off with a wallet containing $260." Although he confessed the crime to his probation officer, he demanded and got a jury trial. Upon conviction, the district attorney's office recommended that he be sent to the Ethan Allen School for Boys. A psychologist said that the crimes did not reflect a pattern of antisocial criminal behavior. The boy had a new judge and was placed on probation again. Seven months later, he was charged with attempted masked robbery of another twenty-seven-year-old woman. When he discovered she only had sixty-five cents, he tried to rape her. His jury trial was delayed by two adjournments. Despite his record, he remained free.

While he was free awaiting trial on the juvenile charges, this young man was accused of attempting another rape. When the woman told him that she was having her period and was a nun, he threatened to kill her. While he was free awaiting trial on the juvenile charges, he was also accused of raping and robbing a seventy-four-year-old woman on the morning of Christmas Eve. While he was free awaiting trial on the juvenile charges, he was also accused of killing his former girlfriend's mother and burning her house to cover it up. Finally, the law caught up with this young man who had received so many breaks. He was sentenced to life plus twenty years for the murder and arson.

He pled guilty to nine additional crimes: three counts of first-degree sexual assault, two counts of attempted second-degree sexual assault, armed robbery, robbery, and two counts of burglary. Pursuant to a plea bargain, the judge added but another twenty years to the man's sentence rather than the 110 years the man faced. He will be eligible for parole less than thirteen years after his initial life-plus-twenty-year sentence. According to an article by *Milwaukee Journal* reporter Dave Hendrickson, this young man who had received so many breaks as a juvenile and who a psychologist said did not display a pattern of antisocial criminal behavior "was able to laugh with his lawyer shortly after he was sentenced" for the nine crimes.

Milwaukee Sentinel reporter John Fauber related how a fifteen-year-old who was already on probation for an armed robbery was placed on "intensive probation" for shooting a boy and wounding him in the shoulder. While he was on this second probation, he shot two other boys during a basketball game.

Fauber also told of another fifteen-year-old. He was placed on "intensive probation" after a record that included burglary, battery to a teacher, and purse-snatching. He was warned that "next time" it would be the state reform school. "Next time" he was charged with retail theft and entry into a locked building. His new judge continued the probation and ordered him to stay away from stores. A month later, he and another boy brutally attacked a seventy-seven-year-old man, taking his watch, car, and a bundle of nonnegotiable bonds.

The post-*Gault* juvenile justice system is overburdened with technicality and procedure. It involves a lot of paper-shuffling as the lawyers, the social workers, and the judges "process" the cases. Unfortunately, the paper-shuffling and the case-processing often take on an overweening significance which obscures the real goal: the public's protection. A juvenile probation officer in Milwaukee once closed her files on a twelve-year-old boy who was charged with battery, theft from auto, and prowling because he didn't show up for his meeting with her. I ran into similar problems during my year as a juvenile court judge.

A sixteen-year-old boy was accused of sexually assaulting his five-year-old niece. Her parents first became suspicious when they noticed an unusual discharge from her vagina. They took her to a hospital. She had gonorrhea. The child told them that the boy had "messed" with her by putting his "dingaling" in her "pussy."

He confessed to the authorities and said he thought he had contracted gonorrhea from an eighteen-year-old woman a couple of months earlier.

I referred the boy to Milwaukee's child and adolescent psychiatric center for evaluation. The boy then denied committing the assault and pointed out that he had been checked for gonorrhea about a week after the incident and was found to be clean. The psychiatrist concluded that he could "find no evidence of serious emotional disturbance or sexual perversion" and saw "no reason for psychiatric intervention in any form at this time."

The boy's "negative" gonorrhea later proved to be positive, and after that came to light he again admitted the crime. Because the psychiatrist had assumed the boy's innocence, I ordered a second evaluation. The psychiatrist submitted a one-paragraph response:

> As a result of the court order . . . I did make contact with the home of [the boy] and requested a follow-up examination. . . . He did not, however show up for the evaluation. . . . Without documentation of repeated contact with this girl or other younger aged children, I cannot find any evidence of serious emotional disturbance or sexual perversion. Unless the boy, himself, wants help because he is experiencing anxiety or guilt, I do not see a reason for psychiatric intervention. I have no basis on which to form further opinions about this case. If as a result of whatever decision the court makes, the boy wishes further psychiatric evaluation or help, please contact [us].

I was astounded. First, the letter seemed to say that the sexual molestation of a five-year-old girl by a sixteen-year-old boy was normal, or at least not abnormal. Second, it predicated psychiatric intervention on the boy's desires. I asked the psychiatrist to come to court and explain. I later commented on his explanation at a court hearing six months later, after I discovered that my order directing psychiatric help for the boy had been largely ignored:

> I think his explanation was that the [American Psychiatric Association] had voted that in order to find a teenager emotionally or psychologically disturbed there has to be a repeated history of sexual abuse of five-year olds or under and that one wasn't enough.

I had ordered the boy to "cooperate fully" with the psychiatrist and stay in the home of a different uncle and aunt, a young couple who had agreed to take him into their home even though they, too, had a young daughter. That was on July 2, 1980.

About a month later, I received a letter from another psychiatrist at the county facility:

> This is to inform you that I am in the process of evaluating [the boy]. If further treatment is indicated, he will continue to be in my care and I will forward my plans for treatment to you. If treatment is not indicated or discontinued, I will inform you of the change of status.

It was not in the psychiatrist's discretion to decide if there was going to be further treatment and I wrote to the prosecutor and the boy's lawyer telling them that. I also directed that the case be brought back to me if there were any problems.

Three months later, I received another letter from the second psychiatrist:

> This letter is concerning [the boy]. I have closed [the boy]'s case [at the county facility]. [The boy] came to his initial appointment and came to an additional appointment in September approximately forty minutes late. He did not come for numerous scheduled appointments. Attached is a copy of a letter I sent to [the boy] on October 9, 1980. [The boy's probation workers] were informed of this.

The letter to the boy told him that the psychiatrist was "closing your case" because "of difficulties in making appointments and because I have not heard from you." It advised him to "please contact us" if there were ever "difficulties that you would like help with in the future." I also learned that the boy's aunt and uncle, whose decision to take him into their home and provide some structure had been one of the reasons I thought the treatment program might work, had separated at the beginning of September, and at that time, the boy began to be truant from school.

The boy's two probation workers, his lawyer, and the chief assistant district attorney at the Children's Court Center listened to my recitation in silence. When I had finished, they all had "reasons" for letting the boy slip by like a ship in a foggy night.

The first probation worker admitted he should have told me my order was being violated, but he pointed out that although he was in touch with the psychiatrist and the other social worker, he only spoke to the boy on the phone. The second probation worker "did not know" whether it had been his "obligation" to tell me, but rather, he felt he was more appropriately "concerned for attempting to encourage [the boy] to survive in spite of the difficulties impacted upon him by his lack of parenting." He then added, "I'm sorry, Your Honor. If there be guilt, I'm going to plead guilty."

It was easy for him to say, but it did not solve the problems—the boy's or the system's. Although by then I was no longer assigned to the Children's Court, I had kept jurisdiction over the case so it would not get lost in a shift of judges. I was clearly frustrated:

> Well, the purpose of this is not to have a litany of *mea culpas*. If this were the only time during the course of my experience with the Children's Court Center that this kind of inattentiveness to judicial orders had surfaced, it could be checked off to human error and accommodated with that kind of response; but, unfortunately, and I know that those of you who have been at the Children's Court Center understand that this has been my feeling for quite some time, this problem seems to be endemic out there; that orders are not complied with; that because the Probation Department is severely understaffed, they cannot see their probationers more frequently than once every three weeks, if that frequently; that there is very little case follow-through, with the attending result that when juveniles turn 18 they feel, on the basis of lessons they have been taught at the Juvenile Court Center, that they can get away with stuff. This, in my view, is a direct contributor of the increasingly serious crime rate in Milwaukee.

Since any other disposition was now impossible, I extended the boy's probation for the maximum possible period of one year and directed that I receive weekly reports on the case's progress. Apparently, it was the only way to insure that my order was being carried out.

As discussed in Chapter 4, the criminal justice system is often a closed universe of back-scratchers in which the public—victims *and* defendants—are generally outsiders. Those in the system who make waves usually just create problems for themselves. A defense lawyer who rubs a prosecutor the wrong way by insisting on going to trial rather than force a plea bargain on an innocent client, for example, may find it impossible to get a good deal for other clients. This could plug the lawyer's main source of income and would reinforce his or her desire to "go along."

Judges, too, are part of the system. When they buck it, some in the system rebel. Judge Charles B. Schudson, one of my colleagues in Milwaukee County, faced such a rebellion in 1983 when he had to decide where to place a young man who had run away from a youth shelter after he threatened its staff. Social workers assigned to the case recommended that he return to the shelter. Judge Schudson disagreed and ordered the boy placed in a different facility. The social workers were not to be so easily thwarted. When the shelter of *their* choice refused to accept the boy because the judge's written order had specified the other facility, one of them scratched out its name from the order and inserted the one they wanted. When he discovered what had happened, Judge Schudson appropriately assessed contempt penalties. Later that year, Judge Schudson was forced to use his contempt powers again.

A sixteen-year-old girl was convicted of forgery. Three other criminal charges were dismissed, apparently as the result of a plea bargain. Judge Schudson placed the girl on probation for a year and, inasmuch as there were serious problems at her home, he directed that she live in a youth shelter. He also directed that she fully cooperate with outpatient drug and alcohol treatment. The alternative to her voluntary cooperation would be a compulsory inpatient program. He made it clear that he expected total compliance with his order:

> One beer is too many. One missed appointment is too many. If you think it is best for you to [undergo the in-patient treatment program], just break these rules and that's where you will go; not as a punishment, but just because it's clear that that's the alternative that we will have to follow.

He then warned the social workers that he wanted the case monitored closely:

> Let it be clear with the Department though, that if there is a violation, you don't have to wait sixty days to come back. If

there is a violation of any of these rules and conditions, then return the case here immediately so we can get started on this in-patient program right away.

It was as if he were talking to stones.

On June 22, 1983, Judge Schudson was told, for the first time, that the girl had run away from the shelter a month and a half earlier, on May 4, and that even her parents had not yet been informed. Indeed, her parents told Judge Schudson that the shelter had billed them, and they had paid for, the post–May 4 period. This failure to appreciate the necessity for swift and certain response to a child's lack of cooperation was, as Judge Schudson noted, "neither isolated nor unusual."

When a judge rules for a particular party in a civil case, that party will make sure that the judge's order is enforced and that it is defended on appeal. If, for example, I order a defendant in a civil lawsuit to make periodic payments to the plaintiff, that plaintiff will be in court the moment one of those payments is missed. In criminal cases, if a judge does something the prosecutor and defense lawyer *both* don't like, such as reject a plea-bargained deal, there is no one to take up the cudgel to see that the judge's order is enforced.

The boy was a nice-looking lad of seventeen and a half. He was charged with confronting a nine-year-old girl in a school bathroom, turning out the lights, pulling her into a stall, rubbing her vaginal area with his hand, and making her touch his exposed penis. He told her she would die if she screamed. When he was arrested, he readily admitted committing the crime and surrendered a box-cutter knife that he used to threaten the girl.

A Children's Court prosecutor charged the boy with first-degree sexual assault, which, in Wisconsin, includes the "sexual contact" of a child under twelve years old. If the boy were kept in the juvenile system, he could be sent to the state reformatory until he was eighteen or be placed on probation for a year. If the juvenile court waived its jurisdiction over the boy and transferred the case to the adult criminal justice system, the maximum penalty would be twenty years in prison and a $10,000 fine.

Despite my known opposition to plea bargaining, the prosecutor told me he had worked out a deal: the boy would plead guilty to fourth-degree sexual assault, a misdemeanor, in return for the state's recommendation of probation until he turned eighteen, some seven months away. Even though I would not be bound by any sentencing recommendation, I wanted more information before accepting or rejecting the proposed guilty plea; I referred the boy to Milwaukee's child and adolescent psychiatric center for evaluation.

Later, I held another hearing. I related what had happened in a written decision:

> The evaluation report, dated March 18, 1980, described the juvenile as a bright but "internally conflicted young man with difficulties in interpersonal relationships especially with women, and sexual identity conflicts" and noted that:
>
> > ". . . there is a prior history of sexual acts, presumably beginning at age 14 with acts of exhibitionism with females. Later charges include reported voyeurism, following a woman in a car and in the Fall of 1979 an incident wherein [the boy] was found naked in a cemetery."
>
> The charges were referred to the Children's Court Center but were handled informally. After the cemetery incident, the boy was referred to a psychologist for therapy. Apparently, the therapy was not successful for the psychiatrist's report noted that the juvenile's problems resulting in increasing pressures of anxiety which "cannot be contained by his usual defense mechanisms and is dealt with through action. The need to reduce anxiety through an act is so strong that it may compromise [the boy's] usual social judgment and lead to sexually deviant acts." The report concluded ominously:
>
> > "As long as the basic intrapsychic, interpersonal and sexual identity conflicts and anxiety continue there will be a potential for further acting-out episodes, even within a treatment process."

I was extremely concerned because the incidents were getting more serious. His lawyer tried to allay my fears:

> The psychiatrist's report states that "there is a potential for further acting out of episodes. A potential is not a probability, not an actuality. What he says is there is a potential. Again, we can't deny a possibility, and I guess what we are all looking at is the best alternative."

He pointed out that the assault happened after the boy had been released from therapy by the psychologist who was treating him in connection with the cemetery incident, and he speculated that if the therapy had continued, "this might not have occurred."

The prosecutor told me that the boy was planning to go to college and that the probation officer "would arrange to transfer his probation out of state, if that became necessary." The boy's lawyer plugged an additional point in his effort to get me to buy the deal: "He has a very bright future and it is only a matter of these episodes that is keeping him from pursuing it." I responded and made reference to a tragic case from Florida involving Theodore Bundy, which was then in the news:

> Well, the fact that [the boy] is real bright, the fact that he wants to go to college, has nothing to do with the underlying problem. We just had a young man who was very bright who was a law student, very personable, who was found guilty of killing a number of coeds in college. The mere fact that he is going to college, the mere fact that he may be bright, doesn't mean that he doesn't have a psychological problem, and what I am trying to do is to help this young man before he reaches that stage. And perhaps if someone had taken the time and effort with the young man in Florida, the coeds would have been spared the tragedies inflicted upon them.

I recalled that, several months before the bathroom assault, the psychologist who had treated the boy after the cemetery incident had said that he was doing well and that he had an active social life. The boy asked to be excused from therapy, and the psychologist, who said the prognosis appeared to be excellent, agreed. I continued:

> Psychology is an inexact science. Predictions may or may not be correct and what disturbs me most about this case is that two months or three months after [the psychologist] made that optimistic prediction, this young man is accused of having sexually assaulted a nine-year old girl. What also concerns me is, as I indicated, the increasing severity of the offenses. You can plot it out on a curve. The curve is rising and I don't know where the dotted line takes us.

I was clearly frustrated, especially at the prosecutor's deadpan response to my concern. Finally, calling the young man a "time bomb" who "can explode and hurt somebody very seriously," I invoked a provision of the Wisconsin Children's Code that permits a judge to institute waiver proceedings if he or she then disqualifies himself from the case. I told the prosecutor that the boy should be tried as an adult so that he would be subject to more than slap-on-the-wrist sanctions but that if his office felt that, because of the proposed plea bargain or otherwise, it could not advocate waiver before the judge to whom the case would be reassigned, I wanted to know so I could have a special prosecutor appointed.

The boy's case was reassigned to another judge who had been on the bench for only a couple of weeks. The prosecutor told him:

> The matter appeared back before Judge Fine on the 21st of March. At the time he indicated he would not accept the guilty plea and—because he was indicating that he believed a waiver appropriate, he disqualified himself from hearing any further proceedings in the matter and referred it to this Court. That is how the matter is appearing before you today, Your Honor.

Of course, I had done more than "indicate" a "belief" that waiver was "appropriate"; I had ordered that waiver proceedings be prosecuted and told the prosecutor that if his office didn't want to do it, I would get a special prosecutor who would. Nevertheless, this is what the assistant district attorney told the new judge:

> I am appearing today on behalf of the District Attorney's office to indicate that if the matter were before us, I would indicate once again to the Court that I believe sufficient safeguards can be provided within the juvenile system for handling this matter and would be asking the Court to accept the admission as well as the prescribed treatment plan—prescribed treatment plan within the juvenile system. Because the prior Court indicated he believed waiver could be considered, I am presenting that although the Court has the matter. I would like the Court to consider hearing the matter in the juvenile system.

The judge then asked to hear from the boy's lawyer, who quite naturally agreed with the prosecutor:

> Your Honor, I agree with what the District Attorney has said regarding the status of this case. I would note that at the

hearing before Judge Fine previously, both the District Attorney's office and the Probation Officer and myself were prepared to recommend a settlement of the case which would involve the juvenile system which would involve strict probationary standards and would also involve intensive psycho-therapy treatment for [the boy]. That was refused and I think on a decision that was not appropriate under the circumstances and certainly not in the best interest of my client.

The judge accepted the bargained settlement and put the young man on probation for a year, subject to the condition that he see the same psychologist who had treated him following the cemetery incident:

I think the young man has gotten some breaks along the way with, first of all, an almost sort of gambling District Attorney's office and second, a psychiatric report which strives to follow the code almost to the letter in the sense of finding the least restrictive disposition; and the Court will honor those recommendations and the professional expertise involved in them.

The judge told the boy that he was "a fortunate young man so far. Let's see if it works."

A year and a half later, the boy, who was by then over the age of eighteen, was convicted of disorderly conduct for exposing himself to an eleven-year-old girl and her younger brother. He pled guilty, was placed on probation for a year, and was ordered to cooperate with "any psychotherapy" the probation department "deems necessary." His juvenile record already protected by a cloak of secrecy, the judge ordered his adult conviction expunged if he successfully completed his term of probation. The assistant district attorney who had ignored my order instituting waiver proceedings ultimately pled guilty to contempt of court after I appointed a special prosecutor to investigate his actions.

Significantly, it was not the first time that that particular prosecutor had circumvented my efforts to instill some credibility into the system. Earlier, I had refused to permit the informal diversion of a young man charged with burglary and had set the case down for trial. While I was away attending my mother's funeral, the prosecutor persuaded the judge sitting in my place to approve the diversion via a so-called "consent decree." When I returned and discovered what he had done, I reiterated as clearly as I could that consent decrees were not to be entered in cases assigned to me without my prior approval. Nevertheless, two weeks before I was scheduled to leave my juvenile court assignment, he attempted another diversion in a burglary case. The following are excerpts from my July 17, 1980, memorandum to the prosecutor—with a copy to his boss, the district attorney:

> I have reviewed the file and find—absent exigent circumstances unknown to me at this time—that a consent decree would not be appropriate. Not only is burglary a serious offense, but the child's attitude and the apparent home life situation referred to by the probation officer in his referral sheet, indicates that a consent decree here would only send the juvenile signals that society's laws can be ignored and that the criminal justice system can be manipulated. This lesson is not only inconsistent with the protection of the public mandate but is against the juvenile's best interest as well. If he is not guilty, he is entitled to an acquittal or a dismissal.

Although the pattern of problems presented by that prosecutor was in many respects unique, it was but an extreme manifestation of deeper and wholesale flaws in the system. Juvenile justice is failing for many of the same reasons adult criminal justice is failing: "business as usual" attitudes bleach both systems of credibility.

A young man with a string of more than thirty robberies against elderly victims was not waived to adult court for an armed rape charge. When he was convicted, he was sent to the reform school for a year. He was released for a weekend furlough and failed to return. Remaining free, he regularly visited his mother and girlfriend. He was never picked up. While at large, he killed a two-year-old boy and raped and killed the boy's pregnant mother, disemboweling her with a butcher knife to get at the baby within.

These stories, buoyed by publicity, bob along the surface while others, equally grotesque, remain hidden beneath the waters of secrecy that obscure most juvenile proceedings. Yet tragically, they are paradigms. Young hoodlums know the law is impotent.

In late 1985, researchers at the University of Pennsylvania announced the results of a massive study of juvenile delinquency that they had conducted with the assistance of a $1.5 million grant from the National Institute for Juvenile Justice and Delinquency Prevention. They followed every one of the 27,000 children born in Philadelphia in 1958 from the ages of ten through seventeen and compared their data with the results of a similar study of almost 10,000 males born in Philadelphia in 1945. They found that although the percentage of delinquency in the two groups was about the same, the crimes committed by those born in 1958 were far more serious. Yet nearly half of the 1958 group who committed as many as four serious crimes were never even placed on probation, let alone locked up. Unlike the group born in 1945, they had all the "advantages" of *Gault*. Paul E. Tracy, one of the researchers and currently a professor of criminology at Boston's Northeastern University, remarked, "The point is, if you let a kid do what he does with impunity, then he's going to continue to do it. So my argument is that we ought to start getting tough with delinquents early."

Roland Hershman, who retired as the head of Wisconsin's maximum security juvenile reformatory in 1985, echoed Professor Tracy's thoughts when he reflected on the system's misguided leniency in a January 1985 interview with *The Milwaukee Journal's* Gary C. Rummler: "The problem is going into court and being told that if you do it again it will be serious and then they do it again and it's not serious. The kids are crying for control. I don't think we get the kids soon enough."

A youngster in Hershman's facility recently told television reporter Gael Garbarino that, ever since his first armed robbery at the age of twelve, he had been constantly threatened that he would be sent to the reform school if he committed another crime. Yet, he was always given "another chance." He told Garbarino that he kept seeing how far he could "stretch it." In retrospect, he reflected, "I wish it [being sent to the reform school] would have happened sooner." As the American Institutes for Research study and Waln Brown's personal experiences have shown, control—firmness in the face of rebellion—can restore a sense of equilibrium to the child and give him or her the stability to resist the temptations of crime.

A few weeks before Christmas 1984, a young man from Chicago's inner city had everything to live for. A star basketball player for his high school team, seventeen-year-old Ben Wilson was being actively recruited by some of the nation's most prestigious colleges. Then one afternoon, as he was walking with two girls during a school lunch break, he apparently brushed against one of two teenagers who were in their path. "Excuse me," he said, but the apology was not sufficient. There was a struggle, and then, according to the police, one of the boys called to the other, "He pushed me. Pop him." The other boy, armed with a .22-caliber pistol, "popped" Wilson, and he died.

In a funeral eulogy, Ben Wilson's high school principal, Ned L. McCray, pointed out that much of the problem with delinquent youth can be blamed on the adults who fail them, "fail them when they are not punished swiftly and surely for their misdeeds." We have failed our children by numbing their pain receptors—we have permitted them to play with fire. We all suffer the resulting inferno.

TEN

Idle Humours

THE YOUNG MAN was charged with rape, robbery, and assault with a deadly weapon. His lawyer argued that he was not guilty by reason of insanity, because he had "an impulse to rape." The psychiatrist disagreed. "It was," he testified, "an impulse to have sexual relations with a lady and if she did not agree with it, why, [he] forced her."

We all recognize that some persons should not be *punished* for their harmful acts. Thus, no one would want to jail a blind man who injures a sleeping baby by inadvertently stumbling into a stroller or a person who takes an ax to a neighbor but who actually believes he is merely chopping wood for the winter. There are two major reasons the law treats these people differently from those who intentionally cause harm. First, it would be wrong to punish someone who didn't know what he or she was doing. Second, as the British jurist Sir Edward Coke (pronounced "cook") explained in the early seventeenth century, the "punishment of a man who is deprived of reason and understanding can not be an example to others." Yet such fine distinctions as the "rape/forced sexual relations" differentiation have tainted attempts to fashion an appropriate mechanism to avoid punishing those who clearly should not be held criminally responsible for their acts and at the same time, prevent the escape of those who should.

The law of insanity—a mistress of both law and medicine—developed slowly. In the centuries following the Norman conquest of England, criminals who were clearly "mad" were pardoned by the King after their conviction. Later, insanity was recognized as a defense that, if successfully established, prevented conviction. Nevertheless, medicine was in its nascent period; both the body and the mind were barely understood. Accordingly, there were few attempts to draw *any* fine lines. As formulated by Coke, for example, the insane person was one who, like a raging beast *(furiosus)*, had no power of the mind *(non compos mentis)*. The focus was generally on whether the defendant knew the difference between "good and evil"—in effect, on whether he knew that what he had done was wrong.

The "good and evil" test was first applied in cases involving children. In the early days of our law's development in England, youngsters under the age of seven could not be punished for any unlawful acts. Those over the age of twelve were treated by the criminal law as adults and, in tenor with the harshness of that era, were severely punished for their crimes.

Children older than seven but younger than twelve could only be punished if they knew the difference between good and evil. Thus, in 1338 a judge ruled that a ten-year-old boy who had killed another lad could be executed because, by concealing the body, he demonstrated he knew that what he had done was wrong. By the seventeenth century, the "good and evil" test was applied to adults.

The "right and wrong" or "good and evil" test was strict. For example, during the trial of Edward Arnold in 1723 for the attempted murder of Lord Thomas Onslow, who, Arnold was convinced, had sent devils to disturb his sleep, the presiding judge warned the jurors considering Arnold's insanity defense that "not every idle humour of a man . . . will exempt him from justice." Rather, the judge explained, he must be "totally deprived of understanding and memory" so that he does "not know what he is doing, no more than an infant, than a brute, or a wild beast." Arnold, who had a history of serious mental problems, was convicted. Although Arnold was sentenced to death, Onslow interceded for his would-be assassin and he spent the rest of his life in prison.

Seventy-seven years later, at the turn of the nineteenth century, an eloquent English lawyer by the name of Thomas Erskine persuaded the court that was trying a man accused of attempting to kill George III that something less than a total deprivation of reason and memory—for example, delusions in a person able to otherwise function in a normal manner—could be enough to avoid criminal responsibility. In those situations, he argued in the colorful language of the time, "reason is not driven from her seat, but distraction sits down upon it along with her, holds her, trembling, upon it, and frightens her from her propriety." The delusions, Erskine argued, were so strong that they could not "be dislodged and shaken by the organs of perception and sense." Erskine's client was James Hadfield, a British army veteran who said he sought martyrdom in order to save the world. Hadfield was acquitted, and although he avoided execution, he spent the rest of his life in an asylum for the insane. Erskine's theme, which for the most part was contemporaneously ignored, was resurrected four decades later when Daniel M'Naghten came to trial.

On January 20, 1843, M'Naghten had waited in ambush for the British Prime Minister, Sir Robert Peel. Suddenly, he saw a man he thought was Peel but who was actually Peel's secretary, Edward Drummond. M'Naghten pulled a pistol from his coat, placed it in Drummond's back, and fired. A nearby policeman jumped M'Naghten and prevented him from getting off another shot. Drummond languished for several months and died on April 25.

At his trial for Drummond's murder, M'Naghten pleaded insanity. His lawyer, taking a chapter from Erskine's defense of Hadfield, argued that M'Naghten was suffering from delusions of persecution and believed that Peel was one of those who were hounding him. The lawyer's argument was based on the theories popularized five years earlier by Isaac Ray, a Maine physician and one of the founders of the American Psychiatric Association. Ray's 1838 book, *A Treatise on the Medical Jurisprudence of Insanity*, contended that a person could be insane in some areas but not others and that antisocial acts were symptoms of mental illness. After hearing nine medical experts for the defense (some of whom did not examine M'Naghten but merely observed him during the course of the trial), the trial judge stopped the proceedings and directed a verdict of acquittal by reason of insanity. Like Hadfield, M'Naghten avoided execution but spent the rest of his life in an insane asylum.

The British were outraged by M'Naghten's acquittal. Queen Victoria, herself the object of assassination attempts and threats, was furious. She wrote Peel an angry letter and complained that she could not understand why M'Naghten was acquitted when "*everybody* is morally *convinced*" that he was "perfectly conscious and aware of what" he had done. "The law may be perfect," she complained, "but how is it that whenever a case for its application arises, it proves to be of no avail?" Queen Victoria suggested that there should be a rule which would be binding in future cases where the insanity defense was raised.

The House of Lords asked the fifteen judges of the King's Bench, the highest court with jurisdiction over criminal cases, to set things right. In response, they formulated a comprehensive set of rules on insanity that are now known as the *M'Naghten* rules, even though they were not applied to M'Naghten. The rules borrowed heavily on the "good and evil" analysis and have been a polestar in the law ever since.

This is the crux of the *M'Naghten* test for determining criminal responsibility:

> Every man is to be presumed to be sane, and to possess a sufficient degree of reason to be responsible for his crimes, until the contrary be proved . . . and that to establish a defence on the ground of insanity, it must be clearly proved that, at the time of committing the act, the party accused was labouring under such a defect of reason, from disease of the mind, as not to know the nature and quality of the act he was doing or, if he did know it, that he did not know he was doing what was wrong.

The focus was "whether the accused at the time of doing the act knew the difference between right and wrong."

If the defendant was, at the time of the crime, suffering from what the judges called a "partial delusion" and was "not in other respects insane," his responsibility was to be fixed "as if the facts with respect to which the delusion exists were real." This is how they explained this latter concept to the House of Lords:

> For example, if under the influence of his delusion he supposes another man to be in the act of attempting to take away his life, and he kills that man, as he supposes in self-defence, he would be exempt from punishment. If his delusion was that the deceased had inflicted a serious injury to his character and fortune, and he killed him in revenge for such supposed injury, he would be liable to punishment.

In some courts, the *M'Naghten* rules were later supplemented by what is known as the "irresistible impulse" defense: an accused would not be criminally responsible for his conduct if he could not control himself, even though he might have known that what he was doing was wrong. Under *M'Naghten,* even as supplemented, the line drawn is sharp: the impairment of knowledge or of control must be complete.

Although the psychiatric profession now generally agrees that the question of criminal responsibility is, as a statement issued by the American Psychiatric Association in December 1982 put it, "a legal issue, not a medical one," the *M'Naghten* formulation was contemporaneously attacked, in the words of the author of a respected 1925 treatise on the subject, "as an attempt to lawyerize a medical concept." The test, critics argued, ignored the "whole man" concept popularized by Ray, thus unduly limiting the circumstances in which the insanity defense could be successfully advanced. They charged that the test also unfairly restricted psychiatric testimony to the question of what the defendant *knew* rather than encompassing also the issue of *why* the defendant acted as he did.

Some psychiatrists wished to usurp the law entirely and impose their own determinism-based morality on society's criminal code. The paradigm of this view was expressed by the eminent American psychiatrist Karl Menninger in 1945: "The modern surgical operating amphitheater developed out of dirty public barber-shops. The physicians took surgery away from the barbers a century ago; now they are taking criminology away from jailers and politicians."

There were others, however, who counseled restraint. For example, a February 1954 editorial in the self-described organ of the American Psychiatric Association, *The American Journal of Psychiatry,* advised:

> Whether the accused is insane in the medical sense is not the question, rather whether he is insane in the legal sense which is quite a different thing; and the doctor in the witness box does well to remember that he is in court and not in the clinic.

Nevertheless, five months after that editorial appeared, the influence of the psychiatric activists hit its high-water mark. In *Durham* v. *United States,* the United States Court of Appeals for

Washington, D.C., declared that no person could be held responsible for his or her crimes unless the prosecution was able to prove, beyond a reasonable doubt, that the unlawful act was not "the product of mental disease or mental defect."

In order to view the complaints lodged against the *M'Naghten* rules in their proper context, as well as to give us the tools with which to analyze the insanity defense's later development, we must consider how the nature of science relates to the study of the mind.

The *sine qua non* of science is replication: two chemicals combined in the same way in the same proportions will always produce the same compound, irrespective of who does the mixing. By the same token, hypotheses in science must not only accurately describe the observations they attempt to explain; they must be predictive as well. As one distinguished science professor at Cambridge has written,

> A theory is to be judged acceptable solely to the extent both that its results accord satisfactorily with the existing data and that future observations predicted on the basis of the theory come to pass with pleasing accuracy.

Scientific disciplines, unlike Minerva, do not spring forth full-grown and fully armed. Rather, they develop—sometimes slowly, occasionally with startling rapidity. For example, humans gazed at the vastness above for millennia and attempted to understand what they saw. At one time, the sky was perceived to be the abdomen of a woman resting on elbows and knees placed at each of the earth's four corners. Later, after the infusion of much sophistication, it was seen as a metal canopy from which were suspended the nocturnal lights. But some of the lights moved in erratic patterns which the theories could not predict. Aristotle, whose articulate wisdom still guides us, tried embedding the lights in concentric transparent spheres which encompassed the earth at their core, much like the layers of an onion. This, too, failed to reflect the movements of the planets or predict their future locations. Some five hundred years later, Ptolemy devised his so-called "ferris wheel" universe, in which the planets rode on epicycles within epicycles in ever-increasing complexity. In the words of John Milton in *Paradise Lost,* this theory, in order "to save appearances," had the earth girded "With centric and eccentric scribbled o'er, / Cycle and epicycle, orb in orb." It was an explanation that, despite Milton's ridicule, lasted for almost 1,500 years, until the age of Copernicus, when he, Kepler, and Galileo, among others, were finally able to come up with theories that worked.

Just as the universe of the cosmos was hidden from the ancient star-watchers, the universe of the mind is largely obscured from us. Mind "science"—which was riding the crest of a phrenology craze at the time Erskine made his successful appeal on behalf of George III's would-be assassin—fails to satisfy the dual prerequisites of any true science: veracity of description and the "pleasing accuracy" of prediction. Rather, as Georgetown University Psychology Professor Daniel N. Robinson has harshly written in a cogent book entitled *Psychology and Law: Can Justice Survive the Social Sciences?,* mind science is "a 'social science,' which is to say it is not a science at all." In Professor Robinson's view, those who presume to testify as experts in the related fields of psychiatry, psychology, and sociology "do not bring to the trial a body of durable knowledge, a set of scientific laws, or even an assortment of reliable measures and procedures. At most, they take a loose collection of question-begging diagnoses that are not beyond dispute even within the small clinical population on which they are based."

The essence of any analysis of the mind sciences' ability to accurately describe and predict what they purport to assess are the fraternal twin concepts of *reliability* and *validity.* Simply stated, a psychiatrist's diagnosis is deemed to be *reliable* if other psychiatrists agree with it. The diagnosis is *valid* if it is, in fact, true. Thus, if ten artists each described light of a certain wavelength as blue, their diagnostic technique—looking—would be reliable *even if the color was actually not blue.* If that were the case, the actual diagnosis—the color description—would be *in*valid even though the diagnostic technique would be reliable.

In my color analysis example, there will usually be absolute agreement or correlation between *reliability* and *validity.* The same is true in metallurgy, for example, where nickel chromium is— to paraphrase Gertrude Stein—nickel chromium is nickel chromium. In the mind sciences, however, Stein's aphorism does not apply; there, a rose may be a rose or a geranium or a tulip, depending on who is looking.

Since there is no absolute way to test the *validity* of mind science diagnoses, *reliability* assumes overarching significance. If all reputable psychiatrists examining a patient concur on the specifics of a diagnosis (as all reputable metallurgists will, for example, when they analyze an alloy), there is some justification in assuming that their analysis is accurate. As a noted psychiatrist has recognized, "There is no guarantee that a reliable system is valid, but assuredly an unreliable system must be invalid."

Although psychiatry clothes itself in the trappings of science and seeks to influence the standards by which we decide criminal responsibility, strict reliability in its diagnoses is rare. One of my favorite examples concerns a seventeen-year-old boy who was accused of strangling another patient while they were both confined in a mental hospital. The boy was observed for about a year in an attempt to determine whether he was competent to stand trial. At the end of that time, the psychiatric staff reported to the court that the youth merely had a "personality disorder" and was not mentally ill. The judge before whom the case was pending was apparently not told that there was vigorous disagreement among the staff members: those favoring the "personality disorder" diagnosis had prevailed over their colleagues, who believed that the boy was a mentally ill schizophrenic, by a *five to four vote*. That case involved pretrial psychiatric evaluation. Such conflicts are also the usual fare when insanity pleas go to trial. Consider the so-called "Yale murder case."

In the early hours of a July 1977 morning, Richard Herrin, a twenty-four-year-old Yale graduate, carefully wrapped a towel around a hammer and then smashed Bonnie Garland's skull as she slept in her parents' suburban New York home. Bonnie Garland was a Yale undergraduate who had dated Herrin since her freshman year. When she wanted to cool their relationship, Herrin, torn by what he called "love" and what the prosecutor called "jealousy," resisted. Ultimately, he killed her. Almost immediately, some in the Yale community rallied round Herrin, a young man from a poor and turbulent background who had come to Yale on a full scholarship. Herrin confessed and was charged with first-degree murder. His supporters, believing "that having lost one life" they must "do what we can to salvage another," raised substantial sums for Herrin's insanity defense.

One of Herrin's psychiatrists testified that at the time of the murder, Herrin "was suffering from a severe mental disease or mental illness" which he characterized as "an adult adjustment problem." He said that people who have this problem

> appear to be relatively normal, in that they have no history of being in mental hospitals, they have no history of attending psychiatrists. And they seem to be getting along quite well except they are relatively unstable, and if one examines them a little more closely, we find these particular individuals are unstable and are not functioning the way we would expect them to.

The psychiatrist pointed out that although Herrin had an IQ of 130, he had only gotten "just passing" grades at Yale. "In people such as this," he testified, "when they are exposed to an overwhelming external stress or situation, they do not have any psychological room to maneuver. Their capacity to adapt is limited. And because of this inability to adapt, whatever adjustments they were making, which were marginal, now become precarious and finally collapse." A prosecution psychiatrist, on the other hand, when asked whether he found any "indication of mental disease or defect in Richard Herrin," replied, "Absolutely none."

Interestingly, the third edition of the American Psychiatric Association's *Diagnostic and Statistical Manual for Mental Disorders*, the Bible of psychiatric diagnostic nomenclature published in 1980, calls adjustment disorders "apparently common."

The prosecution had to prove Herrin was sane beyond a reasonable doubt. The jury did not acquit, or find Herrin not guilty by reason of insanity, but it rejected the first-degree murder charge—killing someone with the intent to do so—and found Herrin guilty of the lesser crime of manslaughter in the first degree—an offense punishable by a maximum term of eight and one-third to twenty-five years. Under New York law, a person is guilty of manslaughter in the first degree if he or she kills another human being "under the influence of extreme emotional disturbance for which there was a reasonable explanation or cause, the reasonableness of which is to be determined from the viewpoint of a person in the defendant's situation under the circumstances the defendant believes them to be." The trial judge sentenced Herrin to the maximum term.

Another example of diagnostic disagreement concerned a man in his midthirties who was accused of twice selling heroin to an undercover agent. According to the trial testimony, after being introduced to the agent by an informer, the defendant quickly got to the point: "I hear you want to buy some heroin." When the agent indicated that he did, the two men agreed on the price and, at the defendant's suggestion, went to a nearby bar to complete the transaction. Five weeks later, they met again and there was another sale. The defendant interposed the defense of insanity at his trial in a New York federal court.

The defendant had a history of alcohol and narcotics abuse. His expert was an associate professor of clinical psychiatry at the New York Medical College and director of psychiatric research at Manhattan State Hospital. As the result of an examination the afternoon before the trial, he concluded that the defendant suffered from impaired mental functioning as well as delusions, hallucinations, epileptic convulsions, and, at times, amnesia. Using the *M'Naghten* test, which then applied, the psychiatrist determined that although the defendant had been aware that he was selling heroin, he was incapable of knowing right from wrong.

The prosecution countered with its own psychiatric expert, a former staff physician at the Payne-Whitney Clinic of New York Hospital who was a clinical instructor in psychiatry at Cornell University. He pointed out that not only was the defendant able to engage in purposeful activity (the illicit sale of narcotics), but he was so fearful of apprehension that he had suggested that one of the transactions take place in the privacy of the bar's men's room. This psychiatrist concluded that the defendant *was* able to distinguish between right and wrong. The defendant was convicted, but the U.S. court of appeals ruled that the *M'Naghten* test was too narrow a standard, and it reversed.

Almost every contested insanity defense trial is an arena for what the American Psychiatric Association has admitted is a "battle of experts." Except in rare instances, the fact of disagreement does not mean that one side or the other is being dishonest. Rather, as was pointed out over fifty years ago in an editorial written in *The Journal of the American Medical Association,* it reflects differences in "point of view and terminology." Indeed, one highly respected outspoken proponent of the use of psychiatric testimony in criminal trials, psychiatrist Bernard Diamond, recently conceded that "psychiatric evaluations are more or less subjective." Similarly, the 1967 edition of a leading medical textbook, *The Technique of Psychotherapy*, calls psychiatric diagnosis "more or less an arbitrary matter." Nevertheless, the jargon-laced battles perplex most who come into contact with the system.

One rape victim who was on trial for killing her attacker, however, was not at all perplexed as she listened to a defense psychiatrist describe her psyche in a rambling stream of consciousness, which reads as if it were cribbed from a William Faulkner first draft:

> In her particular kind of condition, if you trigger off negative feelings about herself which are primarily unconscious and covered over by these reactive formations of being concerned about children's welfare and, you know, what I term a saint-like idealized virgin, if you trigger her into negative feelings, which would be provoked by such an act as rape, being a hysterical person who was striving always to suppress sensuality and aggression, then you could indeed throw her into a state where she is emotionally relating to her own inner conflict.

Finally, the woman could take it no longer and jumped up and shouted, "I killed the motherfucker because I was raped, and I'd kill him again!"

The American Psychiatric Association has recently recognized that "psychiatric disagreements," which highlight the less-than-scientific nature of psychiatry, can be downright embarrassing and do "considerable injustice to psychiatry." It now concedes that the insanity defense, over which some in the profession once sought hegemony, might not be "necessarily 'good for psychiatry.' "

Although the fact that psychiatric diagnoses often conflict with one another was apparently well-known in the mind science field, one of the first widely distributed major explorations of the subject for the legal profession was the exhaustive review of the relevant literature by Bruce J. Ennis, a lawyer, and Thomas R. Litwack, a psychologist. Their article, with the truth-in-packaging title "Psychiatry and the Presumption of Expertise: Flipping Coins in the Courtroom," appeared in a 1974 issue of *The California Law Review*. It included these examples:

- Three psychiatrists jointly interviewed fifty-two patients in a psychiatric clinic. The three agreed on specific diagnoses in 21 percent of the cases. They totally disagreed in 31 percent. When asked to place the patients in general and, therefore, broader categories, they still managed to agree only 46 percent of the time.

- Pairs of psychiatrists diagnosed 427 psychiatric hospital patients. The pairs, which consisted of a psychiatric resident and a chief psychiatrist, were only able to agree about 50 percent of the time when they attempted to arrive at specific diagnoses. When they limited themselves to determining the extremely broad question of whether the patients suffered from organic or nonorganic psychosis, they agreed 90 percent and 80 percent of the time respectively.

- A researcher compared diagnoses of over 6,000 patients at a psychiatric observation unit with subsequent diagnoses made at a mental institution. There was agreement 60 percent of the time, even though the institution's professionals knew of the earlier evaluations.

- A major study found that pairs of psychiatrists agreed on specific diagnoses only 54 percent of the time. The agreement rate jumped to 70 percent when only the major categories of psychosis, neurosis, and character disorder were considered.

- Twenty-seven psychologists, described as "experienced" and "all members of a hospital faculty," used "a standardized set of 565 statements to rate a patient presented to them in a half-hour filmed interview." They were, according to the authors of the study, "unable to agree as to the patient's diagnosis, prognosis, psychodynamics, the causes of her problems, the feeling she was consciously experiencing or the feelings that were latent (unconscious)."

- A psychiatrist who admitted to being concerned by what he termed "the low reliability of psychiatric diagnoses of depression" conducted an experiment in which "two skilled psychiatrists" would diagnose a selected sample of twenty hospital patients. They diagnosed six of the patients as depressed but did not choose the same six!

As a result of their review, Ennis and Litwack determined, in somewhat of an understatement, that "psychiatric judgments are not very reliable."

In another report, also published in 1974, Robert L. Spitzer, the psychiatrist who was in charge of revising the most recent edition of the *Diagnostic and Statistical Manual for Mental Disorders,* and a colleague evaluated six studies that attempted to show how much one psychiatrist's diagnosis of a patient would agree with another's diagnosis of that same patient. The results were similarly disappointing, leading the doctors to lament the "obvious unreliability of psychiatric diagnoses."

The results that Dr. Spitzer and his colleagues obtained with the nomenclature set out in the latest edition of the *Diagnostic and Statistical Manual for Mental Disorders* (DSM-III, 1980) were a little, but not much, better—at least from the law's point of view. Some three hundred clinicians were enlisted for the study, 75 percent of whom, according to the researchers, "identified their main professional activity as the evaluation of patients." Each evaluated at least four patients in conjunction with another clinician, and their independent diagnoses were compared.

Certain clinical psychiatric syndromes and conditions that are presumably easy to spot and diagnose, such as psychosexual disorders (exhibitionism, fetishism, and the like), substance use disorders, organic mental disorders, and mental retardation, had a relatively high percentage of chance-corrected agreement (92 percent, 85 percent, 79 percent, and 80 percent, respectively). Other syndrome and personality disorder diagnoses were significantly less reliable, especially when there was any attempt to hone in on a specific, rather than a general, diagnosis.

Dr. Spitzer and his colleagues defined as "good" a 70 percent "agreement as to whether or not the patient has a disorder within that diagnostic class, even if there is disagreement about the specific disorder within the class." As an example, they pointed out that diagnoses of *paranoid* schizophrenia by one clinician and *catatonic* schizophrenia by another "would be considered agreement on Schizophrenia." Significantly, according to the manual, paranoid schizophrenia is "dominated" by delusions of persecu-

tion, jealousy, or grandeur, while the essential feature of catatonic schizophrenia is "marked psychomotor disturbance" such
as stupor, rigidity, excitement, or posturing. With this ground
rule, not surprisingly, they got an 81 percent "agreement" on
"Schizophrenic Disorders."

Much of the diagnostic unreliability in psychiatry may be built
into the system. An evaluation of 538 first admissions to a psychiatric hospital over a two-year period found that psychiatric
diagnoses often reflected the individual biases of the diagnosti-
cian. The researchers concluded that "clinicians in fact may be
so committed to a particular school of psychiatric thought, that
the patient's diagnosis and treatment is largely predetermined,"
and that psychiatric diagnosis is "so unreliable as to merit very
serious question when classifying, treating and studying patient
behavior and outcome."

A study in the late 1960s by two California psychiatrists
strongly suggests that, unlike other fields, experience in the mind
sciences has little to do with expertise. Detailed histories for thirty-
four patients at the UCLA Neuropsychiatric Institute were given
to ten full-time hospital staff psychiatrists (the group included
full professors of psychiatry), ten second-year psychiatric residents, and ten lay college graduates with varying backgrounds
(accounting, architecture, dentistry, music, and secretarial). Each
of the participants was asked to select one diagnosis for each of
the histories. The results, the researchers concluded, were "only
slightly better than would be expected by chance." Incredibly,
there was no statistical difference between the hit rates of any of
the groups. In sum, the researchers concluded "that the ability
to select the correct diagnosis was not significantly influenced by
the participants' psychiatric experience."

The question of what diagnosis to make when confronted
with a patient with mental problems, of course, is not the same
as determining who has mental problems and who does not. Here,
too, however, the track record is bleak. In the late 1960s, Maurice K. Temerlin and William W. Trousdale, researchers at the
University of Oklahoma, set out to show to what extent, if any,
a diagnosis of mental illness could be influenced by expectations.
They hired an actor and had him memorize a carefully written
"clinical interview" script. The actor played a well-adjusted, happy,
problem-free scientist who was interested in learning more about

psychotherapy. He wanted, according to the script, to see if it could help him enjoy life "even more fully." Five groups, all of whom were to diagnose the man, listened to the taped interview:

- 156 undergraduate students;
- forty advanced law students;
- forty-five graduate students in clinical psychology;
- twenty-five practicing clinical psychologists whose postdoctoral experience averaged six years;
- twenty-five psychiatrists, ten of whom were on the staff of state mental hospitals, six were residents, four were in private practice, and four worked for the Veterans Administration.

Before any of the subjects listened to the tape, however, they were given what Professors Temerlin and Trousdale called a "prestige suggestion." The undergraduates, the clinical psychologists, and the clinical psychology students were casually informed by "a well-known psychologist" that the man to be interviewed "looked neurotic but was actually quite psychotic." A law school instructor mentioned the same thing to the law students. The psychiatrists were treated in a slightly different manner. They were told, "It's very difficult to get psychiatrists to help on research projects because they are very busy people. We were only able to get two so far, both Board members, one also a psychoanalyst, to listen to this tape. Although they agreed that the man looks neurotic but actually is psychotic, two opinions are not enough for a criterion group in a research project."

All the subjects listened to the interview, and following the "prestige suggestion," most concluded that the man was mentally ill: 84 percent of the undergraduates; 90 percent of the law students; 88 percent of the graduate psychology students; 88 percent of the clinical psychologists; and 100 percent of the psychiatrists. One graduate psychology student said he diagnosed a "psychopathic character disorder," even though the man "seemed perfectly normal," because the psychologist had said the man was psychotic, "so I thought he must be very clever at concealing his feelings, like a psychopath often is."

One practicing psychologist described the man—whom, as we will recall, Professors Temerlin and Trousdale imbued with all the attributes of a normal, happy, well-adjusted person free from any psychological problems—as having "An obsessive-compulsive neurosis bordering on paranoid schizophrenia. He is unable to relate himself to others. He is emotionally cold and distant. He seems always to be reacting to and highly sensitive to what the interviewer is saying to him. He seldom exhibited any emotional tone or feeling. Anxiety he attempts to deal with by overorganizing and being rational."

One psychiatrist was less verbose, but equally mistaken: "This individual appears like a boastful, self-reassured, outspoken person, striving to conceal a deep concern for shortcomings which he seems to be partially aware of."

When Professors Temerlin and Trousdale played the same interview tape for a control group of undergraduate students, advanced law students, graduate clinical psychology students, and psychiatrists with the "prestige suggestion" that the patient "looked like a normal healthy man," *all* of them diagnosed him as free from mental illness.

In the early 1970s, David L. Rosenhan, a professor of psychology and law at Stanford University, tested the ability of mind science professionals to sift the sane from the insane with a simple experiment. He and seven others presented themselves for admission to twelve different psychiatric hospitals in five states after first calling for an appointment. They all related the same "complaint": they had heard unfamiliar voices saying "empty," "hollow," and "thud." Although they gave false names and occupations, the eight volunteers told the truth when asked about the significant events in their lives, including their relationships with family and friends. There were three psychologists, a pediatrician, a psychiatrist, a painter, a housewife, and a psychology graduate student in the group. The student, in his twenties, was the youngest; the others were "older and 'established.' " Indeed, according to Professor Rosenhan, in an article published in *Science* magazine, "none of their histories or current behaviors were seriously pathological in any way." Although they all behaved normally after they were admitted, they were ultimately discharged with diagnoses of "schizophrenia in remission." The length of their hospitalization averaged nineteen days, with a range from seven to fifty-two days.

This is how the then-current edition of the *Diagnostic and Statistical Manual for Mental Disorders* defined schizophrenia:

> This large category includes a group of disorders manifested by characteristic disturbances of thinking, mood, and behavior. Disturbances in thinking are marked by alterations of concept formation which may lead to misinterpretation of reality and sometimes to delusions and hallucinations, which frequently appear psychologically self-protective. Corollary mood changes include ambivalence, constricted and inappropriate emotional responsiveness and loss of empathy with others. Behavior may be withdrawn, regressive and bizarre.

All the volunteers openly took copious notes on their experiences. Yet the only observers who seemed to know that there was nothing wrong with them were some of the other patients. According to Rosenhan, in the course of the first three hospitalizations, "35 of a total of 118 patients on the admissions ward voiced their suspicions, some vigorously. 'You're not crazy. You're a journalist or a professor. You're checking up on the hospital.' "

A ninth member of Professor Rosenhan's group but one whose experiences were not included in the *Science* article later wrote about his nineteen days in a hospital:

> At no time did staff suggest that my behavior might be normal. My extensive note taking was viewed as withdrawal from personal contact, despite the fact that I spent the preponderance of my time interacting with both patients and staff. My concern for other patients was taken as a defense against dealing with my own problems. According to the nurses' notes, I demonstrated "shallow affect" and tended to "interact with others on a superficial level." I was also seen as intellectualizing and as defending against genuine emotional responsiveness.

After the experiment was finished, Rosenhan tried a variation. He told the staff at a research and teaching hospital who had heard about his experiment "but doubted that such an error could occur" at their facility that during a three-month period, various ringers would be seeking admission as psychiatric patients. They were asked to see if they could determine who was really suffering from mental illness and who was not.

The results at the end of the period were startling: Forty-one patients were, "with high confidence," thought to be impostors by at least one staff member. Twenty-three patients were labeled phonies by at least one psychiatrist; and nineteen patients were suspected as ringers by one psychiatrist and another staff member. All, it turned out, were real patients; Rosenhan had not sent in any impostors at all. His conclusion was stark: "we cannot distinguish the sane from the insane in psychiatric hospitals."

The problem of how to distinguish the sane from the insane may be even more serious when a person charged with a crime is being evaluated. There is a natural tendency to think, "He's got to be crazy," especially if the crime was particularly heinous or grisly. And it may not be sufficient for a clinician to be aware that a defendant might wish to feign mental illness or, if the threatened criminal penalty is slight, to feign mental health to avoid an insanity diagnosis. Daniel P. Pugh is a psychiatrist who worked at Washington, D.C.'s, facility for the criminally insane, St. Elizabeth's Hospital, in the late 1960s. He reported:

> I believe the malingering is done in both directions, and I suspect that mentally ill defendants reporting a negative psychiatric history usually succeed in being found sane. I believe that most forensic psychiatrists have at some point in their careers confronted this general theoretical problem and have resolved it by deciding that the only malingering that exists is that which they detect, and having thus reassured themselves, they proceed to reassure the courts as well. But I myself have seen so much successful malingering that I cannot reassure myself or anyone else on this point.

According to an article in the April 18, 1978, edition of *The Chicago Tribune*, at least one defendant attempted to run a correspondence course on how to fake mental illness. Thomas Vanda, while awaiting trial for the murder of a young woman, wrote a letter entitled "How To Beat A Murder Rap By Insanity" to another man who was also charged with murder. Vanda suggested to the man that he tell the doctors he was "hearing voices" that "told you to do your crime" and then to "break out in hysterical laughter." Vanda also advised the man to say he saw "two men having sex with each other" if he were shown an inkblot picture. As an apparent clincher, Vanda recommended masturbating while talking to the psychiatrist.

A year before the young woman's murder, Vanda had been released from a mental hospital where he had been sent following his insanity acquittal of the murder of a fifteen-year-old girl. He had spent only ten months in the hospital for that first murder because the staff felt, according to the state's mental health director, that there was "nothing wrong with this guy." Nevertheless, a psychiatrist said the letter was consistent with his earlier conclusion that Vanda was a "paranoid schizophrenic" and was "legally insane."

Much of mind science mystique stems from the belief that psychiatrists and psychologists are able to read our innermost thoughts and feelings by analyzing what we say, how we say it, and how we respond to certain tests. Psychological tests that are often used in the insanity plea context are "projective" tests, such as the Rorschach "inkblot" test that figured in Vanda's letter. In the Rorschach, the most famous of projectives, the patient is asked to describe how he or she perceives various abstract forms. The tests are called "projectives" because, in theory, they make the patient or subject "project" his or her subconscious emotions. The resulting responses are then analyzed to reveal the subject's hidden personality and mental state. Because tests can be "graded"—sometimes by computer—they give the illusion of precision. As a consequence, they carry great weight with lawyers, judges, and juries, even though they often fail to accurately describe what they purport to measure.

An interesting attempt to test the projectives was related by British psychologist H. J. Eyesenk in his 1957 book, *Sense and Nonsense In Psychology*. Batteries of projective tests were administered to prospective U.S. Air Force pilots. The would-be pilots were followed for a number of years, and their records were later placed into two categories. The men in the first group "had unmistakably broken down with neurotic disorders of one kind or another." The men in the other group "had made a spectacularly good adjustment in spite of considerable stress." Responses on the projective tests for the men in both categories were "given to recognized experts in the field," who were instructed to pick out "which records would predict good adjustment and which would predict poor adjustment." According to Dr. Eyesenk, the experts could not do either.

In actual fact, not one of the experts succeeded in predicting with better than chance success the future performance of these airmen. They failed when using a single test; they failed when using all the tests together; they failed when their predictions were combined in all possible ways. Only one single result was statistically significant, and that was significant in the wrong direction!

Another popular projective device is the Thematic Apperception Test, in which the subject is shown a series of pictures and is asked to tell a story based on what he or she sees. The story and the subject's analysis of what the people in the story are thinking, the theory goes, reveals his or her dominant drives, emotions, and personality. Although it has been in use for over forty years, there is little evidence that it works. As a psychology professor at a major American university has noted in a review appearing in the most recent edition of the *Mental Measurements Yearbook,* which is a giant compendium listing and analyzing the thousands of psychological tests on the market, its "reliability and validity seem especially hard to establish." Although he himself uses the test in his practice, the reviewer admitted that if it "were published today with the same amount of information on its reliability, validity, and standardization, it is very doubtful that it would ever attain anywhere near its present popularity."

Draw-A-Person is another popular projective test. As its name indicates, the subject is asked to draw a human form. Here again, the theory is that the subject's unconscious will be revealed in the drawing. One of the scoring manuals for this test advises that "talon-like fingers," "dark piercing eyes," or "emphasized nostrils" betray "aggression." Other manuals say that the nose is a "sexual symbol" and that, if drawn in an unusual way, it can indicate sexual maladjustment. Hair, too, is a sexual symbol; a drawing that emphasizes hair means, according to some of the experts, strivings for virility and compensation for sexual inadequacy. Placing a drawing at the bottom of the page or on a line is thought to reveal feelings of insecurity. According to one manual, the figure's middle is also highly significant:

> Traditionally, the belt, since it separates the upper and lower halves of the body, has been a symbol of control. Physiologically the belt cuts off the upper or intellectually controlling part

of the body from the lower or sexually expressing part of the body. The belt also provides a place for a purse, weapons, or other symbols of power and authority.

As in day-to-day horoscope readings, the suggested analyses can also be self-contradicting. Thus, a manual tells the psychologist that "inadequacy feelings" are displayed by either "very small figures" or "very large, weak or grandiose figures." A very large head may indicate either "strong intellectual strivings" or "feelings of intellectual inadequacy, with compensatory stress on intellectual achievement." An overly large figure may indicate "overwhelming inadequacy with compensatory trying to prove self on paper" or "excessive high self esteem."

A professor of psychology reviewing the Draw-A-Person test for *The Seventh Mental Measurements Yearbook* noted that studies have cast doubt on the test's validity and that there "is also considerable evidence that nonpsychologists, including secretaries and clerk typists, do quite well in interpreting" the drawings as a whole. Indeed, a recently published guide to psychological assessment techniques warns that those who interpret projective tests "run the risk of 'projecting' their own personalities into their interpretations."

A look at how one psychologist used another drawing projective, the House-Tree-Person Test, in a federal court trial in Washington, D.C., gives us a feel for their slippery footing. The defendant, a man by the name of Kent, was charged with housebreaking, robbery, and rape.

Q: And the House-Tree-Person Test—you handed the defendant Kent a pencil and a blank piece of paper, is that right, Doctor?

A: That is correct.

Q: And you asked him to draw a house?

A: Yes.

Q: And what did this tell you about Kent?

A: The absence of a door, and the bars on the windows, indicated he saw the house as a jail, not a home. Also, you will notice it is a side view of the house; he was making it inaccessible.

Q: Isn't it normal to draw a side view of a house? You didn't ask him to draw a front view, did you?

A: No.

Q: And those bars on the windows—could they have been Venetian blinds and not bars? Who called them bars, you or Kent?

A: I did.

Q: Did you ask him what they were?

A: No.

Q: What else did the drawing reveal about Kent?

A: The line in front of the house runs from left to right. This indicates a need for security.

Q: This indicates a need for security! Could it also indicate the contour of the landscape, like a lawn or something?

A: This is not the interpretation I gave it.

Q: And the chimney—what does it indicate?

A: You will notice that the chimney is dark. This indicates disturbed sexual feelings. The smoke indicates inner daydreaming.

Q: Did I understand you correctly? Did you say dark chimneys indicate disturbed sex feelings?

A: Yes.

Q: You then asked Kent to draw a tree. Why?

A: We have discovered that a person often expresses feelings about himself that are on a subconscious level when he draws a tree.

Q: And what does this drawing indicate about Kent's personality?

A: The defendant said it was a sequoia, 1500 years old, and that it was diseased. This indicates a feeling of self-depreciation. Also, the tree has no leaves and it leans to the left. This indicates a lack of contact with the outside world—the absence of leaves.

Q: Don't trees lose their leaves in the winter, Doctor? If you look out the window now, in Washington, do you see leaves on the trees? Perhaps the defendant was drawing a picture of a tree without leaves, as they appear in the winter.

A: The important thing is, however, why did the defendant select this particular tree? He was stripped of leaves, of emotions.

Q: You then asked him to draw a person?

A: Yes.

Q: And he drew a picture of a male?

A: Yes.

Q: And what does this drawing indicate about Kent?

A: The man appears to be running. This indicates anxiety, agitation. He is running, you will notice, to the left. This indicates running away from the environment. If he had been running to the right this would indicate entering the environment.

Q: How about the hands?

A: The sharp fingers may indicate hostility.

Q: Anything else?

A: The head and the body appear to be separated by a dark collar, and the neck is long. This indicates a split between intellect and emotion. The dark hair, dark tie, dark shoes, and dark buckle indicate anxiety about sexual problems.

Q: You then asked Kent to draw a person of the opposite sex. What did this indicate?

A: The dark piercing eyes indicated a feeling of rejection by women, hostility toward women.

The psychologist, presumably relying on these and other tests, diagnosed the man as suffering from schizophrenia and concluded that he was not, therefore, responsible for his crimes.

In the early 1980s, three researchers tested the ability of sixteen Ph.D.-level psychologists to pick out human figure drawings that had been made by thirty-two psychiatric hospital patients (whose average hospitalization was more than seven years) from those drawings that had been made by thirty-two persons with no history of mental illness. Although the psychologists had, on the average, some thirteen years of experience in their profession, their "hit rate" was a mere 58 percent—slightly better than guessing.

Anyone, of course, can guess. Jay Ziskin, an attorney and psychologist, reports in his handbook for lawyers called *Coping With Psychiatric and Psychological Testimony* that laymen are generally able to judge the results of these types of tests as well as, or in some cases even better than, the professionals. Nevertheless, tests that ask subjects to draw figures are very popular diagnostic tools.

The granddaddy of projective tests is, of course, the Rorschach. Yet a psychology professor who reviewed the test for the most recent edition of the *Mental Measurements Yearbook* observed that the "general lack of predictive validity for the Rorschach raises serious question about its continued use in clinical practice." George W. Albee, then the incoming president of the American Psychological Association, expressed similar doubts in a 1970 speech to his group.

Twenty years ago, most of us believed in the art of the Rorschach. The public was fascinated by the magic we owned. Other professions viewed our magic with respect. But along came the hard-nosed scientists, the measurement people, with their questions about reliability and validity, with their split-half techniques, and their demand for public demonstration of the value of our magic under strictly controlled conditions. As a consequence, the Rorschach is quietly disappearing from professional psychology because of our professional sensitivity to the claims of science. Interestingly, the public still believes in the Rorschach.

Perhaps it was "the public" 's continuing faith in the Rorschach that made Dr. Albee's predictions of the test's demise premature. This is how the *Mental Measurements Yearbook* reviewer appraised it:

The Rorschach is gradually declining in popularity but it still continues to be one of the most, if not the most, popular and frequently used assessment procedures for personality-emotional disturbance evaluation.

He observed, however, that "certainly the validity research on the Rorschach does not warrant its popularity." Indeed, one prominent defender of the use of the Rorschach and other projective tests for some purposes, a professor at the Yale University School of Medicine, has recognized that many in the profession look upon them as "no better than reading tea leaves."

Two years after Dr. Albee's speech to the American Psychological Association bemoaning that the "magic" was gone from the Rorschach, the United States Court of Appeals for Washington, D.C., chastised a government prosecutor in an insanity defense case for his "know-nothing appeals to ignorance" because he belittled the famous inkblot test during his cross-examination of a psychologist and closing argument. Apparently, in some circles at least, the magic lingers on.

The Minnesota Multiphasic Personality Inventory, a series of some 560 true/false questions, has fared a little better than some of the other projectives. However, results on the MMPI for the same subject will vary from test session to test session. Dr. Gary Groth-Marnat's *Handbook of Psychological Assessment* concludes that retest consistency "has not proved to be one of the MMPI's strong points."

The simple fact is that projective tests are not magic mirrors of the mind. But because they have the aura of science, the law has given them great weight.

The studies we have discussed concern the *descriptive* ability of the mind sciences: Who is sane? Who is insane? However, the law also enlists their aid in determining whether and when a person who has been acquitted by reason of insanity may be safely released into society.

Almost everyone now agrees that the mind sciences' *predictive* ability is nil. In a brief submitted to the United States Supreme Court, the American Psychiatric Association has conceded that "psychiatrists have no special expertise" in predicting whether a person will or will not be dangerous in the future. Nevertheless, there are psychiatrists who presume to possess that expertise in our courts every day. An interesting and almost archetypal example happened in my court several years ago.

A young man had been acquitted by reason of insanity of "endangering safety by conduct regardless of life": he had held a knife to his mother's throat for forty-five minutes in a confrontation with police who had been called to the home. The trial judge found that he was "presently suffering from mental disease" and was dangerous. Accordingly, the defendant was transferred to a psychiatric hospital. Less than two months later, he wanted out, and the case was assigned to me. A local psychiatrist testified that the young man could be safely released into the community. The young man's lawyer attempted to lock in the doctor's opinion as follows:

Q: Doctor, the opinion you gave before about him being able to be released without danger to himself or others, was that opinion to a reasonable degree of medical certainty?

A: Yes sir.

Since the decision whether to release the defendant was mine, I stepped in with a few questions:

The Court: Doctor, are you familiar with the literature in the field as to the predictive capabilities of psychiatrists with respect to dangerousness?

A: Yes, I am.

The Court: Do you feel that it is generally accepted in the psychiatric community that psychiatrists are able to predict to a reasonable degree of medical certainty the future dangerousness of an individual?

A: Well, psychiatry is a general field. They cannot predict dangerousness any more than any other individual, and the fact that they are psychiatrists doesn't make them any more able to predict such things.

The Court: Well, you just indicated you could make that prediction to a reasonable degree of medical certainty?

A: I'm merely giving an opinion. It certainly doesn't mean I'm bound by the opinion.

The Court: Well, is it an opinion to a reasonable degree of medical certainty?

A: Medical certainty? Oh, I see. Well, it couldn't be.

If the psychiatrist did not think he should be "bound" by his opinion, I wonder who he *did* believe should be bound. As the American Psychiatric Association has admitted, psychiatric testimony on future dangerousness "gives the appearance of being based on expert medical judgment, when in fact no such expertise exists."

The United States Supreme Court has rejected proposals—including those by the American Psychiatric Association—either to prohibit completely or severely restrict psychiatric testimony on the issue of future dangerousness as being "somewhat like asking us to disinvent the wheel." But the Court expressed hope "that the adversary process" would be able to "sort out" the probative evidence from that which is not. Psychiatric presumption of expertise in the legal-insanity/future-dangerousness context—flimsy as that expertise may be—thus remains a significant problem in those many, many cases in which the important questions are *not* asked.

Unfortunately, as we have seen in earlier chapters, the adversary process is often defused by plea bargaining. Psychiatric testimony provides a convenient shield for this practice. Except in notorious cases where there is extensive press coverage, an insanity defense is often agreed to by the prosecutor, the defense lawyer, and the judge. In a study analyzing the insanity defense in one large New Jersey county during a year in the late 1970s, Anne Singer, a lawyer who represented indigent defendants, found that most of the insanity defense trials were "cursory" and that the judicial system professionals involved liked that avenue to resolving criminal cases for their own, basically institutional reasons—part of the same triad of convenience we discussed earlier in Chapter 4. The defense lawyers liked it because it would "absolve" their clients of guilt and because verdicts of "not guilty by reason of insanity" were "wins." The prosecutors and judges went along "in order to save time."

Hospitalization periods are often short. There were forty-six "not guilty by reason of insanity" verdicts during the year Singer studied, and the defendants had been hospitalized, on the average, for just over fourteen months before they were released into the community. For the twelve defendants charged with murder, the average hospitalization period was just over two years.

Statistics elsewhere are equally frightening. In New York, for example, one study showed that from 1965 to 1976, those acquitted of murder by reason of insanity and subsequently released from mental hospitals spent, on the average, 500 days—less than one and a half years—in postacquittal custody, while those acquitted of manslaughter by reason of insanity and later released spent, on the average, only 350 days in the mental hospitals to which they had been committed. A similar study conducted in Florida showed that those who were discharged from mental hospitals following their insanity acquittals of first-degree murder charges spent, on the average, fewer than three years in postacquittal custody, while those who had been convicted of first-degree murder spent, on the average, less than ten years in prison.

I do not know what effect plea bargaining had on the Florida or New York cases, but I assume that many of the commitments were after the same type of "cursory" trials reported by Singer that are common throughout the country. For example, several years ago, a thirty-four-year-old man appeared before me on the felony charge of battery to a police officer. He was accused of slashing a cop in the face with a sharpened screwdriver. He entered a dual plea: not guilty and not guilty by reason of mental disease. As required by the statute, I appointed a psychiatrist to examine him and then set the matter down for trial.

After I moved from the felony division to the civil division, the prosecutor and the defense lawyer agreed to a trial without a jury before a different judge. The defendant pled guilty to the crime but reserved his "not guilty by reason of mental disease" plea. The psychiatrist testified that the defendant had been suffering from paranoid schizophrenia. He arrived at his diagnosis based on what the defendant had done and on the voices the defendant *said* he heard. The prosecutor did not offer any opposing testimony. The judge who presided over this cursory "trial" found the defendant not guilty because of mental disease. He relied on the psychiatrist's opinion that the defendant's illness was "in remission" and released the man into the community that very day on condition that he take some medication.

Like general plea bargaining, cursory insanity-defense trials are common everywhere. Daniel P. Pugh, the psychiatrist mentioned earlier who worked at Washington, D.C.'s, St. Elizabeth's Hospital in the late 1960s, reported that one "judge was so outraged by the deal the prosecution and defendant had made that he could not bring himself to declare the defendant not guilty by reason of insanity." Instead of rejecting the plea and insisting on a trial, the judge transferred the matter "to another judge whose feelings about the case were not so strong."

The law has an extremely difficult job in determining the legal question of whether a particular defendant was or was not criminally responsible at the time of the crime and, if so, when he will be no longer dangerous. It is understandable, therefore, that the legal system should seek all the help it can get. Unfortunately, most lawyers and judges expect the mind sciences to provide answers in neat little packages. That expectation has been nurtured by the mind science community itself; some from that community cannot understand why their "gospel" is challenged. As one psychiatrist peevishly declared, if "society sees fit to appoint neutral experts to determine the sanity of the defendant, then society should demonstrate its faith in those experts and abide fully by their findings." Another has argued that the "clinical judgment" of a properly qualified psychiatrist "must be accepted by the courts to the same extent as the clinical judgment of a surgeon or internist."

Yet as we have seen, mind scientists do not have all the answers and have no magic key to the truth. Indeed, psychiatrist Lee Coleman, founder and head of the Center for the Study of Psychiatric Testimony in Berkeley, California, has flatly charged that psychiatrists are "not scientists at all" and that their often "conflicting and confusing testimony" is "extra nonsense" that should be kept out of court. He puts it this way in his 1984 book about psychiatry, called *The Reign of Error:* "They have no special way of predicting who will commit a criminal act or of determining when a criminal is cured of antisocial tendencies. They have no tests to determine a person's innermost thoughts, even though the courts assume they do." In other words, they "do not have the tools society thinks they have." The mind science disciplines constitute an unsteady foundation upon which to build rules that permit persons to avoid criminal responsibility. Yet as we will see in the next chapter, ever since the *M'Naghten* test was announced in 1843, there have been pressures to expand those rules to encompass almost what the judge in that 1723 case derisively called "every idle humour of a man."

ELEVEN
Real Bite

THE *M'NAGHTEN* TEST for criminal responsibility asks what the defendant knew at the time of the crime or, when it is supplemented with the concept of irresistible impulse, whether he could control himself. Critics believe this ignores what they call "the whole man." One contemporary critic of *M'Naghten* is the highly respected American jurist Irving R. Kaufman. Judge Kaufman sits on the United States Court of Appeals for federal courts in New York, Connecticut, Vermont, and New Hampshire. In 1966, he was instrumental in getting his court to jettison *M'Naghten* for a more liberal rule. After the outrage caused by the acquittal of John W. Hinckley, Jr., in 1982, Judge Kaufman counseled against a return to a stricter standard in an article published in *The New York Times Magazine*. Arguing that the law must punish only those who are called "blameworthy"—the essence of which is "the conscious choice to commit an act warranting moral blame and deserving of punishment"—he contends the law should "absolve from criminal responsibility" those "who—as a result of mental defect, lack of maturity, *or other reasons—differ substantially from the rest of us.*"

I have italicized a portion of Judge Kaufman's comment in order to emphasize the open-ended nature of this view. In my mind, it comes pretty close to the absolutist position held by some that criminal acts are merely symptoms of mental illness, much the way that a cough can be a symptom of bronchitis. That view comes close to excusing *all* criminal activity and is consistent with a philosophy held by those who suggest that few of us are "responsible" for the bad things we do.

Determinists would shift causation—and, therefore, blame—away from the individual not only to his or her psyche but to "society," that person's genes, parents, neighbors, spouse, menstrual period, or even food (as in Dan White's so-called "Twinkie defense" in the slaying of San Francisco Mayor George Moscone and Supervisor Harvey Milk). Columbia Law Professor Herbert Wechsler has noted, in his typical rapier style, that this view is "rooted in a kind of psychiatric crypto-ethics not uncommon in our culture." It rejects the very essence of criminal law, which is founded on the premise that men and women are presumed responsible for their acts. As cogently expressed by the prosecutor in the first insanity defense case in which an expert witness testified, the 1760 trial before the House of Lords of Earl Ferrers for murder, "in some sense every crime proceeds from insanity. All cruelty, all brutality, all revenge, all injustice is insanity. . . . My Lords, the opinion is right in philosophy but dangerous in judicature."

The problem with casting personal beliefs concerning individual responsibility in the folds of scientific garb is that it makes us forget that we are really talking policy, not provable science. As psychiatrist, lawyer, and professor Jonas Robitscher has written, psychiatry "comes to us with the imprimatur of science although it is not always scientific" and "carries the weight of medical authority although it is only occasionally truly medical." Significantly, those who wish to broaden the scope of immunity from punishment recognize that most who will achieve that immunity *are* capable of being deterred and that their actions are, at least to some degree, subject to their free will. Consider this candid admission from a British government report quoted in the landmark insanity defense case *Durham* v. *United States,* that 1954 decision of the United States Court of Appeals for Washington, D.C., that was referred to earlier in Chapter Ten:

> It would be impossible to apply modern methods of care and treatment in mental hospitals, and at the same time to maintain order and discipline, if the great majority of the patients, even among the grossly insane, did not know what is forbidden by the rules and that, if they break them, they are liable to forfeit some privilege.

The need to differentiate those who should from those who should not be held criminally responsible requires that the legal

line be drawn somewhere. Public order makes it necessary that
the line be closely drawn so that the rules that preserve society's
peace apply, in Professor Wechsler's phrase, to "those whose nature or nurture leads them to conform with difficulty no less
than those who find compliance easy." *Durham* rejected this logic.

Like *M'Naghten* 121 years earlier, *Durham* was a watershed in
the law, even though the legal principles articulated in that decision by appeals Judge David L. Bazelon were never widely accepted and, indeed, were ultimately abandoned by his own court.
Before the watershed ran dry, however, its streams nourished an
insanity defense forest. According to psychiatrist Karl Menninger, the decision was "more revolutionary" than *Brown* v. *Board
of Education*, the case in which the Supreme Court outlawed racial segregation in the public schools.

Twenty-six at the time the decision bearing his name was
written, Monte Durham had been in and out of a mental hospital
since his release from the navy as unfit for service at the age of
seventeen. When discharged, he was diagnosed as having "a profound personality disorder." Two years later, Durham was convicted of auto theft and placed on probation for one to three
years. After apparently attempting suicide, he was sent to St.
Elizabeth's Hospital. He was let out after about two months.

Less than a year later, Durham's probation was revoked for
passing bad checks. After a few days in jail, he was given a "lunacy inquiry." A jury found him to be mentally ill, and he was
shipped off to St. Elizabeth's again. This time the diagnosis was
"psychosis with psychopathic personality." After fifteen months,
he was released from the hospital as "recovered." He returned
to jail to serve the balance of his sentence. Paroled a year later,
he quickly got into trouble for some more bad checks. The parole board referred him for another lunacy hearing. The jury
again found that he was mentally ill, and he was again returned
to St. Elizabeth's. This time, the diagnosis was "without mental
disorder, psychopathic personality." Two months later, he was
released from the hospital, and two months after that, he committed the housebreaking for which he was convicted; his insanity defense, under the *M'Naghten* standards, was unsuccessful.

The Court of Appeals for Washington, D.C., reversed Durham's conviction. Judge Bazelon's decision abandoned the
M'Naghten rules' "right and wrong" formulation, supplemented

by the "irresistible impulse" concept, as too limited. As Judge Bazelon explained in an article some twenty years later, he viewed the *M'Naghten* rule as bearing the prejudice of an era "when the dominant perception of human behavior was that people, as rational beings, made free choices informed by conscious consideration." This, he contended, was out of step with the "modern" view that looked on man as an organism pulled in various, often conflicting, directions by subconscious forces. "The psychiatric profession," Bazelon wrote, "was outspokenly critical of" the fundamental assumptions of that earlier era that ignored the "modern dynamic understanding of man as an integrated personality, manifesting nonrational and irrational as well as rational, compulsive as well as volitional, behavior." In establishing a new insanity defense standard for the District of Columbia, the *Durham* rule thus not only broadened a defendant's immunization from criminal responsibility for his unlawful acts but freed expert testimony from what the psychiatrists viewed as the "right and wrong" strait jacket. As Judge Bazelon remembered it in another article almost thirty years later, "Our goal was to expose judges and juries—and through them the community at large— to all that was known and not known about human behavior."

The future United States Supreme Court Justice Abe Fortas, whom the court of appeals appointed to represent Durham, had sought a rule that would have excused *any* mentally ill person from criminal responsibility for his or her acts. Judge Bazelon's court went far, but not that far. Under the *Durham* test, persons would escape criminal punishment unless the prosecution could prove beyond a reasonable doubt that their unlawful acts were not "the product of a mental disease or mental defect." *Disease* was defined as a temporary condition "capable of either improving or deteriorating," while *defect* was a permanent impairment resulting from any one of a variety of causes. The theory was to permit the jury to apply, in Judge Bazelon's words, "our inherited ideas of moral responsibility" after learning all that contemporary psychiatry could tell them about the byzantine world of a particular defendant's psyche.

One of the intellectual pillars upon which *Durham* rested was the work of the nineteenth-century psychiatrist Isaac Ray, whose 1838 book, as we will recall, supported the arguments favoring

M'Naghten's acquittal. This is how Dr. Ray described what he believed was the crux of the problem:

> That the insane mind is not entirely deprived of this moral power of discernment, but in many subjects is perfectly rational and displays the exercise of a sound and well balanced mind is one of those facts now so well established, that to question it would only betray the height of ignorance and presumption.

In short, Dr. Ray and his followers want us to "trust" them when they tell us that there are people who should not be held responsible for their crimes even though they appear to know what they're doing.

The *Durham* decision radically changed the law of insanity in Washington, D.C. Indeed, the test, in Judge Bazelon's words, included "virtually any mode of effective causation." As he later explained, "The illness might have been the source of the defendant's urge to do the act, or it might have exaggerated an otherwise ordinary response to an external threat; it might have impaired his ability to control impulses normally repressed, or it might have impaired his appreciation of the necessity for such control. So long as 'the disease made the effective or decisive difference between doing and not doing the act,' then the act was the product of the disease for the purpose of *Durham*."

Interestingly, the decision purported to write a rule "not unlike" one established by New Hampshire in 1870 that used similar language ("if the homicide was the offspring or product of mental disease in the defendant, he was not guilty by reason of insanity"). But the New Hampshire Supreme Court, unlike *Durham*, required total incapacity to resist as a prerequisite for an insanity acquittal. In fact, in 1871 the New Hampshire Supreme Court rejected the argument of a man who was accused of killing his wife that insanity could be a defense as long as it "*contributed to the crime*" with this explanation:

> If the defendant had an insane impulse to kill his wife, which he could not control, then mental disease produced the act. If he could have controlled it, then his will must have assented to the act, and it was not caused by disease, but by the concurrence of his will, and was therefore crime.

Judge Bazelon and his colleagues, while borrowing the "product" language from the New Hampshire court, rejected its substance.

Two years after the *Durham* decision, Fortas told an American Psychiatric Association meeting that "one may guess" that the *Durham* court "judges suspect that mental disorders may figure in criminal activities with vastly more frequency" than the law then recognized "and that they deliberately began the process of refashioning our legal institutions to take account of this hypothesis." He lauded the decision as "a bill of rights for psychiatry." The American Psychiatric Association apparently agreed and gave Judge Bazelon a certificate of commendation. Psychiatric influence was on a roll.

Although the *Durham* rule was formulated by a three-judge court, it clearly was a *legislative* decision—that is, it was the type of decision that needs the investigation and analysis normally inherent in, and indispensable to, the legislative process, because of the depth of inquiry required and the public policy questions involved. In a very real sense, *Durham* was founded on *ipse dixit* (Latin for "he himself said it," meaning "it is because I say it is"), and it placed unquestioning reliance on those who favored controlling what is essentially a legal issue with psychiatric concepts and theories, what Durham's lawyer, Fortas, candidly referred to as "suspicions" and "hypotheses."

Judge Bazelon had envisioned that a psychiatrist would be able to tell a jury "anything he can about the defendant's behavior and his state of mind," and that the jury would then decide "whether the defendant can justly be held responsible." Much to Judge Bazelon's dismay, however, it did not work out quite that way.

The trust in psychiatry fostered by *Durham* went too far even for Judge Bazelon, who later would accuse the experts of testifying "in boilerplate responses—conclusory, shallow, and overreaching." Confused and perplexed by an overwhelming profusion of arcane concepts and complicated jargon, juries operating under the *Durham* rule—despite Judge Bazelon's hopes that they would be freed from the tyranny of labels—were unable to intelligently sift through the morass, and as a result, they abdicated their fact-finding responsibilities. They too often rubber-stamped the psychiatrists' conclusions, which were frequently based on questions of morality—"Should this person be held criminally responsible?"

In an effort to prevent this abdication, the *Durham* court tinkered with the rule for almost two decades. For example, the legal definition of "mental disease and defect" was limited eight years later to "any abnormal condition of the mind which substantially affects mental or emotional processes and substantially impairs behavior controls"; "product" was refined to require "a relationship between the disease and the criminal act" so "as to justify a reasonable inference that the act would not have been committed if the person had not been suffering from the disease."

Even as modified, however, *Durham* gave psychiatrists broad berth in which to dock their own views as to who should, and who should not, be punished by the criminal law. And, indeed, between 1954, when *Durham* was announced, and 1961, insanity acquittals in the District of Columbia federal court spurted some thirtyfold, from .4 percent to 14.4 percent (one out of seven!) of all defendants. Yet as we have seen, psychiatric insight into the mind falls far short of cogent scientific analysis. Rather, it presents ever-undulating contours whose configurations change with the ebb and flow of theory.

On April 5, 1957, Comer Blocker arrived in Washington, D.C., from his home in Philadelphia to visit Frances, his estranged girlfriend—a woman whom the courts would later call his common-law wife. He came with a recently purchased shotgun. Shortly after 11 P.M., he appeared at Frances's apartment where she lived with her five children. Blocker's fourteen-year-old son, Chester, answered the door. Chester tried, but failed, to keep his father out.

Blocker used the shotgun to push Chester toward the bedroom. Frances, seeing Blocker, tried to close the bedroom door. He shot her through the wood. Then he finished her off with a final blast. When he was arrested, Blocker appeared to be sober.

He explained that he had come from Philadelphia to kill his girlfriend and had done so. That story changed by the time of trial. There, Comer Blocker raised two defenses: one, the shootings were accidental; and two, he was insane at the time.

Three psychiatrists testified at Blocker's trial. Although one testified for the prosecution and the other two for the defense, they were all on the staff of St. Elizabeth's Hospital. Their testimony concerned sociopaths—those amoral individuals whose consciences are mute. Before the 1954 *Durham* decision, the staff at St. Elizabeth's had considered sociopathy to be a mental disorder. Once *Durham* broadened the standard of nonresponsibility, however, they changed their view. Apparently they were concerned that the hospital would be overrun by defendants whose criminal acts would be excused under *Durham* as products of their sociopathy. Accordingly, they announced that they no longer considered sociopathy a disease and began to add the phrase "without mental disorder" to their court reports diagnosing defendants with sociopathic personalities.

The two psychiatrists called by the defense testified that Blocker had a "sociopathic personality disturbance" and was also suffering from chronic alcoholism. The psychiatrist testifying for the prosecution said he could find nothing wrong with the man. All three of them, however, agreed that sociopathy was not mental disease. This is how one of the defense psychiatrists expressed it:

> Now, this is not the same thing as a mental defect or mental illness. It is more a long standing personality disturbance characterized in many cases by a lack of conscience, a lack of moral responsibility, and inability to profit from experience.

Blocker was convicted of first-degree murder and sentenced to death.

On a Monday morning about a month after Blocker's conviction, the St. Elizabeth's assistant superintendent was testifying in another case. He told the judge that he would have to change his previous Friday's testimony when, consistent with the post-*Durham* policy at St. Elizabeth's, he had said that sociopathy was not a mental illness. Over the weekend, he and the superintendent changed their minds; they now believed sociopathy was a mental illness.

As a result of the relabeling, Blocker's attorney sought a new trial. He claimed that the flip-flop amounted to "newly discovered medical evidence." The district judge denied the motion, but the court of appeals reversed. Blocker should get a new trial, two of the three appellate judges reasoned, because he was "entitled to a verdict based upon the most mature expert opinion available." The third judge disagreed, pointing out that the 1952 edition of the American Psychiatric Association's *Diagnostic and Statistical Manual for Mental Disorders* had concluded that sociopathy was a mental disease and that there was no shortage of psychiatrists who could have so testified.

Blocker was tried again. Again, he was convicted of first-degree murder and sentenced to death. Again, the court of appeals reversed his conviction, this time because the trial judge made a mistake in his legal instructions to the jury.

Blocker was tried a third time, and one psychiatrist and two psychologists testified that he was a psychotic and that the murder was the result of his psychosis. A psychiatrist testifying for the government disagreed and said he could find no evidence that Blocker was mentally ill. Blocker was convicted again. This time, however, the jury found him guilty of *second*-degree murder. His sentence: ten years to life. Blocker appealed, and his conviction was affirmed. Finally, on March 29, 1965, some eight years after the murder, the case of Comer Blocker was put to rest when the United States Supreme Court refused further review.

The St. Elizabeth's flip-flop resulted from a confluence of self-interest, the amorphous nature of psychiatric concepts, and the imprecision of the *Durham* rule. As Dr. Pugh, who worked there during the late 1960s, later recalled in an article published in *The Washington University Law Quarterly*, there were similar problems at the hospital:

> A common experience was that a new doctor would find virtually every defendant insane. Some would actually insist that *anyone* who would commit a felony must be insane. However, after being confronted with the task of trying to manage an unselected group of felons in the hospital following their criminal commitment, the new doctor would reverse tack and become very stringent about finding defendants insane. . . . The secretaries who typed reports to the court informed me that one doctor who had been there before I came had never adjusted to these pressures, and switched every few months from

finding everyone insane to finding everyone sane and then back again.

Another famous labeling flip-flop occurred in 1973, when the American Psychiatric Association, after much debate and dissension, deleted homosexuality from its classification of "personality disorders and certain other non-psychotic mental disorders" in the second edition of the *Diagnostic and Statistical Manual for Mental Disorders.* Such divergence of views is not, as we have seen, uncommon. Noted psychiatrist Philip Q. Roche, in his 1958 book *The Criminal Mind* (which won the APA's Isaac Ray Award), concedes that even with "two of the most frequently encountered terms in psychiatry," *psychosis* and *neurosis,* there is "confusion" not only "as to the precise meaning of each term" but also as to the conditions to which they "can be applied." Perhaps Chief Justice Warren Burger put it best when, as a judge on the United States Court of Appeals for Washington, D.C., he was one of the many judges who heard one of Blocker's appeals: "No rule of law can possibly be sound or workable which is dependent upon the terms of another discipline whose members are in profound disagreement about what those terms mean." After all, what self-respecting chemist would call a certain chemical sodium chloride (table salt) one day and sodium hydroxide (lye) the next? And if he did, would you trust him to bring food to a picnic?

In 1972, after almost twenty years of unsuccessful struggle, the United States Court of Appeals for Washington, D.C., finally abandoned the *Durham* rule and embraced an insanity standard drafted by the American Law Institute a decade earlier, and which had been adopted, with various modifications, by almost all the other federal courts of appeals and by about half of the states.

The American Law Institute, a 2,000-member organization of lawyers, law professors, and judges, was founded in the early 1920s, in the words of its charter, to "promote the clarification and simplification of the law and its better adaptation to social needs." It has had a profound impact on the law's development through its various projects, which explain, analyze, and evaluate existing law as well as propose improvements. Starting in the 1950s and under the leadership of Columbia Law Professor Herbert

Wechsler, it tackled the massive task of writing a code in the area of criminal law that could be used as a legislative—or, where appropriate, judicial—model. In 1962, after much study, debate, more study, and more debate, the Institute approved its model penal code. This is how the Institute suggested that the insanity defense be handled:

> (1) A person is not responsible for criminal conduct if at the time of such conduct as a result of mental disease or defect he lacks substantial capacity either to appreciate the criminality [wrongfulness] of his conduct or to conform his conduct to the requirements of law.
> (2) As used in this Article, the terms "mental disease or defect" do not include an abnormality manifested only by repeated criminal or otherwise anti-social conduct.

The rule has two prongs. The first is a weakened version of the *M'Naghten* "right and wrong" test: Did the defendant have " 'substantial capacity' to know his act was criminal, wrong, or was at the time he committed it?" The second expands the "irresistible impulse" modification of the *M'Naghten* rule: Did the defendant lack "substantial capacity" to control himself even if he did know right from wrong?

While Judge Bazelon agreed that it was time for a change, he argued for a standard that he had hoped would have flowed from *Durham:* one that permitted the jury to make its decision based on its perception of what was just under the circumstances. With minor modifications, his formulation was substantially similar to that proposed by Professor Wechsler, but rejected by a majority of the Institute. Judge Bazelon suggested that the jury be told "that a defendant is not responsible if at the time of his unlawful conduct his mental or emotional processes or behavior controls were impaired to such an extent that he cannot be justly held responsible for his act." Under his proposal, the mind science experts would be limited to discussing the nature and extent of any impairment of the defendant's mental or emotional processes or behavior controls. All moral judgments would be made by the jury.

Judge Bazelon's view was rejected by the eight other full-time appeals court judges as dangerously open-ended. As the late Judge Harold Leventhal wrote for the majority,

The thrust of a rule that in essence invites the jury to pon-
der the evidence on impairment of a defendant's capacity and
appreciation, and then do what to them seems just, is to focus
on what seems "just" to the particular individual. Under the
centuries-long pull of the Judeo-Christian ethic, this is likely to
suggest a call for understanding and forgiveness of those who
have committed crimes against society, but plead the influence
of passionate and perhaps justified grievances against society,
perhaps grievances not wholly lacking in merit. In the domain
of morality and religion, the gears may be governed by the particular instance of the individual seeking salvation. The judgment of a court of law must further justice to the community,
and safeguard it against undercutting and evasion from over-
concern for the individual. What this reflects is not the rigidity
of retributive justice—an eye for an eye—but awareness how
justice in the broad may be undermined by an excess of compassion as well as passion.

Although it was better than the more open-ended *Durham*
formulation, the American Law Institute test nonetheless permits juries to play "expert roulette" with society's safety. In contrast to a trial in which experts may testify on various issues
ranging from the electrical safety of a toaster to the standard of
care generally practiced by physicians, in trials involving the insanity defense, juries have no compass of either common sense
or experience with which to guide their judgment when faced
with a conflict in mind science testimony. The most notorious
example of this arose out of the attempted assassination of Ronald Reagan in which the prosecutor had to prove John W.
Hinckley, Jr., sane beyond a reasonable doubt under a version
of the American Law Institute test that was then being used in
the District of Columbia federal court.

Hinckley planned to kill President Reagan as a way of attract-
ing the attention of Jodie Foster, a young movie actress who had
rebuffed him. For months, he brooded and plotted. Finally, on
March 31, 1981, his bullets caught the President, Press Secretary
James Brady, Secret Service Agent Timothy McCarthy, and
Washington, D.C., police officer Thomas Delahanty.

Hinckley's insanity defense was the focus of his eight-week
trial. The mind science experts, who all told charged both the
government and the defense about a half a million dollars in fees

and expenses, could not agree. Government psychiatrists testified that Hinckley was not mentally ill; those hired by the defense swore that he was. A juror in the case later explained their predicament to a Senate subcommittee studying the insanity plea: "If the expert psychiatrists could not decide whether the man was sane, then how are we to decide?"

The government did not carry its heavy burden, and Hinckley was acquitted by reason of insanity. As then–White House Counselor Edwin Meese put it in blasting the law that made the verdict possible, "You couldn't even prove the White House staff sane beyond a reasonable doubt."

Psychiatrist and Columbia University Professor Willard Gaylin, who wrote a book on Bonnie Garland's murder, *The Killing of Bonnie Garland,* believes the law has been too ready to excuse criminal behavior because of alleged insanity. As a result of Hinckley's acquittal, however, all this has changed—at least in the federal courts. To mint a cliché, some sanity has returned to the issue of insanity and the criminal law.

As discussed in Chapter 1, legal principles develop slowly as experience tinctured with logic builds from generation to generation, much like the rings of a tree or layers of coral. Just as dendrochronologists chart the life of trees by analyzing their rings, legal historians can slice through the law and similarly chart its development.

A tree's physical environment, of course, can spur or retard its growth. By the same token, social environment is an important catalyst to the law's evolution. We have seen how twice in the history of the insanity defense cataclysmic events have suddenly altered its course: M'Naghten's attempt to kill British Prime Minister Robert Peel and Hinckley's unsuccessful attempt on the life of President Ronald Reagan.

The *M'Naghten* rules, which focused on what the defendant *knew* at the time of his unlawful act, were clear-cut. Over the years, they were eroded by those who sought to look at "the whole man" through deterministic glasses where everything man does is seen as but the sum of his genes, environment, and experience. The peak of the determinists' influence came with the *Durham* case and its "product" test. The American Law Institute formulation, which was intended to define the insanity defense with more precision than had *Durham,* kept the inquiry almost as broad. The Hinckley acquittal and the outrage that followed have changed the course once more.

The Hinckley verdict shook the public's faith in the criminal justice system, much as M'Naghten's acquittal had almost 140 years earlier. Even the liberal California governor, Jerry Brown, criticized it as the result of a legal system that "totally disregards the issue of guilt or innocence and relies on so-called psychiatric experts to tell us whether a man who committed a deliberate attack should be acquitted because he watched too many movies." As a consequence of the outrage, some twenty bills to abolish or reform the insanity defense were introduced into the Congress.

One of the first groups to feel the sting was the American Psychiatric Association. In its official response to the furor, the association adopted the shield of modesty to deflect criticism and sought to minimize its responsibility for the problems: "Long before there was psychiatry," began its December 1982 statement, "there was the insanity defense." Although it recognized, as we have seen, that "sanity is, of course, a legal issue, not a medical one," the group nevertheless reaffirmed its position that "defendants who lack the ability (the capacity) to rationally control their behavior do not possess free will," and who therefore "cannot be said to have 'chosen to do wrong,'" should not be criminally punished. Although it admitted that "psychiatry is a deterministic discipline that views all human behavior as, to some extent, 'caused,'" the APA, in an important concession, went to the heart of the dilemma facing those who seek to divine criminal responsibility:

> Many psychiatrists, however, believe that psychiatric information relevant to determining whether a defendant understood the nature of his act, and whether he appreciated its wrongfulness, is more reliable and has a stronger scientific basis than, for example, does psychiatric information relevant to whether a defendant was able to control his behavior. The line between an irresistible impulse and an impulse not resisted is probably no sharper than that between twilight and dusk.

After careful analysis and investigation, Congress reformulated the insanity defense for the federal courts. It reads not unlike the British judges' *M'Naghten* test:

(a) It is an affirmative defense to a prosecution under any Federal statute that, at the time of the commission of the acts constituting the offense, the defendant, as a result of a severe mental disease or defect, was unable to appreciate the nature and quality of the wrongfulness of his acts. Mental disease or defect does not otherwise constitute a defense.

(b) The defendant has the burden of proving the defense of insanity by clear and convincing evidence.

The new law makes four significant changes. First, the mental illness must be "severe." In the words of the Senate Judiciary Committee report, this was designed to eliminate such nonpsychotic behavior disorders or neuroses as "inadequate personality" and the like.

Second, the burden of proof when insanity is raised as a defense has been shifted from the prosecution—which was previously required to prove beyond a reasonable doubt that the defendant was sane—to the defense. There are three burdens of proof in the law: the normal burden in civil cases of "by the greater weight, or preponderance of the credible evidence"; the prosecution's burden in criminal cases of "beyond a reasonable doubt"; and the so-called "middle" burden of proof by evidence that is "clear and convincing." This last burden lies between the other two. By placing this relatively high burden of proof on the criminal defendant who raises the insanity defense, Congress intended, in the words of the Judiciary Committee report, to "assure that only those defendants who plainly satisfy the requirements of the defense are exonerated from what is otherwise culpable criminal behavior."

Third, the test in federal courts now focuses solely on what defendants knew, not whether they could have controlled themselves. As Richard J. Bonnie, professor of law and director of the Institute of Law, Psychiatry and Public Policy at the University of Virginia, told the Congress,

Unfortunately, however, there is no scientific basis to measure a person's capacity for self-control or calibrating the impairment of such capacity. There is, in short, no objective basis for distinguishing between offenders who were undeterrable and those who were merely undeterred, between the impulse that was irresistible and the impulse not resisted, or between substantial impairment of capacity and some lesser impairment.

Professor Bonnie concluded that to inquire into a defendant's ability to control his or her behavior "invites fabricated claims, undermines equal administration of the penal law, and compromises its deterrent effect."

Fourth, the Federal Rules of Evidence were changed to prohibit mind science experts in criminal cases from giving their *conclusions* as to whether the defendant had the required "mental state" to commit the crime. It therefore accomplished what the federal appellate courts—at least in the District of Columbia—had been attempting to do for years.

The insanity defense river has meandered its snakelike course ever since it left its *M'Naghten* headwaters a century and a half ago. At least in the federal system, that course is now straight and full. Each of the fifty states, however, has its own criminal justice system. Other than New Hampshire, which apparently retains its strict version of the "product" test, the states are about evenly divided between those that use the *M'Naghten* approach (with or without modification) and those that use the American Law Institute standards.

A dozen states permit juries to compromise between "guilty as charged" and "not guilty by reason of insanity" by returning a "guilty but mentally ill" verdict if they believe the defendant's disturbance does not warrant relieving him of criminal responsibility. Michigan was the first to take this approach. A 1974 decision by the Michigan Supreme Court required that persons acquitted on insanity grounds be released within sixty days unless the state was able to satisfy a judge that they should be committed to a mental hospital under the same standards as would apply to someone with suspected mental illness *who had not done anything unlawful.* Within a year, one of the men released under that ruling killed his wife. Another raped two women. As a result of public outcry, the Michigan legislature changed the law. Now, a "guilty but mentally ill" defendant goes to a mental hospital for as long as he needs treatment, after which, rather than be released, he is transferred to prison to serve the remainder of the sentence.

As of this writing, two states (Idaho and Montana) have abolished the insanity defense entirely. In those states, the defendant's mental condition is a sentencing consideration only. In California, voters overturned that state's court-imposed diminished capacity standard—which had recognized degrees of moral culpability—and substituted a test patterned after the *M'Naghten* rules.

At the time the *M'Naghten* rules were developed, an acquittal on insanity grounds meant that the defendant—although spared execution—would spend the rest of his or her life in an asylum for the criminally insane. Public safety was assured. Then, in the 1950s, appellate courts began to change the law. Today, persons acquitted on insanity grounds—even those who commit murder—may not be held in custody if they are thought to be no longer mentally ill or dangerous. Indeed, prior to the passage of the Comprehensive Crime Control Act of 1984, defendants acquitted on the insanity defense in federal courts everywhere but Washington, D.C., could not be held in custody unless state officials could be persuaded to start civil commitment proceedings. Since an acquittal by reason of insanity can mean rapid freedom, the insanity defense now has some "real bite," in the words of Alan A. Stone, a professor of law and psychiatry at Harvard University and a former president of the American Psychiatric Association.

The major problem with a system that permits early release, especially when crimes of violence are involved, is that *no one* can predict dangerousness with any degree of accuracy. As a result, there have been unspeakable tragedies in which persons who were spared criminal responsibility were freed, only to murder and rape again. Indeed, Idaho eliminated its insanity defense as a direct result of the shooting of a nurse by a man who had been released a year after his insanity acquittal of two rape charges. A 1983 article in *U.S. News & World Report* recounted some additional horrors:

- A man acquitted of killing his wife as the result of his insanity plea was, after three months, released from a mental hospital. Five years later, he was charged with killing his second wife.
- A man acquitted of murder on an insanity plea was later accused of killing four teenagers in an Anchorage, Alaska park.
- A bus hijacker was found unable to understand the charges against him and, therefore, could not be tried. He was re-

leased, and fifteen months later, he was accused of killing his roommate and stuffing the body parts into a freezer.

Put on probation with orders to see a psychiatrist after attempting to hijack an airplane, a man hijacked a plane making the same run three years later. He was killed by federal agents.

There are many other examples. The article reports that defendants acquitted by reason of insanity and sent to mental hospitals are now generally released after less than two years. Although Dr. Bernard Diamond favors what is, in effect, psychiatric intervention in the criminal justice system, he told *U.S. News & World Report* in 1982, "I know of cases where patients deceived their therapists and were released and went out and did very terrible things."

According to Dr. Pugh, inappropriate insanity acquittals have another unfortunate result:

> Still another disaster may occur when a sane man is found not guilty by reason of insanity: he may view himself as being able to escape from justice, and nothing that happens in the hospital is likely to make him less dangerous. He is most likely to be released within two years to resume his career in crime. Statistics tell us that he will probably commit many crimes before being again subjected to an earnest felony prosecution. And when that happens he will have a record of being "criminally insane." The original mistake will be repeated. We had a few such "revolving door" case histories at [St. Elizabeth's] John Howard Pavilion. One of them used to gloat that the doctor who had originally discovered his "schizophrenia" had handed him a "license to do burglaries" which he had made good use of ever since. He referred to St. Elizabeth's hospital as the "headquarters for my operation." John Howard Pavilion was often characterized by the hoodlums spending time there as a "good camp."

While some may argue that the burglar's comments reveal his mental illness, the fact is that he perceives he is beating the system. It is a view that I am sure his victims share.

In its post-Hinckley statement, the American Psychiatric Association admitted the inability of psychiatrists to screen those who are dangerous from those who are not. Accordingly, it urged caution when dealing with defendants who have been acquitted on insanity grounds:

> Their future dangerousness need not be inferred; it may be assumed, at least for a reasonable period of time. The American Psychiatric Association is therefore quite skeptical about procedures now implemented in many states requiring periodic decision making by mental health professionals (or by others) concerning a requirement that insanity acquittees who have committed previous violent offenses be repetitively adjudicated as "dangerous," thereupon provoking their release once future dangerousness cannot be clearly demonstrated in accord with the standard of proof required.

Among other things, the APA was concerned that treatment might mask the danger. The group warns that treatment with drugs, "while clearly helpful in reducing overt signs and symptoms of mental illness, does not necessarily mean, however, that 'cure' has been achieved—nor that a patient's 'nondangerousness' is assured. Continuing, even compelled, psychiatric treatment is often required for this population once the patient is released from the hospital." Unfortunately, as the APA recognizes, few places have the facilities and skilled personnel needed to provide the "long period of conditional release with careful supervision and outpatient treatment" required. Without these resources, the APA cautions, conditional release subjects the public to "great risk." One case I reviewed during my year presiding over felony cases underscores the "revolving door" nature of the current insanity defense system.

In the early-morning hours of the late spring of 1979, a five-year-old girl heard a knock at the door. Standing in the doorway was, as she later related it, "the tallest man I've ever seen." The man, twenty-six years old and six feet, eight inches tall, took the little girl from her home into a neighboring backyard, where he brutally raped her. A police officer would later relate that when she spoke to the child some time after the attack, "the little underpants that she had on were quite fully loaded with blood."

The defendant pleaded insanity before another judge. At the time, Wisconsin handled insanity defense trials in three stages. The jury first had to decide whether the defendant had committed the crime. If they found that he had, they then had to decide whether he had proven, by the greater weight of the credible evidence, that "as a result of mental disease or defect he lacked substantial capacity either to appreciate the wrongfulness of his conduct or conform his conduct to the requirements of law," in the words of the Wisconsin statute (patterned after the American Law Institute test). A "yes" answer to that question resulted in a "not guilty by reason of mental disease or defect" verdict, and the jury then had to decide whether the defendant could be safely discharged or released "without danger to himself or to others." If the answer to this last question was yes, the defendant walked out of the courtroom a free man. If the answer was no, the defendant could be either committed to a mental hospital or released subject to certain conditions.

In this case, the man accused of raping the five-year-old girl gave up his right to a jury trial. After hearing the testimony, the judge changed the charge from rape to "sexual contact" and found that the defendant "lacked substantial capacity to conform his conduct to the requirements of law" as the result of schizophrenia. He was sent off to a state mental hospital for evaluation as to whether he could be safely released. Five weeks later, the defendant was returned to court.

The medical report from the state mental hospital made two points. First, the defendant's schizophrenia was "in remission," and he did not need further hospitalization. The psychiatrist noted with special emphasis that "*psychiatrically,* this man could be managed adequately as a day patient from a custodial psychiatric ward, in a halfway house, or even at home (he says his parents are willing to accept him back home)." Second, honing in on the critical question of whether the defendant could be safely released, the psychiatrist made the following candid comments:

> But regarding his dangerousness, it is foolish for me, or any other psychiatrist—but many are wont to do so—to predict whether [the defendant] will in the future be dangerous or not. We can say that if [the defendant] continues to take his anti-psychotic medicine that he will probably be more aware of what he is doing, and we can say that while here that he has shown no signs at all of being dangerous; in fact he is one of the most passive patients that we have had. But whether [the defendant] would rape a five year old girl again or not is not an answerable question. As long as he is *physically capable* of such it is possible.

The defendant was released for a three-week testing period.

When the defendant returned to court, the judge found that his mental illness was in remission but that he was dangerous. Rather than remove him from society and return him to the mental hospital, however, the judge placed him on a "conditional release" and ordered him to cooperate with the authorities, take his medicine, and stay out of trouble. That, they trusted, would defuse the danger. Presumably, they all crossed their fingers and hoped for the best.

Two years after the defendant's conditional release, the case was assigned to me. He had been charged with violating several of the conditions. Specifically, he was accused of fighting with his sister and breaking her window and, ominously, trailing his earlier rape victim. He also had shaved his eyebrows and bleached his hair. I returned him to the mental hospital for a reevaluation.

After relating that the defendant had been violent during his first week at the facility, the psychiatrist's new report was basically a clone of the one two years earlier:

> We can say that this man *generally* has been reasonable while a patient here, that he has controlled himself more recently (without either verbal or physical outbursts), that he has seemed to improve generally while on a small amount of the neuroleptic drug Haldol, and that from a purely psychiatric viewpoint the man does not need to be an inpatient in a psychiatric hospital further. And as long as he continues to take the tranquilizer Haldol, his mental condition is not likely to change from what it is now.

Not satisfied that the defendant could be safely released from custody even on "conditions," I ordered him recommitted. A little over seven months later, another judge released him subject to the same type of conditions he had previously violated.

Two years later, the defendant went before still another judge for not cooperating with the people who were supposed to be supervising his liberty, and for not taking his medication. Again, he was returned to the mental hospital for reevaluation. This time he was cooperative and told one of the staff that he was "just waiting out my thirty days." This judge, too, placed him on conditional release.

During the next seven months, he was back in court several times for various violations. Each time he was returned to the community on "conditional release." Finally, according to one of the reports, he was recommitted to the psychiatric hospital after he "beat up" his girlfriend. Released again, he was later accused of indecent exposure. As of the time of this writing, that has been the last word on this giant of a man who brutally raped a little five-year-old girl. Thankfully, another real tragedy has not yet happened. The man is, however, to use an overworked but, in the context of this case, especially apt phrase, a ticking time bomb waiting to go off.

Those who seek the early release of persons acquitted by reason of insanity claim that the vast majority never cause any trouble. That may be. However, the fact that tragedies may be few from an analytical perspective does not lessen their impact on the victims—or on their families and friends. The criminal justice system, sadly, often has more compassion for the live criminal than it does for the dead victim or for the future but unknown victims.

All of life—indeed, all of law—is a compromise of competing principles. As the drafters of our Constitution wrote in the letter transmitting that document to Congress, "Individuals entering into society, must give up a share of liberty to preserve the rest." That is the very essence of a cooperative society. If we are to balance the "right" to freedom of those who have committed criminal acts but who are spared the ordeal of criminal responsibility against the right of persons in society to be safe from predators, greater weight must be given to society's protection. A valuable start is the provision of the Comprehensive Crime Control Act of 1984 applicable to criminal trials in the federal courts. It requires that those acquitted by reason of insanity of crimes "involving bodily injury" or "serious" property damage (or "substantial risk of such injury or damage") and who seek freedom, first prove by "clear and convincing evidence" that they can be released without creating "a substantial risk of bodily injury to another person or serious damage to the property of another due to a present mental disease or defect." Given the limited reach of our knowledge, however, even this approach may not be enough to avoid gambles with disaster.

TWELVE

Fairness

JUSTINIAN, THE SIXTH-CENTURY Roman emperor whose codification of law is the foundation for most of civilized jurisprudence, defined *justice* as that "which gives to every man his due."
The core of what is "due" in the criminal law is *fairness,* a brittle
balance between the rights of the accused and the rights of society. An extreme example will help to crystallize this thought: No
one would suggest that we summarily execute all criminal suspects, even though that would do much to eliminate crime, just
as no one would suggest that we repeal all criminal laws, even
though that would prevent the conviction and punishment of
innocent persons.

Unfortunately, as we have seen, the criminal law is often
tainted with expediency, rigidity of application, and inappropriate leniency. The resulting structure fails to protect us from
crime. We saw this when the Massachusetts Supreme Judicial
Court voided the search warrant in *Sheppard* because of what was,
in essence, a typographical error.

And it was also visible in the way the Colorado courts handled Francis Barry Connelly. In August 1983, Connelly approached a policeman in downtown Denver. He told the officer
that he had killed someone. Advised of his *Miranda* rights, Connelly said he understood them and that he wanted to talk anyway. He then told how he had killed a young woman about nine
months earlier. When his story panned out, Connelly, who had
a history of mental problems, was charged with murder. His lawyer tried to suppress both incriminating statements.

A psychiatrist testified that Connelly had told him that he
had had an urge to confess. God, Connelly said, commanded

him to get the crime off of his chest or kill himself. The trial judge threw out both statements. He ruled that neither Connelly's initial, volunteered comment nor his later elaboration could be used against him in court. The first statement had not been voluntary, in the judge's view, because it was "compelled by his illness." The second was suppressed because the judge was not persuaded that Connelly had known what he was doing when he agreed to talk. The Colorado Supreme Court affirmed. Two justices dissented:

> The defendant's statement demonstrated his desire to acknowledge his past crime so that he could purge himself of guilt. The "internal voices" that compelled his confession were part and parcel of his own psychological makeup.

They complained that the majority had thwarted the defendant's conscience and, additionally, required "police officers to close their eyes and ears when openly approached with evidence that a crime has been committed." In January 1986, the United States Supreme Court agreed to review the case.

Some two decades ago, federal trial judge and legal scholar Alexander Holtzoff told a congressional subcommittee that was considering proposed crime control legislation about a man whom he called "a self-confessed murderer whose guilt was not in dispute." Arrested at 5:15 in the evening, the man and his wife were brought to police headquarters fifteen minutes later. His wife remained nearby while he was questioned "for at the most five minutes." When he denied knowing anything about the crime, the officers stopped the interrogation and let him talk to his wife. He then said that he wanted to tell them what had happened. The man was convicted in a trial before Judge Holtzoff, but the conviction was overturned when the United States Court of Appeals in Washington, D.C., ruled that the five minutes of questioning violated a rule that required that every arrested person be taken before a magistrate "as quickly as possible." In frustration, Judge Holtzoff reported that the prosecutor had to free the man because, without the confession, there was no case.

Although a preoccupation with "quiddities" and "quillets" (to borrow from *Hamlet*) may make for enjoyable discourse in the sterile chambers of legal theory and philosophy, it tends to contaminate real-world applications. It serves the interests neither of society nor of the persons involved. It results in neither fairness nor justice.

Several centuries ago, Jeremy Bentham warned, "If rogues did know all the pains that the law has taken for their benefit, honest men would have nothing left they could call their own." More recently, after the creation of appropriate rules to safeguard all of our freedoms, the balance between the rights of the accused and the rights of society has been skewed; the law has taken "pains," many of which benefit *only* the criminal. Unlike in Bentham's time, the rogues of today know the rules and how to exploit them. When John Wayne Gacey was arrested for the murder of scores of young men in Illinois, he recognized that the state did not have capital punishment and bragged to police that the only thing they could get him for was "running a funeral parlor without a license." More recently, in March 1985, three teenagers led police on a high-speed chase from Illinois into Wisconsin. Accused of robbing six people and savagely beating an elderly couple with a bat, they not only bragged about their crimes to the police when they were finally caught but taunted the officers for not being able to shoot at them during the chase because of a *two-day-old* United States Supreme Court decision essentially forbidding police from firing at fleeing felons. As Judge Holtzoff explained to Congress twenty years ago:

> The grapevine of the underworld travels fast, and the members of the underworld, while not familiar with the intricacies of the law, know the general tendencies, and the result is that they become bolder, feeling that there will be some technicality or other which will save them from punishment.

It is no coincidence that the precipitous rise in violent predatory crime has come at a time when the law's credibility has been weakened by the infirmities we have discussed. Not only has the law lost its bite, it has lost most of its bark as well. We have let criminals believe that social factors—not they—are to blame for their crimes; we have permitted the cloth of individual responsibility and accountability to unravel. A judge who bought the "society is to blame" theory of crime once expressed it in verse:

Crime
What factors created,
Developed, related
Character flaws
And breaking of laws?
A weakness inherent
Derived from a parent?
Moral decay
As Moralists say?
A man whose sin
Is his colored skin
Whom no one will hire,
Whose needs are dire
With resentment seethes,
Vengeance breathes;
A criminal he?
Are not we?

As Harvard Professors James Q. Wilson and Richard J. Herrnstein point out in their recent book *Crime and Human Nature* and as Charles Murray explains in his *Losing Ground,* this "society is to blame" theory, although extremely popular in some circles, is wrong. Not only doesn't the theory explain crime, it actually encourages the rampant lawlessness we have been experiencing. On an individual level, the theory defuses conscience, letting the criminal believe that he or she is *entitled* to break the law. On the societal level, it breeds collective guilt, which reinforces those who reject "punishment" and "retribution" as legitimate goals of the criminal justice system. The resulting leniency has fanned the fires of crime.

In 1949, the United States Supreme Court declared that retribution was "no longer the dominant objective of the criminal law" and was being replaced by "reformation and rehabilitation." Yet as we discussed, the alternatives to punishment simply have not worked and, in a number of instances, have been counterproductive.

Punishment and retribution *do* have a criminal justice function. Common sense and the studies demonstrate that crime *can* be reduced if we increase the certainty and severity of punishment, if we make the anticipated penalty outweigh the anticipated gain. Although we should, of course, continue our attack on poverty, unemployment, broken families, and the like, we must also apply the law's sanctions in a firm, fair way. Punishment resets the scales of justice. The threat of punishment deters criminal activity.

The laws against drunk driving in Norway are tough and unremitting. Three weeks in prison is the minimum mandatory penalty for a first offense, and 7,000 persons are imprisoned under the drunk driving code every year. The result is that 78 percent of Norwegians simply do not drink at all when they know they will have to drive. Most of the few drivers who do drink carefully monitor their intake of alcohol.

Closer to home, Charleston, South Carolina, Police Chief Reuben Greenberg told a "60 Minutes" audience in January 1986 (and my "A Fine Point" audience in March 1986) about his visit to New York's Spanish Harlem. Greenberg saw an old woman. She was a bag lady for the area's numbers mob, and she often carried tens of thousands of dollars from one illegal betting spot to another. Yet although she was unguarded the thugs left her alone. As Chief Greenberg pointed out, they understood what would happen to them if they did not: certain, swift, and severe punishment.

An analysis by the federal government's Bureau of Criminal Justice Statistics shows that between 62 percent and 71 percent of all persons imprisoned for the *first time* learn their lesson and never return. There are those, however, who remain dangers to society as long as they are free (or until old age weakens their criminality). The same study showed that 61 percent of those admitted to prison in the year studied (1979) had previously served a term of incarceration, and 46 percent of them *would still have been in prison on the earlier sentence* if they had not been released on parole. The message is clear: deter those who can be deterred; incarcerate those who cannot.

While a credible threat of punishment prevents crime, the punishment itself serves another important function: it restores essential moral equilibrium. As sociologist Ernest van den Haag explains in his book *Punishing Criminals,* "Some are caught when they yield to temptation. Were they not punished, those who did restrain themselves would feel cheated." Justice Potter Stewart made this same point in the context of a decision on capital punishment: "When people begin to believe that organized society is unwilling or unable to impose upon criminal offenders the punishment they 'deserve' then there is sown the seeds of anarchy—or self-help, vigilante justice, and lynch law."

In his book on Bonnie Garland's tragic death, Dr. Willard Gaylin asks what would be the proper sentencing considerations for Adolph Hitler if he were caught today. Protection of society? Hardly, argues Dr. Gaylin; Hitler would be an old man incapable of any further mischief. Deterrence of others? As Dr. Gaylin points out, there is no likelihood that Hitler's personal fate would deter future Hitlers, any more than the fates of other vanquished tyrants deterred Hitler. Rehabilitation? There might be nothing to rehabilitate: "Hitler might well have led a peaceful and fruitful life in retirement," Dr. Gaylin hypothesizes, and he might have even "resumed his painting career."

> Yet, the concept of Hitler in retirement on a ranch in Argentina painting landscapes is simply intolerable. Even if it cannot be justified on purely utilitarian grounds, that man deserves to be punished with all the righteous wrath of an outraged community sensitivity. It cheapens the Holocaust to suggest that his punishment must be justified in terms of prevention of some future pain and destruction.

As I mentioned in the preface, this book's story is "untold" only because no other judge similarly frustrated by the law's fictions, expediencies, and myopic rigidities has bothered to tell it. Everything related here exists in the public record amid myriad siblings. Together, they constitute a mosaic of failure: the criminal justice system's failure to do its job. There have, of course, been successes: juveniles dissuaded from a life of crime and adults who keep their promise to go straight. Sadly, the saplings of success are overshadowed by the forest of failures.

I suspect this will be a controversial book. If some of my colleagues perceive personal criticism, let me assure them that none has been intended. I challenge not their motives but their assumptions and the policies that flow from those assumptions. Unlike most judges—but by no means all—I do not believe that plea bargaining is essential, that leniency will rehabilitate young thugs, or that the insanity defense dance and the rules of exclusion are necessary to prevent governmental oppression. Those who differ on these issues apply their principles in good faith; they do not seek to frustrate justice. Yet as all will concede, justice *has* been frustrated.

I do not labor alone in the vineyard of common sense. All over this nation there are judges who are similarly tormented by, and are trying to change, a system that has all too often been dominated by those who in their good-faith efforts to preserve liberty are actually placing it in grave danger. With only minimal exaggeration they are turning the Constitution into a "suicide pact," to borrow the phrase of Justice Robert H. Jackson, written in another context nearly four decades ago.

Justice Byron White's dissent in *Miranda* warned of the threat:

> In some unknown number of cases the Court's rule will return a killer, a rapist or other criminal to the streets and to the environment which produced him, to repeat his crime whenever it pleases him. As a consequence, there will not be a gain, but a loss, in human dignity. The real concern is . . . the impact on those who rely on the public authority for protection and who without it can only engage in violent self-help with guns, knives and the help of their neighbors similarly inclined.

As predicted, we are coming full circle to the vigilantism that was present at the birth of our legal process a millennium ago. A reflection of this can be seen in our popular culture and the recent spate of movies and television shows glorifying extra-legal means of coping with crime.

Those who live with crime every day, either as citizens entrapped by its frightful horrors or as law enforcement professionals trying to contain it, recognize that much of society has broken down. We are in the throes of social entropy: the de-enervation of civilizing forces. We see it all around us, and we see it in our children. Recently in Chicago, youngsters looted an ice cream wagon after its owner had been shot in a robbery and lay bleeding in the gutter. His pleas for them to stop, his pleas for help, went unheeded. A woman who lives in Milwaukee's inner city and whose home has been repeatedly burglarized and vandalized told *Milwaukee Journal* reporter Gary C. Rummler in August 1984 that "the kids have taken over, and I'm their slave." In March 1985, Rummler reported about a ten-year-old boy who was tormented by thugs almost every day. This fifth grader's solution? "Get a helmet, some shin pads, chest pads, and a shotgun." How sad, how terribly tragic it all is.

Several years ago, a minister was attempting to convey his view of the promise of redemption to a Sunday school class. "Imagine," he told them, "that your mother or father brings home a new watch. Inside the box is a small piece of paper that says that if the watch doesn't work, you can bring it back and get it fixed or replaced for free. Does anyone know what you call that piece of paper?" Several hands went up. "I know," a nine-year-old girl said eagerly, "a lie."

Unfortunately, the criminal justice system has not kept its promise of protection. All over this nation, courthouses, which are supposed to be temples of truth and justice, have by and large become places where criminals learn they can get away with crime. If we are to change this, we must restore credibility and accountability. We must eliminate plea bargaining, eliminate the distorted application of the insanity defense, modify—if not eliminate—the exclusionary rules that suppress highly probative evidence, and restore an equilibrium to community values through the expiation and catharsis of punishment. There should be no "free rides," no free "first bites," and no expediency-driven little fictions that call burglary "receiving stolen property," that call rape "disorderly conduct," and that call murder "manslaughter."

There are signs that after decades of hiding from reality, those who shape our laws are beginning to recognize that what Justice Cardozo once called "gossamer possibilities of prejudice" to a defendant should never derail common-sense realities. We must continue our efforts to restore fairness to our criminal justice system; justice to the accused should never mean injustice either to the victim or to society.

Accountants and business executives are fond of talking about "the bottom line." Other disciplines have borrowed the idiom to such an extent that it has become but another cliché, benumbed of meaning. Nevertheless, I will use it here because no other phrase expresses the thought as well. Sadly, very few among us can enjoy a peaceful nighttime stroll through our neighborhoods, and all too many of us are deprived of that simple pleasure even during the day. Crime and the fear of crime have done what foreign tyrants have failed to do. They have made us unfree. And that, my friends, is a bottom line that we must—and can—change. After all, wouldn't it be nice—wouldn't it be *just*— if every elderly person terrified of the dusk, if *every* man, woman, and child could be as safe from hoodlums in their neighborhoods as that numbers bag lady is in Spanish Harlem?

The final chapter in a book is usually a conclusion. If readers cluck their teeth in agreement at the end of this book but lament their inability to change what needs to be changed, I will have failed, and all the nights, weekends, and holidays I have invested will have been squandered. This last chapter must be a beginning, not an end. It must be a springboard for efforts to accelerate the return to common sense, to do something about the criminals who murder, maim, and imprison our people.

The criminal justice system is not a private preserve for prosecutors, defense lawyers, and judges. We do the public's business, and you have a right to know and to question what we do. If you believe—as do I and many of my colleagues—that the system is failing to protect us from crime, you can help. I offer two practical suggestions:

- Join or form court watch groups to monitor and publicize what the lawyers and judges are doing. While judges must, of course, remain protected from the public clamor, we must never use that rightful insulation as a shield of arrogance. We should be no more immune from criticism than any other group. Accordingly, if you see things you like, let everyone know you approve. If you see things you do not like, complain.

    Many aspects of the criminal justice system such as sentencing and parole policies are controlled by the legislature. Let your legislators know if you believe the laws of your state should be changed.

Undoubtedly, many of you will fashion special solutions to problems that are unique to your own areas. If you speak loudly enough, however, your voices—the voice of the people—will be heard.

Oliver Wendell Holmes once observed that the law appropriately reflects the "felt necessities of the times." We are awash with crime, and something must be done.

While I believe that much in our criminal justice system has to be changed, change must be lawful. Various aspects of change can come from the legislatures in each of our states and from the Congress as well as from each state's highest court and from the United States Supreme Court. Trial judges like myself, however, must apply the law as it is and not as we might think it should be. If we did not obey this hierarchy, anarchy would soon prevail and, ultimately, our nation would have no justice and no fairness.

Each of us in society can help in the struggle against torrential crime. We *can* return to an era when our streets, our neighborhoods, and our homes were as safe and secure as the snuggest harbor. But we must grasp the oars within our reach.

BIBLIOGRAPHY

Akler, Henry A. Review of *Minnesota Multiphasic Personality Inventory. The Eighth Mental Measurements Yearbook* (1978): 931.

Albee, George W. "The Uncertain Future of Clinical Psychology." *American Psychologist* 25 (1970): 1071.

Alschuler, Albert W. "The Changing Plea Bargaining Debate." *California Law Review* 69 (1981): 652.

———. "The Defense Attorney's Role in Plea Bargaining." *Yale Law Journal* 84 (1975): 1179, 1182.

———. "Plea Bargaining and Its History." *Columbia Law Review* 79 (1979): 1.

———. "The Prosecutor's Role in Plea Bargaining." *University of Chicago Law Review* 36 (1968): 50.

———. "Review: *Criminal Violence, Criminal Justice* by Charles E. Silberman." *University of Chicago Law Review* 46 (1979): 1007, 1031.

American Bar Association. *Standards For Criminal Justice: Standard Relating to Pleas of Guilty.* (Approved draft, 1968).

———. *Standards For Criminal Justice.* 2nd ed. (1980).

American Psychiatric Association. *Diagnostic and Statistical Manual for Mental Disorders.* 3rd ed. (1980).

———. *Statement on the Insanity Defense.* (December 1982).

Andenaes, Johannes. *Punishment and Deterrence.* Ann Arbor: University of Michigan Press, 1974.

Bailey, F. Lee and Henry B. Rothblatt. *Crimes of Violence, Rape and Other Sex Crimes.* Rochester, N.Y.: Lawyers Co-Operative Pub. Co., 1973.

Bazelon, David L. "Psychiatrists and the Adversary Process." *Scientific American* 230 (June 1974): 18.

———. "Veils, Values and Social Responsibility." *American Psychologist* 37 (1984): 115, 118.

Beach, Bennett H., and David S. Jackson. "When the Police Blunder a Little." *Time* (March 14, 1983).

Bender, Jeanne Matthews. "After Abolition: The Present State of the Insanity Defense in Montana." *Montana Law Review* 45 (1984): 133.

Berger, Moise. "The Case Against Plea Bargaining." *American Bar Association Journal* 62 (1976): 621.

Besharov, Douglas J. *Juvenile Justice Advocacy*. New York: Practicing Law Institute, 1974.

Biggs, John, Jr. *The Guilty Mind*. New York: Harcourt, Brace & Co., 1955.

Blatt, Sidney J. "The Validity of Projective Techniques and Their Research and Clinical Contribution." *Journal of Personality Assessment* 39 (1975): 327.

Blumberg, Abraham S. "The Practice of Law as Confidence Game." *Law and Society Review* 1 (1967): 15.

Blumstein, Alfred, and Daniel Nagin. "The Deterrent Effect of Legal Sanctions on Draft Evasion." *Stanford Law Review* 29 (1977): 241.

Boffey, Philip M. "Youth Crime Puzzle Defies a Solution." *The New York Times*, March 5, 1982.

Bowen, Catherine Drinker. *Miracle at Philadelphia*. Boston: Little, Brown, 1966.

Branegan, Jay. "Suspect Tells How to Beat Murder Charge." *The Chicago Tribune*, April 18, 1978.

Brill, Steven. "Entrapped?" *The American Lawyer* (January 1983).

Brown, Merry Rubin. "The Exclusionary Rule in Probation Revocation Hearings, *State* v. *Lombardo*." *Wake Forest Law Review* 19 (1983): 845.

Brown, Waln. *The Other Side of Delinquency*. Rutgers University Press, 1983.

Bruske, Ed. "A Law Meets Reality—And Loses." *The Washington Post*, May 11, 1986.

———. "Plea Bargains Erode Drug Law's Intent." *The Washington Post*, May 12, 1986.

———. "D.C. Judges Find Loopholes to Ease Drug Punishment." *The Washington Post*, May 13, 1986.

Calonius, J. Erik. "Just a Bottle of Beer Can Send a Motorist to Prison in Norway." *The Wall Street Journal*, August 16, 1985.

Chapman, Loren J. and Jean P. "Genesis of Popular But Erroneous Psychodiagnostician Observations." *Journal of Abnormal Psychology* 72 (1967): 193.

Church, Thomas W. "In Defense of 'Bargain Justice.'" *Law and Society Review* 13 (1979): 509.

Churchill, Winston. *A History of the English Speaking Peoples.* vol. 3. New York: Dodd, Mead, 1957.

Cleveland, Sidney E. "Reflections on the Rise and Fall of Psycho-diagnosis." *Professional Psychology* 7 (1976): 309.

Coleman, Lee. *The Reign of Error.* Boston: Beacon Press, 1984.

———, and Bernard Diamond. "Pro and Con, Bar Psychiatrists as Trial Witnesses?" *U.S. News & World Report* (June 7, 1982): 57.

"Criminal Irresponsibility." *American Journal of Psychiatry* 110 (1954): 627.

Cressey, Donald R., ed. *Crime and Criminal Justice.* New York: Quadrangle, 1971.

Crown, Sidney. " 'On Being Sane in Insane Places': A Comment From England." *Journal of Abnormal Psychology* 84 (1975): 453.

Dana, Richard H. "Review of the Rorschach test." *The Eighth Mental Measurements Yearbook* (1978): 1040.

Davids, Anthony. "Projective Testing: Some Issues Facing Academicians and Practitioners." *Professional Psychology* 4 (1973): 445.

De Grazia, Edward. "The Distinction of Being Mad." *University of Chicago Law Review* 22 (1955): 339.

Dershowitz, Alan M. *The Best Defense.* New York: Random House, 1982.

Diamond, Bernard L. "Isaac Ray and the Trial of Daniel M'Naghten." *American Journal of Psychiatry* 112 (1956): 651.

Ennis, Bruce J., and Thomas R. Litwack. "Psychiatry and the Presumption of Expertise: Flipping Coins in the Courtroom." *California Law Review* 62 (1974): 693.

Eyesenk, H. J. *Sense and Nonsense in Psychology.* New York: Penguin, 1957.

Fallows, James. "Born to Rob? Why Criminals Do It. Review of *Crime and Human Nature* by James Q. Wilson and Richard J. Herrnstein." *The Washington Monthly* (December 1985).

Feher, Edward, Leon Vandecreek, and Hedwig Teglasi. "The Problem of Art Quality in the Use of Human Figure Drawing Tests." *Journal of Clinical Psychology* 39 (1983): 268.

Fortas, Abe. "Implications of Durham's Case." *American Journal of Psychology* 113 (1957): 577.

Friendly, Henry J. "The Bill of Rights as a Code of Criminal Procedure." *California Law Review* 53 (1965): 929.

Fullin, James, Jr. "The Insanity Defense: Ready for Reform?" *Wisconsin Bar Bulletin* 55 (December 1982).

Gaylin, Willard. *The Killing of Bonnie Garland.* New York: Simon and Schuster, 1982.

Gest, Ted. "Turned Loose Too Soon?" *U.S. News & World Report* (June 27, 1983): 52.

Glueck, Bernard C., Jr. "Changing Concepts in Forensic Psychiatry." *Journal of Criminal Law, Criminology and Police Science* 45 (1954): 123.

Glueck, S. Sheldon. *Mental Disorder and the Criminal Law.* Boston: Little, Brown & Co., 1925.

Grant, J. A. C. "Our Common Law Constitution." *Boston University Law Review* 40 (1960): 1.

Greene, Bob. "The War On Crime: Top Priority in U.S." *The Chicago Tribune,* February 5, 1985, Sec. 2, p. 1.

Greenfield, Lawrence A. *Examining Recidivism.* Special Report, Bureau of Justice Statistics (February 1985).

Grisso, Thomas. "Juveniles' Capacity to Waive *Miranda* Rights: An Empirical Analysis." *California Law Review* 68 (1980): 1134.

Goldsmith, Stephen R., and Arnold Mandell. "The Dynamic Formulation—A Critique of a Psychiatric Ritual." *American Journal of Psychiatry* 125 (1969): 152.

Goldstein, Abraham S. *The Insanity Defense.* Yale University Press, 1967.

Groth-Marnat, Gary. *Handbook of Psychological Assessment.* New York: Van Nostrand, Reinhold, 1984.

Guttmacher, Manfred S. "The Psychiatrist as an Expert Witness." *University of Chicago Law Review* 22 (1955): 325.

———. "The Psychiatric Approach to Crime and Correction." *Law and Contemporary Problems* 28 (1958): 633, 635.

Hagan, John, and Ilene Nagel Bernstein. "The Sentence Bargaining of Upperworld and Underworld Crime in Ten Federal District Courts. *Law and Society Review* 13 (1979): 467.

Hall, Jerome. "The M'Naghten Rules and Proposed Alternatives." *American Bar Association Journal* 49 (1963): 960.

Haller, Mark H. "Plea Bargaining: The Nineteenth Century Context." *Law and Society Review* 13 (1979): 273, 277.

Halpern, Abraham L. "The Fiction of Legal Insanity and the Misuse of Psychiatry." *Journal of Legal Medicine* 2 (1980): 18.

Hakeem, Michael. "A Critique of the Psychiatric Approach to Crime and Correction." *Law and Contemporary Problems* 23 (1958): 651.

Harris, Dale B. "Review, The Draw-A-Person Test." *The Seventh Mental Measurements Yearbook* (1972): 401.

Herbert, W. "MMPI: Redefining Normality for Modern Times." *Science News* 124 (October 8, 1983): 228.

"Hinckley Bombshell: End of Insanity Pleas?" *U.S. News & World Report* (July 5, 1982).

Hughes, Graham. "Pleas Without Bargains." *Rutgers Law Review* 33 (1981): 753.

Hyman, Jonathan M. "Bargaining and Criminal Justice." *Rutgers Law Review* 33 (1980): 3.

"Interrogations in New Haven: The Impact of Miranda." *Yale Law Journal* 76 (1967): 1519.

"The Influence of the Defendant's Plea on Judicial Determination of Sentence." *Yale Law Journal* 66 (1956): 204.

Isaacson, Walter. "Insane on All Counts." *Time* (July 5, 1982): 22.

Jeffery, Ray. "The Psychologist as an Expert Witness on the Issue of Insanity." *American Psychologist* 19 (1964): 838.

Kamisar, Yale. "*Brewer* v. *Williams*—A Hard Look at a Discomfiting Record." *Georgetown Law Journal* 66 (1977): 209.

———. "Fred E. Inbau: The Importance of Being Guilty." *Journal of Criminal Law and Criminology* 68 (1977): 182.

———. "What Is 'Interrogation'? When Does It Matter?" *Georgetown Law Journal* 67 (1978): 1.

———. "Is the Exclusionary Rule An 'Illogical' or 'Unnatural' Interpretation of the Fourth Amendment?" *Judicature* 62 (1978): 66.

Kaplan, John. "Why People Go to the Bad. Review of *Crime and Human Nature* by James Q. Wilson and Richard J. Herrnstein." *The New York Times Book Review*, September 8, 1985.

Katz, Wilber G. "Law Psychiatry, and Free Will." *University of Chicago Law Review* 22 (1955): 397.

Kaufman, Irving R. "Judges Must Speak Out." *The New York Times*, January 30, 1982.

———. "The Insanity Plea on Trial." *The New York Times Magazine*, August 8, 1982 p. 16.

Keilitz, Ingo, and Junius P. Fulton. *The Insanity Defense.* Williamsburg, Va.: National Center for State Courts, 1984.

Kipnis, Kenneth. "Criminal Justice and the Negotiated Plea." *Ethics*

86 (1976): 93. Reprinted in Franklin E. Zimring and Richard S. Frase, *The Criminal Justice System*. Boston: Little, Brown, 1980.

Kitay, Philip M. "Review of the Bender-Gestalt test." *The Seventh Mental Measurements Yearbook* (1972): 394.

Klieman, Rikki J. "The Insanity of the Restriction of the Insanity Defense: Is There An Insanity Defense in 1985?" Paper prepared for the Atlanta Bar Association Superstars of Seminars in Criminal Defense Litigation, June 1984.

Karpman, Benjamin. "An Attempt At a Re-evaluation of Some Concepts of Law and Psychiatry." *Journal of Criminal Law and Criminology* 38 (1947): 206.

———. "Criminality, Insanity and the Law." *Journal of Criminal Law and Criminology* 39 (1949): 584.

Keating, Robert. "The DA's War on Technicalities." *New York* (January 30, 1984).

Koestler, Arthur. *The Sleepwalkers*. New York: Macmillan, 1959.

Lando, Harry A. " 'On Being Sane in Insane Places': A Supplemental Report." *Professional Psychology* 7 (1976): 47.

Langbein, John H. "Torture and Plea Bargaining." *University of Chicago Law Review* 46 (1978): 3.

Langen, Patrick A., and Lawrence A. Greenfield. *The Prevalence of Imprisonment*. Special Report, Bureau of Justice Statistics, July 1985.

Langer, Ellen J., and Robert P. Abelson. "A Patient by Any Other Name." *Journal of Counseling and Clinical Psychology* 42 (1974): 4.

Lauter, David. "Why the Insanity Defense is Breaking Down." *National Law Journal* (May 3, 1982).

"Lawyer Verdict: He Criticizes Own Case." *Time* (June 22, 1981).

Leo, John. "Is The System Guilty?" *Time* (July 5, 1982): 26.

Lowell, A. Lawrence. "The Judicial Use of Torture." *Harvard Law Review* 11 (1897): 220, 290.

Lyttleton, R.A. "The Nature of Knowledge." In Ronald Duncan and Miranda Weston-Smith, eds. *The Encyclopedia of Ignorance*. New York: Pergamon Press, 1977.

Mack, Julian W. "The Juvenile Court." *Harvard Law Review* 23 (1909): 104.

Maeder, Thomas. *Crime and Madness*. New York: Harper & Row, 1985.

Maitland, F. W. *The Constitutional History of England*. Cambridge University Press, 1908/1961.

Malinowski, Bronislaw. *Crime and Custom in Savage Society.* London: Routledge and Kegan Paul, 1926.

Meyer, Peter. *The Yale Murder.* New York: Empire Books, 1982.

Millon, Theodore. "Reflections on Rosenhan's 'On Being Sane in Insane Places.' " *Journal of Abnormal Psychology* 84 (1975): 456.

Moley, Raymond. "The Vanishing Jury." *Southern California Law Review* 2 (1928): 97, 120.

Monaghan, Henry P. "The Supreme Court, 1974 Term Forward: Constitutional Common Law." *Harvard Law Review* 89 (1975): 1.

Moreland, Kevin. "Diagnostic Validity of the MMPI and Two Short Forms." *Journal of Personality Assessment* 47 (1983): 492.

Morris, Norval. *Madness and the Criminal Law.* University of Chicago Press, 1982.

Murray, Charles. *Losing Ground.* New York: Basic Books, 1984.

Oaks, Dallin H. "Studying the Exclusionary Rule in Search and Seizure." *University of Chicago Law Review* 37 (1970): 665.

Pasamanick, Benjamin, Simon Dinitz, and Mark Lefton. "Psychiatric Orientation and its Relation Diagnosis and Treatment in a Mental Hospital." *American Journal of Psychiatry* 116 (1959): 127.

Penn, Stanley. "Seeking Justice." *The Wall Street Journal,* September 5, 1985.

Peterson, Rolf A. "Review, The Rorschach Test." *The Eighth Mental Measurements Yearbook* (1978): 1042.

Platt, Anthony, and Bernard Diamond. "The Origins of the 'Right and Wrong' Test of Criminal Responsibility and its Subsequent Development in the United States: An Historical Survey." *California Law Review* 54 (1966): 1227.

Pollock, Frederick. "The King's Peace in the Middle Ages." *Harvard Law Review* 13 (1900): 177.

———, and Frederic William Maitland. *The History of English Law.* 2 vols. Cambridge: Cambridge University Press, 1899.

Pound, Roscoe. *Criminal Justice in America.* New York: Holt, 1930.

President's Commission on Law Enforcement. *The Challenge of Crime in a Free Society.* Washington, D.C.: GPO, 1967.

Press, Aric, and Peggy Clausen. "Not Guilty Because of PMS?" *Newsweek* (November 11, 1982).

"Psychiatry in Relation to Crime." *Journal of the American Medical Association* 95 (1930): 346.

Pugh, Daniel P. "The Insanity Defense in Operation: A Practicing Psychiatrist Views Durham and Brawner." *Washington University Law Quarterly* 1973 (1973): 87.

Ranii, David. "A Furor Over an Alternative Sentence." *The National Law Journal* (December 5, 1983): 8.

Regnery, Alfred S. "Getting Away With Murder." *Policy Review* (Fall 1986).

Reik, Louis E. "The Doe-Ray Correspondence: A Pioneer Collaboration in the Jurisprudence of Mental Disease." *Yale Law Journal* 63 (1953): 183.

Reik, Theodor. *The Compulsion to Confess.* New York: Farrar, Straus & Cudahy, 1959.

Ricks, Thomas E. "Stalking Killers: Two Homicide Sleuths Win Some, Lose Some on Streets of Miami." *The Wall Street Journal,* October 16, 1985.

Rembar, Charles. *The Law of the Land.* New York: Simon and Schuster, 1980.

Riordon, William L. *Plunkitt of Tammany Hall.* New York: Dutton, 1963.

Roberts, Sam. "For One Zealous Judge, Hard Bargaining Pushes Cases Through the Courts." *The New York Times,* April 29, 1985, p. 13.

Robinson, Daniel N. *Psychology and the Law: Can Justice Survive the Social Sciences?* Oxford University Press, 1980.

Robitscher, Jonas. *The Powers of Psychiatry.* Boston: Houghton, Mifflin, 1980.

Roche, Philip Q. "Criminality and Mental Illness—Two Faces of the Same Coin." *University of Chicago Law Review* 22 (1955): 320.

Rogge, O. John. *Why Men Confess.* New York: Nelson, 1959.

Rosenhan, David L. "On Being Sane in Insane Places." *Science* 179 (1973): 250–58.

———. "The Contextual Nature of Psychiatric Diagnosis." *Journal of Abnormal Psychology* 84 (1975): 462.

Rowe, Jonathan. "Why Liberals Should Hate the Insanity Defense." *The Washington Monthly* (May 1984): 39.

Royko, Mike. "When You Wish Upon A Death . . ." *The Chicago Tribune,* January 21, 1985.

Rubinstein, Michael L. *Alaska Bans Plea Bargaining.* National Institute of Justice, 1980.

———, and Teresa J. White. "Alaska Bans Plea Bargaining." *Law and Society Review* 13 (1979): 367.

———. "Plea Bargaining: Can Alaska Live Without It?" *Judicature* 62 (1979): 266.

Shaffer, John Whitcomb, Karen Rose Duszynski, and Caroline Bedell Thomas. "A Comparison of Three Methods For Scoring Figure Drawings." *Journal of Personality Assessment* 48 (1984): 245.

Schlesinger, Steven R. "Excluding the Exclusionary Rule." In Patrick B. McGuigan and Randall R. Rader, eds. *Criminal Justice Reform.* Chicago: Regnery, 1983.

———. *Exclusionary Injustice.* New York: Marcel Dekker, 1977.

———, and Elizabeth A. Malloy. "Plea Bargaining and the Judiciary: An Argument for Reform." *Drake Law Review* 30 (1981): 581.

Schwartz, Bernard. *Super Chief: Earl Warren and his Supreme Court— A Judicial Biography.* New York: New York University Press, 1983.

Seeburger, Richard H., and R. Stanton Wettick, Jr. "Miranda in Pittsburgh: A Statistical Study." *University of Pennsylvania Law Review* 29 (1967): 1.

Silberman, Charles E. *Criminal Violence, Criminal Justice.* New York: Random House, 1978.

Singer, Anne C. "Insanity Acquittals in the Seventies." *Mental Disability Law Reporter* 2 (Jan.–Feb. 1978): 406.

Slovenko, Ralph. "The Insanity Defense in the Wake of the Hinckley Trial." *Rutgers Law Journal* 14 (1982): 373.

Spitzer, Robert L. "On Pseudoscience in Science, Logic in Remission and Psychiatric Diagnosis: A Critique on Rosenhan's 'On Being Sane in Insane Places.' " *Journal of Abnormal Psychology* 84 (1975): 442.

———, and Joseph L. Fleiss. "A Re-Analysis of the Reliability of Psychiatric Diagnoses." *British Journal of Psychiatry* 125 (1974): 341.

———, J. B. W. Forman, and J. Nee. "DSM–III Field Trials: Initial Interrater Diagnostic Reliability." *American Journal of Psychiatry* 136 (1979): 815.

———, and Janet B. W. Williams. "DSM–III Field Trials: Interrater Reliability and List of Project Staff and Participants." *Diagnostic and Statistical Manual for Mental Disorders.* 3rd ed. (1980).

"Statutory Discretion of the District Attorney in Wisconsin." *Wisconsin Law Review* 1953 (1953): 170.

Steadman, Henry J. "Insanity Acquittals in New York State, 1965–1978." *American Journal of Psychiatry* 137 (1980): 321.

Stern, Herbert J. "Review: *The Passive Judiciary* by Abraham S. Goldstein." *Columbia Law Review* 82 (1982): 1275.

Stewart, Potter. "The Road to *Mapp* v *Ohio* and Beyond: The Origins, Development and Future of the Exclusionary Rule in Search and Seizure Cases." *Columbia Law Review* 83 (1983): 1365.

Strasburg, Paul A. "Recent National Trends in Serious Juvenile Crime." In *Violent Juvenile Offender, An Anthology.* San Francisco: National Council on Crime and Delinquency, 1984.

Swartz, Jon D. "Review of the Thematic Apperception Test." *The Eighth Mental Measurements Yearbook* (1978): 1127.

Tarter, Ralph E., Donald I. Templer, and Charlotte Hardy. "Reliability of Psychiatric Diagnosis." *Diseases of the Nervous System* 36 (1975): 30.

Taylor, Stuart Jr. "Too Much Justice." *Harper's* (September 1982).

Temerlin, Maurice K., and William Trousdale. "The Social Psychology of Clinical Diagnosis." *Psychotherapy: Theory, Research and Practice* 6 (1969): 24.

Thau, Jonathan. "How Lawyers Can Benefit From Trends in Collateral Estoppel." *The National Law Journal* (November 7, 1983): 22.

Tucker, William. *Vigilante.* New York: Stein & Day, 1985.

U.S. Congress. Senate. Committee on the Judiciary. *Hearings on the Comprehensive Crime Control Act of 1983.* S. Hrg. No. 98–503. 98th Cong., 1st sess., May 4, 11, 18, 19, & 23, 1983.

U.S. Congress. Senate. Committee on the Judiciary. *Report on the Comprehensive Crime Control Act of 1983.* S. Rep. No. 98–225. 98th Cong., 1st sess., September 14, 1983.

U.S. Department of Justice. Federal Bureau of Investigation. *Uniform Crime Reports for the United States.* Washington, D.C.: GPO, 1983.

U.S. Department of Justice. Federal Bureau of Investigation. *Uniform Crime Reports, Crime in the United States—1982.* Washington, D.C.: GPO. Released 9/11/83.

U.S. Department of Justice. *Households Touched by Crime, 1983.* Bureau of Justice Statistics Bulletin. Washington, D.C.: GPO, 1984.

U.S. Department of Justice. *Report to the Nation on Crime and Jus-*

tice: The Data. Bureau of Justice Statistics, 1983.
U.S. National Advisory Commission on Criminal Justice. *A National Strategy to Reduce Crime.* (1973).
————. *Criminal Justice Standards and Goals.* (1976).
————. *Criminal Justice System.* (1973).
————. *Courts.* (1973).
————. *Juvenile Justice and Delinquency Prevention.* (1973).
Van den Haag, Ernest. *Punishing Criminals.* New York: Basic Books, 1975.
————. "Limiting Plea Bargaining and Prosecutorial Discretion." *Cumberland Law Review* 15 (1984): 1.
Warden, Karl P. "Miranda—Some History, Some Observations, and Some Questions." *Vanderbilt Law Review* 20 (1966): 39.
Wechsler, Herbert. "The Criteria of Criminal Responsibility." *University of Chicago Law Review* 32 (1955): 367.
Weihofen, Henry. "The Flowering of New Hampshire." *University of Chicago Law Review* 22 (1955): 356.
Weiner, Bernard. " 'On Being Sane in Insane Places': A Process (Attributional) Analysis and Critique." *Journal of Abnormal Psychology* 84 (1975): 433.
Weintraub, Joseph. "Criminal Responsibility: Psychiatry Alone Cannot Determine It." *American Bar Association Journal* 49 (1963): 1075.
Wertham, Fredric. "Psychoauthoritarianism and the Law." *University of Chicago Law Review* 22 (1955): 336.
White, Welsh S. "Police Trickery in Inducing Confession." *University of Pennsylvania Law Review* 127 (1979): 581.
Wildman, Robert W., and Robert W. Wildman, II. "An Investigation Into the Comparative Validity of Several Diagnostic Tests and Test Batteries." *Journal of Clinical Psychology* 31 (1975): 455.
Wilkey, Malcom Richard. "The Exclusionary Rule: Why Suppress Valid Evidence?" *Judicature* 62 (1978): 215.
Wilson, James Q. "Thinking About Crime." *The Atlantic Monthly* (September 1983): 72.
————. *Thinking About Crime.* Rev. ed. New York: Basic Books, 1983.
————, and Richard J. Herrnstein. *Crime and Human Nature.* New York: Simon and Schuster, 1985.
Wingo, Harvey. "Growing Disillusionment with the Exclusion-

ary Rule." *Southwestern Law Review* 25 (1971): 573.

Wise, Stuart M., ed. "A Fine Way to Give to Charity." *The National Law Journal* (November 26, 1984): 47.

Yunker, Conrad E. "Bar Sanctioning Cut in Oregon Cases." *National Law Journal* (August 26, 1985).

Woodward, Bob, and Scott Armstrong. *The Brethren.* New York: Simon and Schuster, 1979.

Zilboorg, Gregory. "A Step Toward Enlightened Justice." *University of Chicago Law Review* 22 (1955): 331.

Ziskin, Jay. "Coping With Psychiatric and Psychological Testimony." Marina Del Rey: Law and Psychiatry Press, 1975.

INDEX